THE SUMMER OF
1876

THE SUMMER OF
1876

OUTLAWS, LAWMEN, AND LEGENDS IN THE SEASON THAT DEFINED THE AMERICAN WEST

CHRIS WIMMER

ST. MARTIN'S GRIFFIN
NEW YORK

Published in the United States by St. Martin's Griffin,
an imprint of St. Martin's Publishing Group

THE SUMMER OF 1876. Copyright © 2023 by Chris Wimmer. All rights reserved.
Printed in the United States of America. For information, address
St. Martin's Publishing Group, 120 Broadway, New York, NY 10271.

www.stmartins.com

Map illustrations by Billy Roberts of Bad Hoss Ventures

Designed by Michelle McMillian

The Library of Congress has cataloged the hardcover edition as follows:

Names: Wimmer, Chris, author.
Title: The summer of 1876 : outlaws, lawmen, and legends in the season that
    defined the American West / Chris Wimmer.
Description: New York : St. Martin's Press, 2023. | Includes bibliographical
    references and index.
Identifiers: LCCN 2023002013 | ISBN 9781250280893 (hardcover) |
    ISBN 9781250280909 (ebook)
Subjects: LCSH: West (U.S.)—History—1860–1890. | Outlaws—West (U.S.)—
    Biography. | Peace officers—West (U.S.)—Biography. | Frontier and pioneer
    life—West (U.S.) | West (U.S.)—Biography.
Classification: LCC F594 .W74 2023 | DDC 978/.02—dc23/eng/20230208
LC record available at https://lccn.loc.gov/2023002013

ISBN 978-1-250-84347-0 (trade paperback)

Our books may be purchased in bulk for promotional, educational, or business use.
Please contact your local bookseller or the Macmillan Corporate and
Premium Sales Department at 1-800-221-7945, extension 5442, or
by email at MacmillanSpecialMarkets@macmillan.com.

First St. Martin's Griffin Edition: 2024

10 9 8 7 6 5 4 3 2 1

CONTENTS

MAP OF CENTRAL
✶ United States ✶
with Canada and Mexico

Scale of Miles

0   100   200   300

CANADA

Brandon   Winnipeg

Spokane

International Falls   Th

Missoula   Great Falls   *Missouri River*   Minot

Helena

MONTANA   NORTH DAKOTA   Fort Lincoln   Fargo

Yellowstone R.

MINNESOTA

Fort Ellis
Battle of the Little Bighorn   ✕   Battle of Slim Buttes ✕

IDAHO   Battle of the Rosebud   *Cheyenne R.*   SOUTH DAKOTA

James R.   Minneapolis

WISCONSI

Deadwood   Northfield

Snake River   WYOMING   Sioux Falls

Des Moines R.

Red Cloud Agency   James-Younger escape route   IOWA   Des Moines

Fort Laramie

Cheyenne   *N. Platte*   NEBRASKA   Omaha   *Missouri R.*

Salt Lake City   *Platte River*

S. Platte   Kearney

UTAH   Denver   *Republican River*   Topeka   Kansas City   MISSOURI   St.

Colorado Springs

COLORADO   Abilene   KANSAS

Dodge City   *Arkansas River*   Granby

ILLI

White River

Santa Fe   *Canadian R.*   Sweetwater ✕   Battle of the Washita   *Mississippi R.*

Flagstaff

Albuquerque   Oklahoma City   ARKANSAS

ARIZONA   NEW MEXICO   Amarillo   OKLAHOMA

Phoenix

Gila River   *Pecos River*   *Red River*

Tucson   *Rio Grande*   Ft. Worth   Dallas   Shreveport   MISS

Nogales   El Paso   *Sabine R.*

TEXAS   *Brazos River*   *Red River*   Baton

Hermosillo   Austin   Houston   LOUISIANA

Guaymas   San Antonio

Chihuahua

MEXICO   Corpus Christi

Laredo   *Gulf of Mexico*

Nuevo Laredo

Culiacan   Monterrey   Matamoros

MONTANA

Dakota Column

Fort Abraham Lincoln

NORTH DAKOTA

Fort Rice

Fort Ellis

Montana Column

Yellowstone River

Bighorn River

Tongue River

Powder River

Little Bighorn Battlefield

Rosebud Battlefield

Slim Buttes Battle

Belle Fourche

Deadwood

SOUTH DAKOTA

Camp Cloud Peak

Fetterman Massacre

Bighorn Mountains

Black Hills

Cheyenne River

White River

Wyoming Column

WYOMING

Fort Fetterman

Yellow Hair Fight

Red Cloud Agency

Niobrara River

Great Wood

Fort Laramie

NEBRASKA

North Platte River

Laramie River

North Platte River

BATTLE OF THE
⋆ Little Bighorn ⋆
Regional Perspective
1876

Laramie

Cheyenne

Scale of Miles

0   30   60

South Platte River

Last Stand Hill

Calhoun Hill

LITTLE BIGHORN
⋆ Battlefield ⋆
Landmarks
1876

Northern Cheyenne

Sans Arc

Scale of Miles

Oglala

Brule

Minniconjou

0   1   2

Blackfoot

Hunkpapa

Weir Point

Reno's Second Position

Reno's First Position

Little Bighorn River

Reno's Entrenchment
(Reno Hill)

☀ The Northfield Raid ☀
by the James–Younger Gang
September 7, 1876

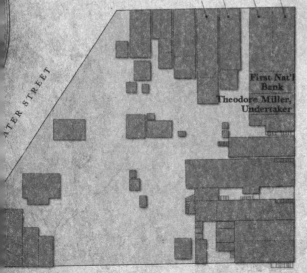

IRON BRIDGE

River

Cannon

Ames
Mill

MILL
SQUARE

4TH STREET

DIVISION STREET

Lee & Hitchcock General Store
Hiram Scriver Dry Goods
Manning Hardware
J. S. Allen Hardware

First Nat'l
Bank
Theodore Miller,
Undertaker

ATER STREET

DIVISION STREET

5TH STREET

Dampier
Hotel

Wheeler & Blackman
Drugstore

PREFACE

The summer of 1876 was a transformative time in the Old West era and American history in general. In a ninety-day period from mid-June to mid-September, three major events happened: the Battle of the Little Bighorn, the murder of Wild Bill Hickok, and the Northfield Raid. Moving parallel to those events, Wyatt Earp and Bat Masterson patrolled the streets of Dodge City together for the first time; Deadwood, the richest and one of the most notorious boomtowns in American history, exploded into life; and the National League of Base Ball Clubs played its first season.

A full understanding of the effects of that summer, and the whole of 1876, would only be possible many years later when they could be viewed in full historical context. But the gravity of at least one event, the Battle of the Little Bighorn, was obvious in its own time. The American military had never suffered a loss to a Native American army like it did at the Little Bighorn. And the American psyche had never suffered a blow like it suffered when it learned that one of its heroes had been killed in such disastrous fashion.

But then, as now, America was a vast nation. Most people and institutions were not directly affected by the Battle of the Little Bighorn, or any of the other battles in the spring, summer, and fall of 1876. Miners in Deadwood were solely focused on becoming rich. Lawmen in Dodge City were solely focused on corralling rowdy Texas cowboys. Baseball players in the East were solely focused on beating their opponents, and so on and so on.

Everyone who could read devoured newspaper stories about the army's campaign against the "hostiles" that summer, but they also devoured stories about bank robberies and the upcoming presidential election and the World's Fair in Philadelphia and a myriad of other fascinating things.

The goal of this book is to weave all those threads into a single narrative. It is intended to be an entertaining journey through the pivotal events of the summer of 1876. It is intentionally lean and fast-paced. And, as such, it is *not* intended to be a deep dive into any one subject. I relied heavily on wonderful books that were written by great authors, and you'll see their works in the bibliography. Those books provide all the detail you could ever want. Please find them wherever you buy your books.

For those who want to continue with this journey, strap in. It's a wild ride.

RED CLOUD'S WAR

Lakota war chief Red Cloud stood on the hill like a commanding general and surveyed the engagement below with a critical eye. This was a test and a sizable gamble for the forty-five-year-old Oglala leader. He had persuaded hundreds of Lakota and Cheyenne warriors to remain on the high plains of northern Wyoming when the weather turned frigid rather than retreat to their traditional winter camps in the Black Hills. But that wasn't Red Cloud's only feat of salesmanship in the winter of 1866. Next, he convinced the warriors to try a limited attack *before* an all-out assault. As always, the younger warriors wanted immediate action. They had little patience for talk and planning and incremental maneuvers. They craved chances for glory. But the war chief's voice carried weight, and Red Cloud won the debate. They would run a test before committing to a full-scale battle. And now, Red Cloud stood on a hill in the freezing December weather and watched the test.

One hundred warriors attacked a group of U.S. Army soldiers on a knob of land dubbed Piney Island. The nickname was straightforward: the small chunk of land was nearly encircled by creeks and was covered with dense pine trees. It was at the base of the Bighorn Mountains four miles west of the soldiers' base at Fort Phil Kearny. To build the fort, the soldiers first constructed a crude lumber mill on Piney Island. For the previous six months, detachments of infantrymen loaded into wagons and trudged to the lumber mill to produce the materials that were needed to build their home for the foreseeable future. All summer, the soldiers hacked and sawed and felled the ninety-foot trees on Piney Island.

The destruction of the forest infuriated Red Cloud. As a consequence, warriors attacked the lumber mill on Piney Island and the wagon trains that rolled between the mill and the fort. But despite continual harassment, work on the fort continued.

Colonel Henry Carrington had led seven hundred infantrymen into a region that had been closed for a year. His mission was to reopen the Bozeman Trail and build a string of forts to protect it. The trail was the northernmost road to the West, and it had existed for three years when Carrington arrived in Wyoming to secure it for white travelers. John Bozeman charted the course in 1863 and led the first wagon trains along the road in 1864. But by the summer of the 1865, the passage was too dangerous to use. That April, Red Cloud had vowed that he would fight to the death to protect the land around the road.

The unique aspect of the Bozeman Trail was that it sliced right through the homeland and the hunting grounds of the Lakota and Cheyenne. The tribes had not attacked travelers in 1864, but in 1865, warriors harassed nearly everything that moved. The U.S. Army chased the warriors all summer and fall but failed to quell the resistance. And then Colonel Carrington arrived in Wyoming in mid-June 1866 with orders to refurbish a decrepit camp north of Fort Laramie and build two more forts in the heartland of the Lakota and Cheyenne.

Carrington had convened a meeting at Fort Laramie to explain to the chiefs and prominent warriors that he came in peace. But before he could deliver his mission statement, the chiefs enumerated a long list of grievances against the army and the U.S. government. At the end of the litany, Red Cloud rose and said, "The Great Father sends us presents and wants a new road. But the White Chief already goes with soldiers to steal the road before the Indian says yes or no. I will talk with you no more. I will go now, and I will fight you. As long as I live, I will fight you for the last hunting grounds."

Red Cloud immediately made good on his promise. When Carrington led his men 150 miles north to a run-down outpost called Camp Connor, Red Cloud's warriors shadowed them the whole way and stole horses at every opportunity. The soldiers rebuilt the installation and named it Fort Reno, and then continued about 40 miles north to the site of their next fort. They arrived at a plateau near the Bighorn Mountains on July 20, 1866, and erected a tent city to live in while they constructed Fort Phil Kearny. The next day, the Lakota stole 175 army horses. And when the soldiers built the lumber mill on Piney Island, the real attacks began.

For the next five weeks, warriors hit the wagon train that moved back and forth between the fort and the lumber mill; they hit the lumber mill itself; and they stole horses and cattle and killed civilians who dared to enter the territory. The Lakota and Cheyenne paused the attacks for three weeks at the end of the summer, probably to conduct the autumn buffalo hunt. But in the second week of September, they started up again.

The soldiers at Fort Phil Kearny felt besieged. Leaving the fort for any reason was a life-and-death proposition. And yet, they continued to build their outpost, as well as a smaller fort 90 miles farther north that would be called Fort C. F. Smith. By mid-October, the work on Fort Phil Kearny was nearly complete.

In the camps of the Lakota and Cheyenne, a war council was under way. Despite constant attacks, the soldiers remained at their posts. Red Cloud advocated a plan that had never been tried on this scale on the northern plains: winter warfare. When heavy snowfall made travel and communication impossible, the forts would be isolated and vulnerable. Red Cloud wanted the warriors to stay in the area instead of moving to their traditional winter camps in the Black Hills. When the time was right, they would kill all the soldiers and burn the forts to the ground. The congregation agreed and the camps remained in place, but the patience of the younger warriors was tested on the final day of the month.

The soldiers at Fort Phil Kearny had been working and suffering nonstop since mid-July, and on the final day of October, they proudly raised the American flag over their fort. They celebrated until lookouts spotted horsemen in the distance. A twenty-year-old warrior named Crazy Horse and members of an elite warrior society called the Strong Hearts were patrolling the hills when they heard cannon fire from the fort. They didn't understand the activity in the fort, but it was clear that something had changed. That night, Crazy Horse and the Strong Hearts crept into a village of tents outside the fort. The tents were the homes of forty miners who had moved closer to the army for safety. Crazy Horse and the warriors fired a volley of arrows into the tents and then slipped away into the darkness.

The surprise attack created chaos in the tent city. Miners burst from their shelters and fired in all directions, but the warriors were long gone. Later that night, the residents in and around the fort saw bonfires in the hills. The warriors danced and sang and tried to intimidate the soldiers. The message was simple: the Lakota and Cheyenne weren't going anywhere. In response, Colonel Carrington ordered the cannons to target the bonfires. The artillerymen hit their marks. Shells exploded around the bonfires and killed several warriors. That was when Red Cloud was forced to perform his second feat of salesmanship.

The warriors shouted for immediate revenge, but Red Cloud counseled patience. His scouts told him there were more soldiers on the way. This would probably be the final delivery of supplies and manpower before the onset of winter. If the warriors could wait a little longer, they would have the right conditions for a campaign that could wipe out the occupants of Fort Phil Kearny. The warriors tentatively accepted Red Cloud's plan.

Four days later, the predicted reinforcements arrived. Captain William Fetterman led 65 men into the fort and quickly learned about the shocking events of the past few months. One hundred fifty soldiers and civilians had died. More than 450 people had been wounded. And worst of all in Fetterman's mind, Colonel Carrington hadn't conducted a single offensive action against the tribes. Fetterman intended to break that streak, but he had no way of knowing that his first engagement against Red Cloud's forces was a test that would ultimately lead to his demise.

On the morning of December 6, 1866, Red Cloud mounted his best warhorse and led hundreds of warriors out of their camp on the Tongue River northwest of Fort Phil Kearny. They rode to within a few miles of the outpost and then split into their assigned groups for the attack. Red Cloud stationed himself on a hill above the prospective battleground to observe the actions of the warriors and the reactions of the soldiers.

Warriors crept into the timber around Piney Island where the woodcutters were hard at work. Moments later, the warriors leaped from their hiding spots and attacked the woodcutters. A soldier galloped to the fort to get help. Colonel Carrington and Captain Fetterman led about seventy-five men on a rescue mission to Piney Island. The brief engagement that followed was messy and confusing, but it resulted in the death of just one soldier. Overall, Carrington could view it as a success, even though his men clearly needed better discipline.

On the other side of the equation, Red Cloud also viewed the engagement as a success. The goal wasn't to inflict maximum damage; it was to learn the tendencies of the soldiers. To that end, Red Cloud now possessed the necessary knowledge. He had wanted to wait until the deepest part of winter when the soldiers had used most of their supplies and were weak from hunger, but that was no longer an option. Crazy Horse and other prominent warriors who had been in the thick of the action gave their reports to Red Cloud. They advocated for a major strike as soon as possible, and it was agreed that the attack would happen on the first good day after the next full moon. The opportunity arrived ten days later.

On the morning of December 21, 1866, more than one thousand Lakota, Cheyenne, and Arapaho warriors silently stationed themselves in the hills around Fort Phil Kearny. The basic plan was unchanged: attack the soldiers at Piney Island, lure the rest out of the fort, and annihilate them. It worked nearly as well as Red Cloud hoped.

Yellow Eagle and forty warriors attacked the lumber mill. Captain Fetterman led fifty-three soldiers out of the fort in an exercise that was a replay of the engagement two weeks earlier, except this time the soldiers were outnumbered more than ten to one. Two more detachments raced out of the fort to help the soldiers who quickly discovered that the hills and valleys were swarming with warriors. Crazy Horse and the Strong Hearts helped lure the soldiers into a trap, and hundreds of warriors launched themselves at the bluecoats in a screaming, frenzied mass. As the warriors overwhelmed the soldiers, the fighting became brutal hand-to-hand combat. The great Lakota chief American Horse was credited with killing Captain Fetterman with a knife.

Red Cloud supervised the battle from his position on the hill. When he saw an army unit leave the fort with field cannons, he and his spotters signaled the warriors with mirrors to finish the fight and leave the area. The war party hadn't wiped out the entire force at the outpost, but it had killed every trooper on the battlefield. The warriors returned to their camp on the Tongue River, likely singing songs of glory all the way home. The assault and unprecedented victory were enough to satiate the appetite of every Lakota, Cheyenne, and Arapaho. The camp moved to the base of the Bighorn Mountains many miles north of the U.S. Army forts and settled in for the winter.

At Fort Phil Kearny, Colonel Carrington and the remaining men of his regiment buried the eighty-one soldiers who died in the engagement that would be called Fetterman's Fight or the Fetterman Massacre. Less than a month later, Carrington was replaced as the commander of Fort Phil Kearny. His successor, Colonel Henry Wessells, fared no better. Red Cloud's forces resumed their attacks in the spring of 1867 and kept them going until October, when the U.S. government finally decided it was too costly to keep fighting. One American commander said it would take twenty thousand men to stop Red Cloud. That was one-third of the entire U.S. Army, and that wasn't an option. The only solution was a peace treaty.

Negotiations began in October of 1867, but Red Cloud refused to sign the agreement until his demands were met. In May of 1868, the United States gave him what he wanted. It closed the Bozeman Trail forever. It closed the three forts along the trail: Fort Reno, Fort Phil Kearny, and Fort C. F. Smith. And it deeded to the Lakota a quadrant of land from the Missouri River in the east to the Bighorn Mountains in the west and from the Nebraska border in the south to the Canadian border in the north.

In the final week of August 1868, the last wagons rolled out of the three forts along the Bozeman Trail. Red Cloud did as he had promised: he and his warriors burned them to the ground. *Then* he signed the Fort Laramie Treaty of 1868. It was the proudest moment of Red Cloud's life. He secured the last remaining hunting grounds on the northern plains for his people. He secured their most sacred land, the Black Hills, on the eastern edge of the territory. And he stopped the advancement of white civilization into his homeland. He accomplished something no Native American leader in history accomplished: he forced the United States to sign a peace treaty on *his* terms. But of course, neither he nor any other chief could fully comprehend the complex legal jargon that was used to explain those terms in writing. He didn't realize the document gave the U.S. government the freedom to send virtually anyone who was deemed an employee onto Lakota land for virtually any reason.

Within three years, railroad survey crews began moving through the hunting grounds Red Cloud fought so hard to protect. Within four years, the U.S. Army authorized expeditions into the Black Hills, the first of which was led by a flamboyant lieutenant colonel with long blond hair. And within six years, another historic battle was fought just a few miles west of the spot where Red Cloud's force crushed Captain Fetterman's command.

The summer of the great battle was the peak of a transformative year for both American and Native American societies. Red Cloud almost certainly had not heard of Jesse James or Wyatt Earp or Bat Masterson or James Butler Hickok. He had never played baseball, though he may have glimpsed the game on trips east in 1870 or 1875. Or he may have seen soldiers playing it on the frontier. He likely knew little of the milestones of the United States in 1876 or of the adventures, many dangerous and deadly, of the men and women who achieved legendary status in the lore of the American West. But if he cared to hear the stories, he might have been entertained. It was one hell of a year.

THE SWEETWATER SHOOTOUT

Bat Masterson was twenty-two years old and already a hero on the day he nearly died. He was sojourning in the hamlet of Sweetwater in the Texas panhandle when the trouble started. It was late January of 1876, and Masterson had recently completed his final season as a buffalo hunter. The best time to hunt buffalo was in the fall and early winter, when the animals' coats were thick to protect against the dropping temperatures, and Bat had finished one last run as a hunter before his life took an unexpected turn.

Sweetwater was a rowdy town about seventy-five miles north-west of Amarillo. It was the social hub of the area for buffalo hunters and soldiers who wandered in from a nearby army outpost called Cantonment Sweetwater. Today, Sweetwater is the village of Mobeetie, whose population is significantly smaller than it was on the night Bat almost died in Charlie Norton's saloon. In 1876, the town was booming. It quickly rose from a dirty buffalo camp to a bustling frontier community that boasted a shop, a restaurant, a hotel, a laundry, and a bevy of saloons. The most popular joint in town was the Lady Gay Saloon, owned and operated by Henry Fleming and Billy Thompson. Fleming doesn't figure prominently into the history of the American West, but Billy Thompson and his older brother, Ben, crossed paths with some major players.

The brothers were born in England but grew up in Austin, Texas. They served with the Texas Mounted Rifles in the Confederate army during the Civil War, despite the fact that Billy was just sixteen years old at the time. After the war, Ben drifted down to Mexico as a soldier of fortune. Billy stayed in Texas and began a long career as a troublemaker. In March of 1868, he shot and killed the chief clerk in the U.S. adjutant general's office in Austin following a drunken dispute. Two months later, he killed an eighteen-year-old stable hand in Rockport, Texas, after the young man slapped his horse. After two killings in as many months, Billy spent the next few years on the run.

While Billy lay low to avoid murder warrants, Ben returned to the United States and headed for the biggest cow town on the plains, Abilene, Kansas. In May of 1871, Ben teamed up with Phil Coe to start the Bull's Head Tavern, a raucous saloon on the outskirts of town that became a favorite of Texas cowboys. Coe and Thompson likely met as mercenaries for Emperor Maximilian during the Mexican revolution and then reunited in Kansas. Coe was born and raised in Gonzales, Texas, about fifty miles southeast of Thompson's adopted hometown of Austin. Like Thompson, Coe served with a Texas cavalry unit in the Civil War before heading to Mexico.

Tension began immediately between the saloon owners and the townsfolk of Abilene. The job of policing the cowboys in *all* the saloons rested with Abilene's new marshal, Wild Bill Hickok. One month before Coe and Thompson opened their saloon, city leaders hired the famous lawman to replace the previous marshal after the man had been killed while trying to serve a warrant with the county sheriff. Throughout the summer of 1871, Hickok butted heads with Coe and Thompson, and the trouble peaked in the first week of October.

It was the final week of the cattle season, and the remaining cowboys in town staged a last hurrah in the form of an Old West bar crawl. Ironically, the bar crawl wasn't the problem. While the cowboys celebrated at the Novelty Theatre, a shot rang out from a neighboring street. Hickok rushed to the scene and found Phil Coe with a pistol in his hand. Coe claimed he had shot a dog, but even if the claim were true and he hadn't harmed another person, it was illegal to carry a firearm in town. Hickok seemed inclined to let the infraction slide to avoid a confrontation in the middle of the street, but Coe turned the gun toward the marshal. Without hesitation, Hickok pulled both pistols and fired. His bullets hit Coe in the stomach and knocked the saloon owner into the dirt.

Hickok then caught a flash of movement out of the corner of his eye. He spun and fired at a man who ran into the street. The man died instantly. A few moments later, Hickok realized he had killed his friend and deputy, Mike Williams. The accidental killing deeply affected Hickok, and after the town fathers decided, at the end of the year, they no longer needed Hickok's services, he never wore a badge again.

Phil Coe lingered in agony for four days before succumbing to his gunshot wounds. At that point, his business partner, Ben Thompson, decided it was time to move along. Two years later, Ben and his brother, Billy, clashed, to some extent, with soon-to-be marshal Wyatt Earp in Ellsworth, Kansas. Billy killed the county sheriff with a shotgun in an incident that was ultimately ruled a drunken accident. Two years later, the brothers were back in their home state

of Texas. Billy co-owned the Lady Gay Saloon in Sweetwater, and
Ben was a faro dealer. When Bat Masterson breezed into town
in the summer of 1875, he spent plenty of time at the Lady Gay
and became friends with Ben Thompson. A few months later, that
friendship helped save his life.

After Bat spent the fall and early winter of 1875 hunting buffalo,
he settled into a routine of gambling and merriment in Sweetwater. He had certainly earned it. It was an understatement to call the
past year of his life an adventure. Since he left the family farm in
eastern Kansas in 1871 at the age of eighteen, he had been hunting
buffalo or working for railroad crews in the vicinity of Dodge City,
the growing settlement that was destined to be the next big cow
town in Kansas. In June of 1874, he left Dodge with a collection of
buffalo hunters, and they traveled south to the abandoned trading
post of Adobe Walls in the Texas panhandle. Almost exactly ten
years earlier, famous frontiersman Kit Carson narrowly survived an
engagement with the Kiowa and Comanche at Adobe Walls, and
now Bat and the crew from Dodge were about to star in a repeat
performance. The panhandle was the last stronghold of Comanche
chief Quanah Parker, and it didn't take him long to realize the buffalo hunters had set up camps in the area of Adobe Walls.

On June 26, 1874, Parker led an estimated force of seven hundred warriors in an attack on the hunters. A battle raged for two
hours, during which Bat performed heroically. When the warriors
broke off the attack and melted back into the dry, flat landscape,
the hunters decided they needed to send a rescue party back to
Dodge City. Bat Masterson and a handful of others slipped away
from Adobe Walls and made the 150-mile trek to southwestern
Kansas. When they arrived, they learned Colonel Nelson Miles
was preparing to lead an army column down to the panhandle.

Bat and his friend Billy Dixon signed on as scouts for the campaign. When Bat, Billy, and a detachment of soldiers returned to Adobe Walls two months later, they found the hunters in fine shape. There had been no further attacks. Bat was happy for the safety of his friends, but he still had a job to do. The army's mission had changed twice since Colonel Miles organized the campaign, and Bat agreed to stay with the soldiers for the long haul.

The initial goal was a basic punitive expedition against the remaining Kiowa and Comanche holdouts under Quanah Parker, who refused to move to reservations. Then Bat and his friends added a rescue component when they informed Miles of the situation at Adobe Walls. And then, just as the mission seemed to be complete, Miles learned that four sisters had been kidnapped by Cheyenne Dog Soldiers. The family of the four girls was headed to Colorado in search of its dream life. But in central Kansas, just east of Hays City, where Wild Bill Hickok had been the marshal four years earlier, the girls watched in horror as their parents, their brother, and their two older sisters were killed and scalped. Colonel Miles's intelligence said the captors were moving south toward Texas with the sisters. It took seven months, but the army column recovered all four girls, and Bat Masterson played a critical role in the recovery effort.

Over the course of ten months, Bat rode hundreds of miles, fought in the second battle of Adobe Walls, and helped rescue the four kidnapped sisters. He was viewed as a hero, and he was just twenty-two years old. With his service complete in the spring of 1875, he mustered out of the army and returned to civilian life. He was in no hurry to return to Dodge City, so he drifted into the small community of Sweetwater, which was a decision he would narrowly live to regret.

Bat spent most of his time drinking and gambling at Billy Thompson's saloon, the Lady Gay. Bat became good friends with Ben Thompson and developed a relationship with a girl named Mollie Brennan. Mollie ended up in Sweetwater courtesy of Billy Thompson. She had been in Ellsworth, Kansas, when Billy killed the county sheriff. She was married to a saloonkeeper named Joe Brennan, but she fell hard for the gunman from Texas. When Billy fled Kansas after the killing, Mollie went with him. She was a dance hall girl and possibly a prostitute, and by the time Bat arrived in Sweetwater, she was working as an entertainer in Charlie Norton's saloon. Whatever the nature of her previous relationship with Billy Thompson, it didn't get in the way of a budding romance with the dashing, dark-haired hero who was fresh off a campaign that saved four kidnapped girls.

But there was a problem. As Bat and Mollie spent more time together, their blossoming relationship angered "Sergeant Melvin King." King was an unhinged, hot-tempered soldier who was stationed at nearby Cantonment Sweetwater. He was a Civil War veteran, a noted gunslinger, and a bully. He was said to have killed several men in barroom gunfights—gunfights *he* provoked. And his name wasn't Melvin King, nor was he currently a sergeant. His real name was Anthony Cook, and he had risen to the rank of sergeant before he was dishonorably discharged after a host of problems that included drunkenness, brawling, insubordination, and assaulting a fellow soldier. Several months after he was kicked out of the army, he reenlisted under the name Melvin A. King, and by the time he was stationed at Cantonment Sweetwater, he was a corporal.

On the night of January 24, Corporal King was already drunk when he showed up at the Lady Gay Saloon and sat down at the poker table with Bat Masterson, and matters deteriorated from there. King lost several hands, and his mood darkened.

While the game was in progress, saloon owner Charlie Norton strolled into the Lady Gay with a few of his employees. Charlie's joint was closed that night, and he escorted Mollie Brennan, Kate Elder (future girlfriend of Doc Holliday), and a few others to the Lady Gay for the evening. Corporal King continued to lose, and his irritation grew, no doubt fueled by seeing Bat and Mollie in proximity. When King lost all his money, he bowed out of the game and exited the saloon.

By midnight, Bat, Charlie, and Mollie decided they wanted a change of venue. Charlie offered to pour a couple of drinks at his place, and the trio headed for his saloon. Charlie unlocked the door, ushered the couple to a table, and closed the door behind them. He stepped behind the bar to produce their beverages, but before he finished pouring, the door shuddered loudly. Someone pounded on it and demanded entry. Bat opened the door, and Corporal King barged in with a pistol in his hand.

King raved and shouted, and before Bat could subdue him or even understand the problem, King pulled the trigger. The bullet bored into Bat's groin and broke his hip. He crashed to the floor as King fired again. At the same moment, Mollie threw herself in front of Bat. She took the full impact of King's second shot and collapsed to the floor next to Bat. Bat pulled his pistol and returned fire. He shot King in the chest, and King crumpled to the floor near Mollie.

The sounds of gunshots drew soldiers and civilians to Norton's saloon. When they burst inside, they found Bat Masterson, Melvin King, and Mollie Brennan bleeding on the floor. Masterson and King were gravely injured, but alive. Mollie was not. The soldiers seemed ready to kill Bat for his role in the fight, but then the most hotly debated part of the night happened.

In a version of the story that was told years later by Wyatt Earp, Ben Thompson rushed into the saloon, leaped onto a table, pulled two pistols, and kept the soldiers back while friends carried Bat to his room at the nearby hotel. In other versions, Billy Thompson is credited with the daring act. Whichever Thompson came to Bat's aid, he likely saved Bat's life in the short term. But Bat's prospects for survival in the long run were dim. The doctor from Cantonment Sweetwater examined Bat and informed him that only time would tell. If Bat didn't develop blood poisoning, he had a chance to live. But many before him had died of similar wounds. Bat could do nothing but lie in bed and hope for the best.

The next day, January 25, Corporal Anthony Cook—alias Melvin King—succumbed to his gunshot wound and was buried at Cantonment Sweetwater. The next month, in February 1876, the outpost was officially named Fort Elliott in honor of Major Joel Elliott, the man who commanded a company of scouts for Lieutenant Colonel George Armstrong Custer at the Battle of the Washita in 1868. Elliott and his entire detachment were killed in the engagement, a tragedy for which Captain Frederick Benteen never forgave Custer. The deaths of Elliott and his men would factor into Benteen's decision-making process in a historic battle exactly six months later. But to set the stage for the battle, the U.S. government needed to issue a declaration that had been in the works for months. In essence, it was a declaration of war.

On February 1, one week after the Sweetwater shootout, the U.S. Department of the Interior declared all Native Americans who were not on reservations "hostile." The designation was largely the brainchild of General Phil Sheridan, the commander of the Department of the Missouri. Sheridan oversaw all the territory from the Missouri River to the Rocky Mountains and from Texas to Canada. In essence, he supervised all the land of the Plains Indians. By 1876, virtually all the members of the tribes of the southern plains had been subdued and pushed onto reservations. But their northern brethren in the Dakota, Wyoming, and Montana Territories still maintained the ability to roam freely, though that was about to change.

The overarching goal was to obtain the Black Hills region that was on the border of Dakota Territory. There was gold in the Hills, and speculation ran rampant that the quantity could be unparalleled. Rumors of gold in the area had persisted for decades, but they were confirmed in the summer of 1874 when Custer led more than one thousand soldiers into the Hills. On paper, the mission was to scout a site for a fort. But the underlying reason for the expedition was to see if the rumors were true. In August of 1874, newspapers shouted the confirmation, and prospectors immediately headed for the Black Hills. For the next year and a half, the U.S. Army forcibly removed miners from the region because America didn't own the land, but that was about to change, as well.

The Fort Laramie Treaty of 1868 deeded the Black Hills to the Lakota for all time. But when the Panic of 1873 spread financial ruin across the country, and the existence of gold was confirmed in 1874, President Ulysses S. Grant tried to buy the Black Hills twice in 1875. He failed both times. By November of 1875, Grant felt he was out of options. He didn't want to rip up the agreement, but the nation screamed for the annexation of the Black Hills, and prospectors were going to continue to flood the area regardless of treaties. Grant resigned himself to the course of action that General Sheridan had preached for years.

Whether or not Sheridan knew of the concept of Manifest Destiny or had heard the term, he was a believer. Newspaper editor John O'Sullivan popularized the idea in 1839 when he made the case for America's expansion westward. He wrote an article called "The Great Nation of Futurity," which eloquently explained the political, economic, and moral reasons why Americans should go forth and spread across the North American continent. The words *destiny* and *progress* are prevalent in the piece, and a central tenet of progress was to civilize the Native American tribes, who were seen as archaic and savage. The idea of civilizing the tribes seemed noble at the time, but it was destructive at its core.

O'Sullivan's missive stated, in part, ". . . We are a nation of progress, of individual freedom . . . freedom of conscience, freedom of person, freedom of trade and business pursuits, universality of freedom and equality." The great irony of Manifest Destiny, of course, was that universal freedom applied only to the white population. Slavery still flourished in the South, and the only way to civilize the Native American tribes was to destroy their way of life and convert them to the white man's customs and the Christian religion.

In 1845, six years after O'Sullivan wrote his article, he rallied support for the annexation of Texas and wrote the quote that gave a name to America's guiding principle of westward expansion. O'Sullivan said that it was Americans' "manifest destiny to overspread the continent allotted by Providence for the free development of our yearly multiplying millions."

Westward expansion accelerated in the 1840s and 1850s with the addition of Texas, Kansas, and Nebraska to the Union, and the discovery of gold in California. After the Civil War, Americans raced to blaze new trails to and through the West, and then ditch those old wagon roads as soon as possible for the faster, safer, and easier mode of travel, the railroad.

All of that progress required the subjugation of Native American tribes and their removal from their ancestral lands. Naturally, they wouldn't leave without a fight. And by the late 1860s, General Phil Sheridan and General William Tecumseh Sherman were advocating all-out war against the tribes. If the tribes wouldn't submit peacefully and agree to live on the most desolate, undesirable pieces of land on the continent, they would be killed. To the generals' way of thinking, violent conflict was inevitable. So America might as well be the aggressor and get it over with. The faster it was done, the faster America could say that the West was simultaneously safe and open for business.

While Red Cloud fought his war on the northern plains, members of the tribes of the southern plains signed the Medicine Lodge Treaty of 1867. But, as always, the treaty did little to stop the fighting between the tribes and the soldiers who tried to secure roads to the West for settlers. By the autumn of 1868, General Sheridan was ready to take the first major, coordinated step toward removing or annihilating the Plains Indians.

Sheridan devised a strategy that used three army columns from three different forts on the southern plains. The columns would strike from different directions and use speed and surprise to kill or capture the enemy. But the first stage of the plan featured just one column in action: the Seventh Cavalry led by Lieutenant Colonel Custer. The other two columns, one of which included scouts Wild Bill Hickok and Buffalo Bill Cody, were waylaid by early winter snowstorms.

Custer's men still called him "General" to honor his brevet rank during the Civil War, but in the smaller postwar army, he was bumped back to lieutenant colonel. Less than a week after Custer's column departed Fort Dodge in Kansas, his detachment of scouts, led by Major Joel Elliott, found the trail of a Cheyenne village that was led by Chief Black Kettle. Black Kettle had survived the Sand Creek massacre in southern Colorado four years earlier, an event that helped spark Red Cloud's War. But he would not survive Custer's assault.

On November 27, 1868, Custer's men attacked the village along the Washita River near present-day Cheyenne, Oklahoma. The cavalry burned the village, killed combatants and noncombatants alike, and captured 53 women and children. But during the attack, Major Elliott's detachment of 17 men advanced beyond the main assault force and ran headlong into a charging horde of more than one thousand Kiowa and Arapaho warriors. Black Kettle's village was small, maybe 250 people total. But beyond his village, tucked into a loop of the Washita River, were two larger villages. Warriors from the Kiowa and Arapaho villages rushed toward the fight at Black Kettle's village and swarmed Major Elliott's detachment.

When Custer saw the wave of warriors racing toward his men, he withdrew across the Washita River and marched back to the camp that acted as a staging area for the attack. Custer claimed victory, but he made no attempt to rescue Major Elliott's detachment or recover the bodies in a timely fashion, and those decisions infuriated Captain Frederick Benteen. Benteen was a close friend of Major Elliott, and Benteen believed Custer cared more for personal glory than the safety of his men. This campaign would seem eerily familiar to Benteen in the future.

Seven years after the Battle of the Washita, General Sheridan stood in President Grant's office and said it was time to try the same tactic against the tribes of the northern plains who refused to sign treaties or set foot on reservations. Grant reluctantly agreed, but with a caveat: he wanted legal cover for the action. He needed to justify the campaign by saying the tribes broke the Fort Laramie Treaty.

Grant was in a tight spot. He seemed like a man who genuinely appreciated the destructive history of America toward Native American tribes. He didn't want to continue the policies of previous generations that forced the tribes onto reservations or killed them in the attempt. But most of the country cried out for more land and more resources—namely, gold. And Americans had clearly proven that they were going to move west regardless of Grant's feelings or opinions. So, Grant talked himself into approving Sheridan's plan by finding a tepid middle ground. By 1876, it was clear that certain groups within a few tribes were not going to sign a treaty or live on a reservation. Grant could ask for all the legal cover he wanted, and his administration could state as many righteous goals for the campaign as it desired, but Grant had to know that there was a high likelihood of significant bloodshed. Grant had tried to buy the Black Hills, but failed. And he couldn't hold back the flood of westward expansion. His only choice was to compartmentalize his inner turmoil and give Sheridan the green light.

Sheridan worked quickly. One week after the meeting in late November 1875, an Indian inspector in the Interior Department wrote a report that enumerated a list of grievances against the Lakota and Cheyenne of the northern plains. The list was full of exaggerations and outright lies. In fact, the year of 1875 had been the most peaceful in recent memory. Grant must have cringed when he read it, but he was past the point of no return. In late December, runners went out to the winter camps with a message: be on a reservation by January 31, 1876, or the U.S. Army would wage war.

For most tribes, the time frame was a joke. In the dead of winter, the majority couldn't make it by the deadline even if they'd wanted to. The handful of tribes who wanted to and *could* make it, did. But many didn't try because it was impossible. And a third group had no intention of complying with any order or request by the American government.

General Sheridan put his plan into motion. He wanted to attack while snow was still on the ground. If the weather warmed, and the scattered winter camps merged into large summer villages, and Native American warriors and their ponies returned to full strength, the odds of a victory for the U.S. Army decreased dramatically. It was imperative for the cavalry to strike now, while the tribes were at their weakest and most vulnerable. Sheridan organized the same three-pronged strategy he used against the tribes of the southern plains.

In the 1876 version, Lieutenant Colonel Custer would lead the Seventh Cavalry west from its current home at Fort Lincoln near Bismarck in Dakota Territory. General George Crook would lead a column north from Fort Fetterman in Wyoming Territory. And Colonel John Gibbon would lead a column east from Fort Ellis near Bozeman in Montana Territory. The three forces would locate and attack the winter camps of the Lakota and Cheyenne that were expected to be somewhere in eastern Dakota Territory or southern Montana Territory.

On February 1, the day after the deadline in the declaration, General Sheridan had full authorization to carry out his mission. He wanted to strike that very month. From his headquarters in Chicago, he urged his field commanders to get started. But he was about to experience a series of disappointments. If he felt a sense of momentum, it wouldn't last. His grand strategy would experience setbacks. His commanders would underperform in the field. And it would all culminate in a catastrophic loss of life for the U.S. Army in a little more than three months.

On February 2, 1876, while Sheridan organized the conquest of the northern plains and Bat Masterson slowly recovered in Sweetwater, eight men met in New York City to formalize the first major sports agreement in American history. The men owned eight successful baseball clubs, and they gathered in a room at the Grand Central Hotel in Manhattan to form a new professional baseball league. It wasn't the first professional league in baseball history, but it would be the first to stand the test of time. They called it the National League of Professional Base Ball Clubs. "Baseball," as a single word, was not yet common, and the league was soon referred to simply as *the National League.*

The effort was spearheaded by William Hulbert, the owner of the Chicago White Stockings. He was frustrated by the previous entity, the National Association of Base Ball Players. Hulbert wanted the new league to improve the structure, organization, and business of the sport. Six clubs carried over from the old NA: the Chicago White Stockings, the Philadelphia Athletics, the Boston Red Stockings, the Hartford Dark Blues, the New York Mutuals, and the St. Louis Brown Stockings. They added two new franchises for the one and only season that the original eight would be together: the Cincinnati Red Stockings and the Louisville Grays.

That same month, Al Spalding, the twenty-five-year-old starting pitcher for the Chicago White Stockings, opened a sporting goods store with his brother Walter in Chicago. It was called A. G. Spalding & Brothers, and the company quickly developed the official baseball for the National League. When the American League began in 1901, Spalding's company provided the baseballs for it, as well. For one hundred years, Spalding supplied baseballs to the major leagues.

Opening day was scheduled for April 22, and the clubs agreed to play seventy games over the course of the 1876 season. There were four eastern teams—New York, Boston, Hartford, Philadelphia—and four western teams—Chicago, Cincinnati, St. Louis, Louisville—and each club played ten games against the others. At the end of the season, the club with the most wins would be declared the champion. On that frigid day in early February, America's national pastime was truly born.

Unbeknownst to the baseball owners in New York, General Sheridan hollered for action from his headquarters in Chicago. It would take nearly six weeks for the army to strike a target. And when it did, the strike didn't send a signal of impending doom to the tribes. It acted as a rallying cry that produced the exact situation that Sheridan wanted to avoid.

— 2 —

THE POWDER RIVER FIGHT

I n the first five days of March of 1876, three things happened that varied in notoriety at the time but produced monumental ripple effects throughout the year. On March 1, General George Crook began the campaign to "chastise" the tribes of the northern plains. On March 2, the U.S. House of Representatives impeached Secretary of War William Belknap. And on March 5, Wild Bill Hickok got married.

General Sheridan wanted his commanders to be in the field in February, but that didn't happen. Custer's Seventh Cavalry was stationed at Fort Lincoln, south of Bismarck, in modern-day North Dakota. Bismarck is just 150 miles from the Canadian border. In February, the blizzards and subzero temperatures made travel impossible, which was the predominant reason why an extensive winter campaign had never been attempted. Conditions were not much better in northern Wyoming or eastern Montana, and the three army columns remained at their posts. Sheridan likely fumed, but all he could do was wait. His wait ended exactly one month after the "hostile" declaration when General Crook led four hundred cavalrymen north from Fort Fetterman in east-central Wyoming Territory.

The fort was located near the current town of Douglas and was named for Captain William Fetterman, who was killed with the rest of his command in the major battle of Red Cloud's War ten years earlier. For the next two weeks, Crook's force followed the old Bozeman Trail and trekked through snow and bitterly cold temperatures toward southern Montana.

While the column marched, politics in Washington, D.C., exploded and further ruined Sheridan's hope of a decisive winter campaign.

The day after Crook's column departed, Secretary of War William Belknap sprinted to the White House and handed his resignation to President Grant. The House of Representatives was about to vote on articles of impeachment against Belknap, and the secretary hoped he could avoid the consequences if he were no longer in office. He quickly discovered he was wrong. Six years of graft and fraud had been uncovered, and he would face the charges whether or not he was in office. Later that day, the House voted unanimously to impeach Belknap for "criminally disregarding his duty as Secretary of War and basely prostituting his high office to his lust for private gain."

The juicy wording referred to a scheme to receive kickbacks from the trading post at Fort Sill in Indian Territory. For six years, Belknap received regular quarterly payments that totaled more than $20,000. In Washington, D.C., he threw lavish parties and provided his first and second wives with extravagant luxuries. Many wondered how he could afford the indulgences on a government salary of $8,000 per year, and the questions eventually grew into an investigation. When the truth was revealed, he rushed to Grant's office to resign his post before he could be impeached by the House and tried by the Senate. He dodged neither outcome, and his Senate trial helped delay General Sheridan's battle plans on the northern plains. The delay would prove devastating for the U.S. Army.

Three days after Secretary Belknap began the worst six months of his life, Wild Bill Hickok began one of the happiest days of his. He was in Cheyenne, Wyoming, roughly 250 miles south of General Crook's column, and he was about to marry Agnes Lake. Their courtship had been long and intermittent, but they were finally ready to tie the knot. They met in the summer of 1871 when Hickok was the marshal of Abilene. Agnes arrived with her circus for a three-night stint in the most prominent of the Kansas cow towns. Hickok attended at least one of the performances and met the proprietor while she was in town.

Agnes, whose name at birth is still debated, was born in Europe in 1826. Her family moved to America when she was six years old. When she was nineteen, she fell in love with a circus performer named William Lake Thatcher. William called himself Bill Lake professionally, and when Agnes ran away with him and married him, she became Agnes Lake. She joined his circus troupe, and they eventually started their own show under the odd name of the Hippo-Olympiad and Mammoth Circus.

William was tragically killed in 1869, and Agnes inherited the show. At that time, she became the first woman to own and operate a circus. From April to October, she and her troupe traveled the country and performed in small towns and big cities. But by the spring of

1876, she was thinking about retirement. She was forty-nine years old, her children were adults, and she was on the verge of becoming a grandmother. Agnes had known the most famous lawman in the West for five years, and they'd been exchanging letters regularly since a reunion in Rochester, New York, in the spring of 1874. But, to use Henry Wadsworth Longfellow's words from that same year, Agnes and Bill were "ships that pass in the night." They felt a connection, but they couldn't get together.

When Bill arrived in Rochester that spring, he was in town for what turned out to be his final performance as an actor. In the fall of 1873, he joined his friends Buffalo Bill Cody and Texas Jack Omohundro in the cast of a play called *Scouts of the Plains*. It was a long-winded, melodramatic production that mostly featured the three well-known scouts sitting around a campfire telling stories about their adventures on the plains. The original version of the play was written by popular newspaperman and novelist Ned Buntline and was titled *Scouts of the Prairie*.

Buntline was a notorious drunk and a liar. No one knows for sure how many women he married and abandoned, but the number could be in the double digits. And he singlehandedly started two deadly riots, the second of which would still be the worst riot in the history of New York City if not for the Civil War draft riot of 1863. By the fall of 1873, Cody had forced Buntline out of the production, hired his friend Wild Bill as a replacement, and changed the name of the play.

Scouts of the Plains was trashed by critics and loved by viewers. But one of the many problems with the production, especially in the mind of Wild Bill Hickok, was that the audience loved it for the wrong reasons. The play was supposed to be serious. It was supposed to give eastern audiences a glimpse of life in the West. But Buntline's writing was so over-the-top and so out of character for three men who were real, legendary scouts of the plains that audiences ended up laughing through the entire show.

Hickok hated acting; he knew he was bad at it, and he despised the laughter. But the play raked in cash. Despite the quality of the writing and the acting, audiences packed the theater at Niblo's Garden on Broadway and Prince Street in Manhattan for every show in the fall of 1873 and the winter of 1874/75.

By the spring of 1874, Cody decided it was time to take the show on the road. When the production stopped in Rochester, Hickok hit his breaking point. He quit in the middle of a performance and walked out of the venue. It was an abrupt end to his short career in show business, but the timing was fortuitous. Agnes Lake was in Rochester at the same time to start the touring season. It's reasonable to assume that Agnes and Bill spent time together, but details are elusive. Neither was willing to commit to the lifestyle of the other at the time, but they began corresponding regularly from that point forward. Two years later, in the spring of 1876, the time was right. Agnes wanted to stop her heavy travel schedule, and Bill was ready to commit to marriage. She was forty-nine years old, and he was two months shy of his thirty-ninth birthday.

Bill and Agnes married in Cheyenne on March 5 and took an eastbound train to St. Louis that very night. They arrived in her hometown of Cincinnati, Ohio, a few days later to begin a two-week honeymoon . . . right around the time General Crook's column crossed into Montana Territory. Crook was about to provide General Sheridan with the offensive action he craved, but it would only leave Sheridan feeling more exasperated.

* * *

In mid-March, the four hundred cavalrymen of Crook's column marched north along the Tongue River, one of the major waterways in southern Montana. They turned back south and east toward the Powder River, and Crook's scouts spotted signs of a small village. The Powder River country of southeastern Montana had been home to the Lakota and Cheyenne for generations, and as Crook advanced into the region, he attacked the first available target.

A village of approximately sixty-five lodges sat on the banks of the Powder River just inside the border of Montana Territory. Early in the morning on March 17, a detachment of troops charged into the village as its inhabitants slept. In the frenzy of thundering horses and gunshots and shouts, the villagers fled. Their lodges were at the mercy of the soldiers, and Crook's men began burning the village.

Approximately 150 warriors regrouped and found high ground on some bluffs above the camp. They fired at the soldiers and eventually drove them out of the village, but the damage was done. The villagers suffered two dead and several wounded, and their homes and possessions now smoldered in the snow. They had no choice but to abandon the site and try to find help at another village. As it happened, the nearest village was led by Crazy Horse, and he and his band were camped forty miles south of Sitting Bull.

Crook had hoped to find Crazy Horse's village, but he missed. By attacking the Cheyenne village, he succeeded in setting off a chain reaction that united Crazy Horse and Sitting Bull and helped them build an army.

The brief engagement was technically a success for the cavalry. Crook's detachment had located a village, attacked it, and destroyed it. But the action was a disappointment to both Crook and Sheridan. By the time Crook's column found the village, his men were cold, hungry, and miserable. A sustained campaign wasn't possible, and the village was largely inconsequential, relative to the overall mission. But Crook's attack proved to be very consequential for the tribes of the northern plains. It served as a call to arms for Sitting Bull and Crazy Horse.

Crook probably didn't know it at the time, but the village was a Cheyenne group led by Chief Old Bear that also included some visiting Oglala and Minneconjou of the Lakota. The visiting Oglala offered to guide the entire camp to the village of Crazy Horse, which was situated several miles to the northeast on the East Fork of the Little Powder River. While Crook's force endured the long march back to Fort Fetterman, the refugees tromped through the snow for four days toward Crazy Horse's village.

When they arrived, they told their story, and the Oglala villagers offered as much aid as possible. But Crazy Horse's village was also relatively small. It wasn't equipped to house and feed roughly two hundred extra people. The entire camp packed and began the trek to Sitting Bull's village. The Hunkpapa medicine man and his people were about forty miles north on the banks of Spring Creek, a tributary of the Powder River. The journey took the rest of the month, but the weather was warming and travel was becoming easier—and those were the conditions that worried General Sheridan above all others.

While Crazy Horse's new village moved toward Sitting Bull's village, Wild Bill Hickok returned to Cheyenne, Wyoming, with a plan to begin the journey that would be the last of his life. He had spent two weeks in Cincinnati meeting his wife's friends and family, and then he stopped by his own family's home in Troy Grove, Illinois, to visit his mother. He hadn't been home since 1869 when he surprised his family by showing up with the spearhead of a Cheyenne lance lodged in his leg.

At that point in his life, he was a messenger and a freighter for the army. He was delivering dispatches from Fort Wallace in western Kansas to Fort Lyon in eastern Colorado. During the 150-mile trip, he killed a buffalo and cooked some of the meat. A small group of Cheyenne warriors spotted the smoke from his cook fire and attacked. He killed or wounded six of the seven, but not before one of them stabbed him with a lance. He barely survived the rest of the trip to Fort Lyon, and the post's doctor confessed that he wasn't qualified to remove the part of the spearhead that was deeply embedded in Hickok's leg. The doctor recommended amputation, and Bill said absolutely not.

Hickok took a train to Illinois and placed himself in the care of a surgeon he trusted. The doctor successfully withdrew the remainder of the weapon without severing an artery or amputating the leg. Bill spent about six weeks recuperating at his family's home and then returned to the West to continue his adventures.

That was seven years earlier, and so much had happened since then. Whatever Bill chose to share with his family, he did it in limited fashion. He stayed just two days before boarding a train to St. Louis. He was a man on a mission, and he needed to get to work. He and Agnes had decided on a plan during their honeymoon: Bill would follow the gold rush to the Black Hills, and Agnes would wait in Cincinnati for word of his success. Hopefully, he would return to Cincinnati with bags of gold or he would send word for her to join him in the Hills. Either result was fine with her, but he needed to get started.

In St. Louis, Hickok tried to recruit prospectors to join him on a grand expedition to the Black Hills to strike it rich. Somewhat surprisingly, he found no volunteers. Maybe they were reticent because of the journey. It was a long and difficult trip to Deadwood Gulch, the headquarters of the gold rush. But throughout human history, physical hardship had never been a major obstacle in the pursuit of gold. Indeed, at the moment, a thriving community was erupting at breakneck speed from the mud and muck of the gulch. So maybe the problem was Hickok himself. Maybe his star had faded more than he'd realized. He was once the most famous lawman in the West, maybe in the entire country. Hundreds, or possibly thousands, of dime novels had been written about him, despite the fact that he had worn a badge for a grand total of about thirteen months: he had been the marshal of Hays City, Kansas, for about four months and the marshal of Abilene for nine months.

Hickok had killed at least three men while cleaning up Hays City and famously killed saloon owner Phil Coe in Abilene. He had killed or mortally wounded three men in Nebraska while defending the family of an agent of the Overland Stage Company. He had killed Davis Tutt in Springfield, Missouri, in July of 1865, an event that is commonly referred to as the first recorded quick-draw gunfight in the American West. He survived numerous engagements with Cheyenne war parties. He had been a scout, a spy, and a sharpshooter in the Civil War. And he had staged shooting exhibitions in which he dazzled paying customers with his speed and accuracy with a gun. But by March of 1876, the exploits that made him famous must have felt like ancient history.

Since the bulk of Wild Bill's famous activities, he had been arrested for vagrancy in Kansas City and then in Cheyenne. He had produced a live show called *The Daring Buffalo Chase of the Plains* that was a comical failure. He had suffered through a miserable experience in the stage play *Scouts of the Plains*. He had developed a problem with his eyes. There was no formal diagnosis, but his vision was failing, and his eyes were constantly irritated and sensitive to light. He now wore glasses with blue lenses. He carried a cane made from a billiard cue. And he rarely attempted to display his talents with a gun. He had survived for the past two years on his ability at the poker table, and that was a tough way to make a living. He wasn't an old man—he was two months shy of thirty-nine years old—but he felt like one.

In St. Louis, Hickok didn't dwell on the reason for the lack of interest from potential prospectors. He boarded the train again and continued to Cheyenne. He made it back to his temporary home in late March and reunited with his good friend Colorado Charlie Utter. Charlie was succeeding where Bill failed. Charlie was organizing a wagon train to head for the Black Hills later that spring or early in the summer. Hickok readily joined the group and helped Charlie make preparations.

While the two old friends prepped for the trip, forces aligned themselves throughout the West for the historic events of the summer: a major development in Deadwood turned the steady stream of gold seekers into a flood; Crazy Horse delivered his refugees to Sitting Bull's camp, and together, they formed the nucleus of the army that would fight along the banks of the Little Bighorn River in two months' time; Bat Masterson returned to Kansas at the perfect moment to join his friend Wyatt Earp in the wickedest cow town on the plains; and Lieutenant Colonel George Armstrong Custer became mired in politics in Washington, D.C., and caused yet more delays to the expedition that was supposed to be the last great campaign against the Native American tribes.

3

A POLITICAL FIASCO

Custer spent a good portion of the winter of 1876 enjoying a long furlough with his wife, Libbie, in New York City. Even if the weather in February and early March hadn't hindered the Seventh Cavalry's attempts to begin Sheridan's campaign, the mission would have been delayed because Custer wasn't at his post to lead the unit. In March, Custer appealed to General Sheridan to extend the furlough yet again, and Sheridan denied the request. Custer needed to get back to Fort Lincoln, prepare his men, and get into the field while the tribes were still in their winter camps. With mixed feelings, Custer and Libbie returned to the fort. Custer was excited about the action of the upcoming campaign, but he also loved the nonstop attention he received in New York as America's number one Indian fighter.

No sooner had Custer arrived at Fort Lincoln than he received a summons to report to Washington. He was called to testify before a House of Representatives committee led by Congressman Hiester Clymer. Custer sat for the committee on March 29 and explained everything he knew about the scandal involving Secretary Belknap. Custer's testimony was convincing and damning, though he freely admitted he had no proof to support his statements.

At that point in the process, the lack of proof wasn't a problem. The committee was still investigating; the Senate trial hadn't started; and the publicity around Custer's testimony helped the impeachment cause almost as much as the testimony itself. *The New York Times* reported, "Gen. Custer's testimony before Clymer's committee to-day reveals some of the bold rascalities of Indian and Army traders, and reflects severely upon the late Secretary of War."

Custer would sit for the committee again on April 4, but between his appearances, pivotal decisions were made on the northern plains. The tribes who were viewed as hostile renegades by the U.S. government coalesced around Sitting Bull. They strengthened their numbers and prepared for the war that was threatened by American leaders in the East.

While Custer met with military officers and elected officials during his downtime in Washington, Crazy Horse delivered the Cheyenne refugees to Sitting Bull's camp. The previous summer, during a Sun Dance, Sitting Bull had bonded with a Cheyenne medicine man. They pledged themselves to an alliance and swore that their people would help and protect each other. Now, Sitting Bull lived up to his side of the pledge. His Hunkpapa welcomed the Cheyenne refugees and gave them food, blankets, and new lodges.

When the members of Crazy Horse's village and Old Bear's Cheyenne village had settled into their new camp, the chiefs of the new combined settlement convened a meeting. For three days, they sat around council fires and debated the situation on the high plains.

They were all familiar with the order from the white man's government in the East. Most in the group had no intention of delivering themselves to reservations, or "agencies" as they were called at the time. But one of the sad parts of Old Bear's story was that he was leading his village toward an agency to comply with the order when it was attacked by General Crook. Old Bear had been following his own timeline, and he made no attempt to rush to an agency by the January 31 deadline, but he was going nonetheless. And then his village had been destroyed. Now, Old Bear and his people were in Sitting Bull's village, and Sitting Bull vowed to help.

Sitting Bull advocated a course of patience and avoidance. He would never make peace with white men, but he didn't want to initiate a fight, either. He would fight if he had to, without question. But for the moment, he said their new combined village should move north and west, farther away from white society. He also said they should send runners to the agencies. The weather was warming, and warriors at the agencies would soon leave to go hunting. Sitting Bull wanted them to bring their families to his camp. He wanted strength and safety in numbers.

In the wake of General Crook's attack, the Cheyenne considered themselves at war with the white population. Sitting Bull's Hunkpapa band and Crazy Horse's Oglala band agreed to support their Cheyenne friends, and they needed more warriors for the effort. The recruits would soon stream in by the hundreds, but before the runners even had the chance to arrive at the agencies, new additions arrived every day.

News of the army's attack on Old Bear's village spread rapidly across the northern plains, and seemingly every small group in the area plotted a course for Sitting Bull's camp. The order from Washington promised a fight if the tribes did not comply, and if it was going to happen, the Lakota and Cheyenne wanted to be ready. To protect the village while it grew in strength and size, Sitting Bull led the people deeper into the heart of southern Montana.

Custer's second appearance before Congressman Clymer's committee did nothing to help his status with his bosses. A portion of Custer's combined testimony infuriated General Phil Sheridan. And then Custer outdid himself by infuriating the president of the United States. A month earlier, right after impeachment proceedings began in the House of Representatives, President Grant's brother Orvil admitted complicity in the scandal. It was a body blow to Grant, who seemed to be absorbing punches from all angles those days. And now Custer, oblivious as always to the consequences of his actions, added criticism of Orvil Grant to his testimony.

Custer's salacious testimony prompted some newspapers to speculate that a court-martial might be in the works. Custer didn't believe he had done anything wrong, and he was stunned to discover, as the month progressed, that some of the most powerful men in the country were angry with him. He thought his trip to the East Coast would be quick, but now the congressional committee refused to release him to return to his unit.

And while he sat in Washington, stranded and confused, four miners struck the mother lode near Deadwood. It was a mineral deposit that contained more wealth than many nations on Earth. It is probably a safe bet to say that the discovery of riches in the Homestake Mine directly and indirectly impacted more people in the United States than any other event in 1876.

The now legendary Homestake Mine was owned and operated by Hank Harney, Alexander Engh, and brothers Fred and Moses

Manuel. Less than a week after Custer testified for the second time, the miners struck one of the richest gold deposits in history.

The original ore was found on April 9 in Bobtail Gulch, two miles from Deadwood. But the mine began as a simple operation, like all the others in the Black Hills. The men panned in the creek and chipped away at the surface. After a relatively short period of work, they realized they had a big one on their hands. The veins of gold and silver kept going deeper into the earth. The miners carved trenches, and then expanded the trenches, and then dug shafts. The operation was starting to look like a genuine bonanza, and a rough community had been in place in Deadwood Gulch for only a little more than a month.

Prospectors had been poking around the Black Hills for forty years, and they had been rushing to the area since the fall of 1874, when the existence of gold was widely reported by the newspapermen who accompanied Custer's expedition. It is commonly believed that one or two groups of miners "discovered" Deadwood Gulch in November of 1875, and by March of 1876, a crude settlement was rising along the banks of Whitewood Creek. The creek runs through the bottom of the narrow gulch and carved it over millennia.

Through the winter of 1875/76, miners staked claims in the gulch and then started building cabins, shops, and saloons out of canvas and rough-hewn timber. The pace of construction was dizzying. By the end of April 1876, the town of Deadwood had been laid out and a provisional government was in place, with merchant E. B. Farnum as the chairman of the first citizens committee of Deadwood.

Deadwood was officially open for business, despite its status as an illegal community. The Black Hills still belonged to the Lakota, though the bloody conflict that would settle the debate over ownership was just two months away.

While Deadwood raced into existence, and Sitting Bull led his expanding village away from the Powder River, Custer was finally released from further testimony by the congressional committee. He had been hanging out in Washington for more than two weeks since his second appearance before the committee, but now he hurried to New York to attend to some business before he caught a train back to Fort Lincoln on April 24.

The trip to Fort Lincoln didn't happen. Instead, he received a summons to return to Washington to potentially testify in front of the Senate. Custer thought the investment in the impeachment proceedings would be a week, or ten days at most. Now, he had been on the East Coast for more than a month. Somehow, he had managed to anger both General Sheridan and President Grant, and it was about to get worse.

The day after Custer returned to Washington, Grant removed him from command of the Dakota Column for the long-delayed campaign against the tribes of the northern plains. Custer was devastated. He sought advice from General Sherman. Sherman told him to seek an audience with Grant. Custer replied that he had tried to see the president twice and had been rebuffed both times, but he would try again. He went to the White House and settled into a chair outside the president's office. He waited, and waited, and waited. After five hours, Grant sent word that he would not see Custer. Custer thought he was out of options. He acquired the requisite permissions to leave the city and began the thirteen-hundred-mile trip back to Dakota Territory.

The day before Custer was released by Congressman Clymer's committee, the city council of Wichita, Kansas, denied the reinstatement of deputy marshal Wyatt Earp. A little more than two weeks earlier, at the same time as Crazy Horse's village arrived at Sitting Bull's camp, Deputy Earp punched the former marshal.

That April, Wichita was in the middle of election season. The former marshal, Bill Smith, wanted his old job back. He was running against the current marshal, Mike Meagher. Meagher and Smith had traded the badge back and forth for the past couple of years, and in Smith's latest bid to return to office, he might have made some disparaging remarks about Wyatt's family. Wyatt's older brother Jim worked in saloons in Wichita, and Jim's wife, Bessie, ran a brothel and had been repeatedly prosecuted for prostitution. The slandering of Wyatt's family has always been a theory without evidence, but *something* made Wyatt snap. On April 2, the day before impeachment proceedings began in the Senate and one week before the Homestake Mine was founded, Wyatt tracked down Bill Smith and started a fight.

Marshal Meagher caught his deputy in the middle of the altercation and had no choice but to fire Wyatt on the spot and arrest him for disturbing the peace. A little more than two weeks later, the city council sat in judgment of the young officer and denied his reinstatement to the force by a vote of 6–2. A second vote resulted in a 4–4 tie that still kept Wyatt out of service. But it was now late April, and the cattle season was ramping up. Apparently, Wyatt was allowed to stay on as a temporary deputy because the council approved a payment of forty dollars for twenty days of work. But after that, he was done in Wichita.

Wyatt had been a deputy marshal for exactly one year, and it was the latest of several brief stints as a lawman for the twenty-seven-year-old. The first was as a constable in Lamar, Missouri. The second will always be a matter of debate, but it's possible that

Wyatt served as the marshal of Ellsworth for a short time in 1873 during its rowdy heyday as a Kansas cow town. In Stuart Lake's fanciful biography of Wyatt in 1931, Lake claimed that Wyatt singlehandedly backed down a group of Texas cowboys that included Ben Thompson. Ben's younger brother, Billy, had drunkenly shot the county sheriff with a shotgun, and the town of Ellsworth seemed primed for an all-out gun battle between Texas cowboys and the city lawmen.

The shootout didn't happen, and it's possible that Wyatt—a relative unknown in Ellsworth at the time—stepped in, talked to Ben Thompson, and helped cool the situation. Thompson was arrested without incident, possibly by Wyatt. If so, it seems likely that the arrest was Wyatt's only action as a spontaneous lawman in Ellsworth.

With the benefit of hindsight, Ben Thompson could boast an impressive list of run-ins with legendary lawmen between 1871 and 1876. He spent the cattle season of 1871 in Abilene running the Bull's Head Tavern while Wild Bill Hickok was the marshal. When Hickok killed Thompson's business partner, Phil Coe, Thompson wisely moved away. Two years later, in August 1873, he crossed paths with Wyatt Earp in Ellsworth. Three and a half years after that, he played a role in helping Bat Masterson in Sweetwater.

Now, in April of 1876, the Thompson brothers were in Texas, and Bat had returned to his family's home near Wichita, Kansas. He had spent two months in Sweetwater recovering from his gunshot wound and then journeyed to the family farm to rest in a more peaceful environment.

The Masterson clan started in Quebec, Canada, before moving to New York, Illinois, and finally Kansas. Bat was saddled with the lengthy handle of Bartholomew William Barclay Masterson at birth. By the time he was eighteen and ready to leave the family farm, he had settled on the nickname "Bat." In the fall of 1871, Bat and his older brother, Ed, who was nineteen, traded the backbreaking labor of farming in eastern Kansas for the backbreaking and bloody work of buffalo hunting in western Kansas. According to Bat's friend Billy Dixon, who was at the Second Battle of Adobe Walls and on the campaign to save the four kidnapped girls, that first hunting season was when Bat met Wyatt Earp. The two friends spent the next five years on separate adventures, but they were about to reunite in Dodge City, the new hub for Texas cattle that would soon be called the Queen of the Cow Towns.

That spring, Bat Masterson wasn't the only legendary figure who returned home to the Midwest. The nation's most famous outlaw, Jesse James, had been lying low after a prolonged battle with the Pinkerton National Detective Agency, but now he was back home in Kearney, Missouri, and anxious to rob a train.

It had been a hell of a year for Jesse James. More accurately, it had been a hell of a two-year stretch. In fact, there was no reason to limit it to two years. The entire ten-year span of Jesse's outlaw career had been a wild ride of ups and downs.

Jesse and his older brother, Frank, rode with Quantrill's Raiders during the Civil War. The irregular militia unit wasn't officially part of the Confederate army, but it fought for the South anyway. Quantrill's Raiders—organized by William Quantrill—were guerilla fighters. In parlance of the times, they were bushwhackers. They specialized in terrorizing towns and murdering Union soldiers in a variety of ways. By the end of the war, the group was arguably the most notorious and savage unit in either army.

In February 1866, ten months after the end of the war, a dozen men robbed the Clay County Savings Association in Liberty, Missouri. It was the first daylight peacetime bank robbery in American history, and it was almost certainly perpetrated by men who rode with Quantrill's Raiders. There will never be conclusive evidence about the identities of the robbers, but it's widely accepted that the heist was the work of the men who went on to form the James-Younger Gang.

Over the next six years, various configurations of the gang robbed banks, trains, and stagecoaches. Their crime spree spread across Iowa, Missouri, Kentucky, Arkansas, Louisiana, and possibly West Virginia. Along the way, a newspaper editor named John Newman Edwards made them famous. He worshipped the old Missouri guerilla raiders, and he dedicated pages of both *The Kansas City Times* and the *St. Louis Dispatch* to romanticizing their exploits during the Civil War and justifying and defending their exploits as outlaws. But the notoriety, and, of course, the robberies themselves, drew heightened attention from the law.

Local posses routinely failed to catch the bandits, and eventually the Pinkerton National Detective Agency was hired to stop them. The agency was founded by Allan Pinkerton, the man who was responsible for providing protection for President Abraham Lincoln during the Civil War and running the Union's network of spies. Pinkerton assigned his son Robert to apprehend Jesse James, but Robert failed, as well.

The turning point came in January 1874 with the Gads Hill train robbery. Gads Hill was a hamlet in southwestern Missouri that was an ideal spot for a train robbery. It was a tiny, isolated community that could be easily overpowered by a small group of aggressive men. By the time of the Gads Hill job, Jesse loved the attention from the media so much that he wrote his own press release about the robbery. The outlaws successfully escaped with their money, as always, but the Gads Hill heist prompted more strenuous efforts to catch the gang than had been undertaken in the past. The Adams Express Company hired the Pinkerton agency to stop the gang once and for all.

With the rise of the railroads after the Civil War and the heavy migration of white society westward, companies were created to move money and other valuables safely and securely from place to place. The Adams Express Company was one of the largest. It had contracts with railroads to transport safes that held money, papers, and other valuable property. The express company sent a man to supervise the delivery of each safe. He was called an express messenger, and in the earliest days of train robberies, he was more of a chaperone than an armed guard. The James-Younger Gang rarely had trouble subduing and forcing the cooperation of the express messenger.

After the Gads Hill robbery, the Pinkerton agency was back on the case. This time, there would be a yearlong war between the gang and the agency, and Allan Pinkerton was determined to win at all costs. But within three months, the cost would prove too high for the president of the Adams Express Company.

Pinkerton's first plan was to do what his company did best: undercover infiltration. He sent three detectives to Missouri to get close to the gang, and two of the three didn't come back alive. In March of 1874, the body of the first was found by the side of a road with a note pinned to his clothing that read, "This to all detectives." The commonly held belief is that Jesse James, Arthur McCoy, and Jim Anderson murdered the detective. McCoy was part of the Gads Hill robbery, and Anderson was the younger brother of Bloody Bill Anderson, an infamous lieutenant of William Quantrill.

One week after the body of the first detective was found, a pair of detectives ended up in a shootout with Jim and John Younger. The detectives were guided by a local man, a former deputy sheriff. The deputy and one of the detectives died in the gunfight. The other detective narrowly escaped. But in the process, they struck a blow for the agency. John Younger also died in the shootout. He was the first gang member to fall.

The four Younger brothers—Cole, John, Jim, and Bob—grew up in Jackson County, Missouri, one of the four counties in the western part of the state that formed the stronghold of the James-Younger Gang. Directly north of Jackson County was Clay County, the home of the James boys. The two sets of brothers, along with the other miscellaneous members of the gang, rode together at different times during the Civil War. They were the core of the most famous outlaw gang in America, and they had just suffered their first fatality.

The murders of two detectives and a deputy sheriff caused the president of the Adams Express Company to stop his pursuit of the outlaws. The chase became too bloody for the president, but it stoked Allan Pinkerton's fire for revenge. He said, "My blood was spilt, and they must repay. There is no use talking. They must die."

Pinkerton's second plan was essentially the same as his first—infiltrate the gang—but now he took his time with it. He sent undercover operatives to western Missouri and slowly built a small network of sympathizers. The outlaws were loved by some in the area but feared by many others. Not everyone viewed them as heroes who struck at institutions that were viewed as Northern oppressors.

On January 25, 1875, ten months after the murders of the detectives, a unit of Pinkertons attacked the home of Jesse's mother and stepfather. Allan Pinkerton's instructions were explicit: "Above everything, destroy the house. Blot it from the face of the Earth."

The agency received a report from one of its informants in Clay County that Jesse, Frank, and longtime friend Clell Miller were at the house that night. The intelligence was accurate, but the outlaws slipped away before the Pinkertons could organize their assault.

In the middle of the night, while eight people slept in the house, the Pinkertons attacked. They tried to burn the house and then threw an incendiary device through a window. Jesse's stepfather, Reuben Samuel, shoved the foreign object into the fireplace to get it out of the living room. The flames heated the device, and it exploded like a bomb. A piece of shrapnel sliced through the right arm of Jesse's mother, Zerelda. Another hit Jesse's eight-year-old half brother, Archie. Archie was Zerelda's final child, and Jesse had persuaded his mother to name the boy after his good friend, Archie Clement, a member of Quantrill's Raiders who was killed in 1866.

Archie Samuel died before sunrise. A doctor amputated Zerelda's arm below the elbow without anesthetic. And Jesse James went looking for revenge.

The Pinkertons worked with three informants in Clay County. The first was a local lawyer. The second was the postmaster in Kearney, the nearest town to the James family farm. Both men fled the county in fear for their lives when they heard about the disastrous attack. The third informant was Daniel Askew, who owned a farm next to the James family. He had allowed a Pinkerton operative to work on his farm for months while monitoring the Jameses' farm. Askew's property was also the staging ground for the assault. Unlike the lawyer and the postmaster, Askew refused to run.

On the night of April 12, 1875, Askew walked out of his house to draw a bucket of water from his well. A mystery man confronted him in the darkness and shot him three times in the head. Askew's wife heard the gunshots, but she couldn't identify the killer, though it didn't require much imagination to narrow the list of suspects to a single name.

Sometime that spring, Jesse and his wife, also named Zerelda, moved to a small town outside Nashville, Tennessee. They may have traveled as far away as Baltimore, Maryland, while they allowed the heat to die down in Missouri after the year of battling the Pinkertons. In August 1875, Zee gave birth to their first child, Jesse Edwards James. Young Jesse's middle name honored John Newman Edwards, the newspaper editor who helped make the elder Jesse famous.

Less than a week after the birth of Jesse's son, four men robbed the Bank of Huntington in Huntington, West Virginia. It was carried out with the swift precision of the James-Younger Gang, though the identities of the four robbers are still in question. The description of one of the robbers matched Cole Younger, which made Frank James a likely candidate for one of the others. Jesse probably wasn't involved, thanks to the birth of his child.

A few months later, in the spring of 1876, Jesse thought it was safe to return home, and he moved his family back to Missouri. According to Hobbs Kerry, a young man who was desperate to meet him, Jesse was anxious to get back to business. Hobbs would spend the next couple of months trying to get close to the James-Younger Gang so that he could pitch an idea for a robbery. When the gang finally let him into the inner circle, it turned out to be a terrible mistake. It led to the only time in ten years when the authorities learned credible evidence about the gang, and it helped push the outlaws to attempt the robbery that destroyed the gang.

It likely went unnoticed by Jesse James, as he resettled in Missouri; and Bat Masterson, as he focused on his recovery; and Wyatt Earp, as he dwelt on the uncertainty of his job in Wichita, but the first baseball game of the new National League was played on April 22. The Philadelphia Athletics hosted the Boston Red Stockings at the Jefferson Grounds in Philadelphia. The home team lost the inaugural contest 6–5, and it was a bad omen for the Athletics. They were in for a rough season, one that ended in a fashion that would have grabbed nationwide headlines in the modern era.

4

NEW LAW IN DODGE

Custer waited anxiously for a reply from President Grant, and on the morning of May 8, it arrived. It had been a week since Custer sat outside the president's office for nearly half a day in a desperate attempt to gain reinstatement before the upcoming campaign on the northern plains. Grant refused an audience. Dejected and seemingly out of options, Custer left the White House and began collecting the necessary permissions to return to his post at Fort Lincoln. The U.S. Senate, the inspector general at the War Department, and General Sherman all granted Custer's request to leave Washington. But, as Custer soon learned, he was one permission short of a full list.

On the evening that Grant refused to see Custer, Custer boarded a train and headed east. He stopped in Monroe, Michigan, and visited his parents and some friends. He also picked up three traveling companions, two of whom were slated to join the upcoming campaign. One was Custer's favorite nephew, Autie Reed, who recently turned eighteen years old. The other was Dick Roberts, the brother of one of Libbie Custer's closest friends. The third new member of the trip was Autie's younger sister Emma. She was scheduled to spend the summer with Libbie. And while a summer at the fort was an exciting adventure for Emma, the same scenario was a prison sentence for Custer.

Back in March, Custer had been raring to go. He thought he would command one of the three columns on an expedition that the military and the press believed would be the last major campaign against Native American tribes. Now, six weeks later, he had been removed from command and sidelined indefinitely.

After his stop in Monroe, Custer and his three companions continued to Chicago. In Chicago, as they sat on a train bound for St. Paul, Minnesota, and the headquarters of General Alfred Terry, a colonel from General Sheridan's headquarters approached Custer. He handed Custer a message from General Sherman that was clearly a command from President Grant. It informed Custer that he improperly exited Washington without the permission of Grant or Sherman, and he was therefore ordered to stay in Chicago until he received further instructions.

Custer couldn't believe it. He *did* have Sherman's permission, and he tried repeatedly to see the president. Custer was stranded in Chicago, and he pleaded his case in waves of telegrams to Sherman. He received no response to his protests of innocence, but Sherman granted Custer permission to complete his trip home to Fort Lincoln and *then* begin a period of indefinite confinement.

Custer arrived in St. Paul on May 6 believing that he would be trapped at the fort with his wife and niece while his men marched out on the last great campaign against the tribes. He was greeted by General Terry, who was sympathetic to Custer's plight for more than one reason. Terry was the forty-eight-year-old commander of the Department of Dakota. He was tall, soft-spoken, and kind, and he was a bachelor who lived with his mother and four sisters. He was a great administrator who had grown accustomed to a desk job and a life of relative ease and routine. And because of the current calamity with Custer, he had just been ordered to lead the Dakota Column and to supervise the entire expedition.

Terry had no interest in trotting out onto the plains with thousands of men and animals in search of a battle against some of the best horse soldiers in human history. He would be on the trail for weeks and would endure bone-dry days under the blistering sun and periods of torrential rain that turned the ground into an impassable morass. Terry couldn't change his orders, but he *could* lobby for Custer's reinstatement as the most senior officer with experience against Native American warriors. When Custer begged Terry for help, Terry assisted the lieutenant colonel in composing a telegram to Sherman and Grant that was a last-ditch effort to appeal Custer's suspension. Custer wrote:

> *To His Excellency the President, through Military Channels.*
> *I have seen your order, transmitted through the General of the army, directing that I not be permitted to accompany the expedition about to move against the hostile Indians. As my entire regiment forms a part of the proposed expedition, and as I am the senior officer of the regiment on duty in this Department, I respectfully but most earnestly request that while not allowed to go in command of the expedition, I may be permitted to serve with my regiment in the field.*

I appeal to you as a soldier to spare me the humiliation of watching my regiment march to meet the enemy and I not share in its dangers.

(Signed) G. A. Custer
Bvt. Maj. Gen. U.S. Army

The telegram was a masterstroke and bore the influence of a gifted lawyer and wordsmith like General Terry. Terry helped write the Fort Laramie Treaty in 1868, a document that was filled to bursting with vague double-talk and incomprehensible legal jargon. Here, he coached Custer on the opposite approach. In three sentences, Custer stated that he was the senior officer of the Seventh Cavalry; he humbly asked permission to merely accompany his regiment, not command it; and he begged for the chance to share in the danger of battle with his comrades, a desire that was in the heart of every true soldier. Lastly, he signed it with his rank from the Civil War, brevet major general, instead of his current rank of lieutenant colonel. It was one last reminder that he was probably the best soldier in the Department of Dakota.

And it worked. Or it might have helped. There is no way to know Grant's thought process for certain, but he changed his mind on May 8. He had received constant criticism in the press for his tactics against Custer, which were viewed as petty retaliation, and that probably factored into his decision. And the appeal to Grant's sense of duty probably added to the equation. But there was another factor, as well. In the end, Grant simply couldn't afford to lose Custer's experience. Custer fought on the southern plains in the late 1860s, highlighted by the Battle of the Washita. When his regiment was transferred north to Dakota, he led one of two missions along the Yellowstone River in the early 1870s.

Four short years after the signing of the Fort Laramie Treaty, the Northern Pacific Railroad started sending survey crews onto land that was termed "unceded" in the agreement. In theory, that land still belong to the Lakota and the Cheyenne. In practice, it was available for development by the American government. And, more specifically, the treaty allowed for railroad construction virtually anywhere in tribal territory. But, of course, leaders like Sitting Bull and Crazy Horse didn't sign the treaty. They had no intention of allowing railroad tracks to tear up the heart of their country.

The goal of the Northern Pacific was to run parallel to the historic transcontinental railroad and connect Minneapolis, Minnesota, to Seattle, Washington. Construction began in Minnesota in 1870, and workers completed a spur up to Duluth on the banks of Lake Superior and simultaneously built a line to the west. By 1872, the line trekked across Dakota Territory with an eye toward a stop in Bismarck. In August, a survey crew rode out of Fort Rice, south of Bismarck, to scout the next section of track, which would follow the course of the Yellowstone River. The crew was guarded by several hundred soldiers, and they unknowingly picked a bad time to march into the southwest corner of Montana Territory.

Two thousand Lakota, Cheyenne, and Arapaho gathered on the banks of the Powder River south of the Yellowstone for the annual summer Sun Dance ceremony. It was the same area where Sitting Bull would participate in the most impactful Sun Dance of his life four years later. When the tribes discovered the soldiers and surveyors, more than one thousand warriors raced up the Powder River to intercept the encroaching force. The confrontation provided the setting for moments of bravery that added to the legends of Sitting Bull and Crazy Horse.

The warriors and the soldiers opened fire, and Crazy Horse charged forward to distinguish himself. The Oglala leader had been on a roller-coaster ride of ups and downs since he had earned widespread fame among the tribes during Red Cloud's War. At the end of the conflict in 1868, he was a prestigious Shirt Wearer in the honored warrior society called the Strong Hearts. But then he fell in love with a young woman who was already married. They ran away together, but her husband tracked them down and attacked Crazy Horse. The husband fired a gun at Crazy Horse's face at close range. The bullet tore through Crazy Horse's left cheek and broke his jaw. The husband returned to camp with his wife, and Crazy Horse returned with a shattered reputation. He was humiliated, and he lost his Shirt Wearer status.

Shortly after that episode, his only brother was killed in an attack on some miners, and a close friend was killed in a poorly planned raid on a group of Shoshone. The following year, in 1871, Crazy Horse married a woman named Black Shawl, possibly more from a sense of obligation than true love. Until the marriage, he was a thirty-year-old warrior without a wife or children. But by the end of the year, he had both. Black Shawl gave birth to a daughter whom they called They Are Afraid of Her.

Crazy Horse began to rebuild his status through his fierce opposition to white settlers from the East, and around the time that his daughter was born, he met a man with identical beliefs: Sitting Bull.

The Hunkpapa chief and medicine man had led his band south and west from the area around Fort Rice in Dakota Territory. They settled in the Powder River country of southeastern Montana, the home of Crazy Horse's Oglala band. And then, a year later, in August of 1872, Crazy Horse and Sitting Bull led one thousand warriors to fight back the railroad survey crew and its military escort along the Yellowstone.

After the two sides exchanged volleys of fire that did little damage, they settled into a stalemate. Crazy Horse galloped out beyond the warriors and rode back and forth in front of the soldiers. He was armed only with a lance, and as he held it aloft, he challenged the soldiers to fire. He survived the daring ride and earned new acclaim for his bravery, and he might have inspired Sitting Bull to go one step further.

Sitting Bull dismounted and walked forward from the warriors' line of battle. He slowly, nonchalantly strolled two hundred yards ahead of his comrades and picked a spot on the open plain. He was within easy range of the soldiers as he calmly sat down, took out his pipe, lit it, and began to smoke. Four more warriors joined him, but they fidgeted nervously as soldiers fired at the impromptu gathering. Bullets kicked up dust around the little party, but Sitting Bull coolly smoked his pipe as if he sat around a fire in camp and gazed up at the stars in the night sky. The pipe passed from man to man, and when it was finished, Sitting Bull rose and walked back to the main body of warriors. His casual gait taunted the soldiers, but they still couldn't hit him. He completed the action without a scratch and solidified his status as a fearless warrior and leader.

After that, the survey crew refused to continue its assignment. The railroad men and the soldiers returned to Fort Rice to regroup, and they soon learned that further survey work was postponed. The Northern Pacific Railroad was in a financial nightmare and was fighting for survival. Within a year, the company would collapse, and its failure would spark the Panic of 1873. But right before the end, the railroad sent another survey crew to the Yellowstone. This time, the military escort was the Seventh Cavalry under the command of Lieutenant Colonel George Armstrong Custer.

Custer's success on the southern plains prompted General Sheridan to send the regiment north to subdue the last remaining holdouts of the Lakota and Cheyenne. While workers constructed the regiment's new home, Fort Abraham Lincoln, on the western bank of the Missouri River five miles south of Bismarck, Custer led an expedition of nearly two thousand men into Montana. They clashed twice with the combined force of Sitting Bull and Crazy Horse, and both skirmishes featured elements that would be previews of the great battle to come.

On August 4, 1873, Custer led two companies of cavalry to scout ahead of the main column. In typical Custer fashion, he then rode ahead of his advance scouts and found himself alone on the plains. The Lakota sent a decoy party to lure the soldiers into a trap. Custer took the bait and galloped after the decoys. Just before it was too late, he wheeled his horse around and avoided near-certain death. He rushed back to the safety of his scouts, and they were able to hold back the warriors until the main column arrived. At the sight of the bluecoat reinforcements, the warriors broke off the attack and retreated to their camps. That skirmish earned Custer the name "Long Hair" from the Lakota and Cheyenne. Custer would cut his long blond hair before their final meeting in 1876, but here in 1873, the tribes knew him by his distinctive flowing locks.

One week later, warriors assaulted the army camp and spent a full day engaged with the soldiers. It was the first time the Lakota and Cheyenne heard the old Irish tune "Garry Owen," which had been adopted as the song of the Seventh Cavalry. Custer traveled everywhere with his regimental band. Its commander, Felix Vinatieri, kept the musicians playing through the continuous clash of mounted men and the roar of cannon from the infantry. When the action ended and the warriors once again returned to their camps, Custer believed the withdrawal was due to a lack of fighting spirit instead of a calculated retreat. It was neither the first nor the last time he misjudged an opponent.

Five years earlier, at the Battle of the Washita, he had launched an attack without knowing the full strength of the enemy. Here on the northern plains, his small force of scouts had been in danger of being overrun by a larger force, and then he believed his enemies lacked the will to fight in a sustained engagement. If there were lessons to be learned from the experiences, Custer hadn't learned them by May of 1876 when he heard the good news from General Terry.

President Grant authorized General Sherman to reinstate Custer to active duty with the Seventh Cavalry. The reason was simple: Custer was the only senior officer with experience against Native American warriors. General Terry still commanded the overall mission, but he had been an office administrator for his entire post–Civil War career and had never fought warriors of any nation. Colonel Samuel Sturgis, Custer's superior and the commander of the Seventh Cavalry, hadn't led a campaign in the field since the Civil War and had been on recruiting duty in St. Louis for several years.

Custer's senior subordinate, Major Marcus Reno, lobbied for command of the Dakota Column. He had commanded Fort Lincoln for the better part of six months while Custer enjoyed his extended furlough in New York City and then spent weeks in Washington during the impeachment fiasco. But Terry refused Reno's request. Reno, like the other candidates for command, had no experience against Native American warriors. That left Custer as the only suitable leader.

In Terry's mind, if he had to supervise this campaign, he needed Custer, even with the baggage of Custer's arrogance and recklessness. President Grant still wouldn't authorize command responsibilities for Custer, but that didn't matter when the column was out on the high plains and cut off from the rest of the world—and Custer knew it.

Custer, Terry, Custer's young traveling companions, and Terry's staff members boarded a train in St. Paul and arrived at Fort Lincoln on May 10. Custer picked up where he had left off seven weeks earlier and finished preparations for the expedition. For the next five days, Fort Lincoln would be a hive of frenzied activity as the Seventh Cavalry readied itself for the last great campaign against the hostile Indians.

On the same day Custer and Terry arrived at Fort Lincoln, President Grant stepped up to a podium in Philadelphia and welcomed the world to the Centennial Exposition. The World's Fair was a shining example of progress as Americans saw it. If Sitting Bull and Crazy Horse had strolled through the pavilions and witnessed the new inventions for communication, agriculture, warfare, travel, and a hundred other things, they certainly would have held different opinions. But they might also have experienced the same feeling that Red Cloud experienced when he traveled to Washington, D.C., to meet with government officials: resignation.

When Red Cloud saw the size and scale of the capital city, and the technology that most people took for granted, he knew the Lakota's days were numbered. Sitting Bull and Crazy Horse likely would have felt the same way. But just as likely, they would not have surrendered without a fight.

The Centennial Exposition was the first World's Fair on U.S. soil, and it celebrated the one hundredth anniversary of the signing of the Declaration of Independence and the founding of the United States of America. It was the culmination of four years of work, and it truly dazzled the world. In addition to the monumental size and scope of the buildings and the grounds, it featured a spectacular array of new inventions. Alexander Graham Bell showcased a new device that he believed would replace the telegraph. It allowed people to talk to each other over long distances and in real time, and he called it the telephone. Thomas Edison brought a machine that allowed people to play recorded music in their own homes. He called it a phonograph, and it was the forerunner to the record player.

Samuel Colt set up a dizzying display of his firearms. In a massive glass case, he mounted 230 handguns in the shape of a giant pinwheel. Three concentric circles worked their way in to the centerpiece. Smaller guns were on the outer rings, and they grew larger as they moved toward the eighteen specially engraved single-action revolvers in the middle.

The Winchester Repeating Arms Company performed a similar feat. It displayed more than two hundred rifles and debuted the new Winchester 1876 Model. The 1876 was an upgrade of the famous 1873 Model and featured the ability to fire longer distances with larger ammunition, which made it ideal for big-game hunting. It soon became the favorite rifle of future president Teddy Roosevelt.

Nearly ten million people attended the expo during its six-month run from May 10 to November 10, including General Sherman and General Sheridan. They were at the fair when they learned of the historic battle in southern Montana and the devastation of the Seventh Cavalry. Also in attendance later that summer was a bank employee from Northfield, Minnesota, and his vacation to Philadelphia might have saved his life. But two people who didn't attend the expo were Wyatt Earp and Bat Masterson. They were busy with new jobs, and Bat had the additional task of adjusting to the use of a cane that he now needed to help him walk.

It had been five months since Bat was shot in Charlie Norton's saloon in Sweetwater, and it was abundantly clear that it would be an agonizingly slow recovery process. But neither the cane nor the lingering pain and discomfort in his abdomen stopped him from joining Wyatt in Dodge City.

Dodge had a short but exceptionally bloody history before Wyatt and Bat arrived. It began life as a crude camp along the Arkansas River called Buffalo City. It was roughly five miles from Fort Dodge, and it acted as a gathering spot for buffalo hunters and a drinking spot for soldiers who were restricted from consuming alcohol inside the fort. By the fall of 1872, the Atchison, Topeka, & Santa Fe Railway had worked its way west across Kansas to Dodge City. Bat Masterson and his older brother, Ed, had labored on a crew that helped grade the final stretch of land for the tracks. Their work added one of the early highlights to Bat's growing reputation.

Bat and Ed spent the winter of 1871/72 hunting buffalo. When the season ended in the spring, they took jobs on a crew that graded the five miles of land between Fort Dodge and newly named Dodge City. They were hired by a man named Raymond Ritter, who was a subcontractor for the railroad. When Bat and Ed finished the project, they received a hard lesson in shady business practices. Ritter skipped town without paying the $300 he owed them for their work.

Bat, who was eighteen years old, and Ed, who was nineteen, were furious. Bat's anger simmered for a year, and then he learned that Ritter would be passing through Dodge on the train. Bat rushed through town to the train depot. He boarded the train and searched the cars for Ritter. News circulated through town that there might be a rumble at the depot, and people hurried to watch the show. Bat found Ritter and forced him out of the train car and onto the platform on the end of the car. As they stood outside the door, a crowd gathered on the ground below them.

Bat instructed Ritter to pay the money. Ritter appealed to the crowd for help. He shouted that he was being robbed, but the crowd just gawked at the spectacle. Finally, Ritter peeled off $300 from a roll of cash and handed it to Bat. With the debt collected, Bat bought a round of drinks for the townsfolk and impressed them as a generous young man who was also a cool customer under pressure. He had steel nerves and he'd threatened violence, but he hadn't had to use it.

By the end of 1872, there were reportedly fifteen graves in the small cemetery on a grassy hilltop north of Dodge City. The location of the cemetery on the treeless knoll was entirely circumstantial. Two cowboys had camped on the spot, and when a fight broke out between them, one shot and killed the other. The survivor fled, and when townspeople discovered the unknown dead man the next day, they buried him on the spot. He was still wearing his boots, and his resting place became known as Boot Hill. He was quickly and regularly joined by others who met violent ends in Dodge City during the largely lawless years between 1872 and 1875.

The population of Dodge rose rapidly, and new businesses practically leaped up from the dusty prairie. Countinghouses, banks, and shops of all kinds opened along the expanding network of streets. Holding pens for cattle were built outside town. Merchants, lawyers, and preachers soon arrived with their wives and children and nannies. The sod structures and canvas tents of the old camp were replaced with wood buildings for offices, schools, churches, stores, hotels, saloons, and restaurants. And then some of the wood buildings were reconstructed with brick. A few notable businesses would feature prominently on the hit TV show *Gunsmoke* eighty years in the future: the Dodge House hotel, the Long Branch Saloon, and Delmonico's restaurant.

Leading business owners did their best to make the community safe and habitable for families, even though Dodge was an unincorporated town in an unformed county in southwestern Kansas. Early efforts produced disastrous results. In 1873, a group of men, many of whom were little better than outlaws themselves, formed a vigilance committee that they named, creatively, the Society of Vigilantes. It wasn't long before the vigilance committee sparked a showdown with the U.S. Army.

Colonel Richard Dodge, commander of Fort Dodge, sent his servant, William Taylor, to town to buy supplies. While Taylor waited in a dry-goods shop, he saw two men try to steal his wagon. He ran out of the store and shouted at the men to stop. In response, they shot him dead. The killers were members of the vigilante society, and when Colonel Dodge learned of the murder, he wired the governor. He asked for authorization to ride into town and apprehend the murderers. The governor gave his permission, and Colonel Dodge didn't hold back. He saddled a squad of cavalry and roared into Dodge City with guns blazing. The members of the vigilance committee had declared that they wouldn't be taken by the army, but they weren't prepared for soldiers who charged down the streets and opened fire with rifles and pistols. Committee members dove for cover and tried to return fire, but they were woefully outmanned by trained shooters with purpose and motivation. The army caught the two killers and dragged them back to the fort to stand trial.

Shortly after that episode, two things changed in Dodge—one good and one bad. The good was that Kansas organized Ford County and made Dodge City the county seat. The governor appointed Charlie Bassett, a steady, competent lawman, as the first county sheriff. Bassett was headquartered in Dodge, but he was responsible for the entire county, so he couldn't spend all his time in town. To bolster the local law effort, business leaders took up a collection to pay a man to be an informal marshal, and that was the bad change that came to Dodge in the summer of 1873.

The men hired Bill "Bully" Brooks to be the first "marshal" of Dodge. Brooks had been a marshal in Newton, Kansas, but he was also a hotheaded, shoot-first maniac who was already responsible for one of the graves on Boot Hill. In Brooks's first month on the job, he killed or wounded more than a dozen men. In one incident, Brooks killed a man who had four brothers, and the brothers came to town to exact revenge. Brooks stood in the middle of Front Street with a pistol in each hand. As the brothers rounded a corner and confronted the marshal, Brooks opened fire and killed all four. The five brothers were buried next to each other on Boot Hill.

Most times, Brooks was quick to act, usually with deadly force. Other times, he refused to act, which also produced deadly results. Saloon owner Tom Sherman argued with one of his customers and then chased the man out into the street. Sherman shot and killed the customer in cold blood, and Brooks declined to arrest the saloonkeeper.

The tenure of Bill Brooks finally ended when he started showing too much interest in a dance hall girl. The girl already had an admirer, and the man surprised Brooks on Front Street. The admirer opened fire and forced Brooks to dive behind a water barrel. The admirer thought he'd killed the marshal and returned to his business in town. Brooks was alive, but he seemed chastened after the near-death experience, and the people of Dodge decided it was time for Brooks to leave.

Bill Brooks lived for less than a year after his time in Dodge ended. He and two friends stole horses and mules from a stagecoach company. The three men were caught and thrown in jail, and a mob soon decided that it was the perfect opportunity to dispose of Bill Brooks for good. On July 29, 1874, the mob broke into the jail, dragged Brooks outside, and lynched him.

In Dodge, Billy Rivers took over for Bill Brooks, but Rivers didn't last long as the town's second marshal. He left for unknown reasons. By that time, Dodge was organizing for incorporation and preparing to hire its first official peacekeeper. The town was slowly becoming a destination for Texas cattle, which meant the population continued to rise, new businesses continued to open, and rambunctious Texas cowboys started packing the saloons and gambling dens. All of that meant more money flowed into Dodge, which, in turn, meant political factions began to take shape.

On one side was the group that became known as the Dodge City Gang. They were prominent men with interests in saloons, restaurants, dance halls, gambling establishments, and brothels (which operated unofficially and outside the law). By supporting those business interests, the Dodge City Gang also supported the men who frequented them—namely, the cowboys. Texas cattlemen all but demanded that Dodge be declared an "open city," which would allow the cowboys to do pretty much anything. The trail bosses threatened to take their herds to other towns if they felt their cowhands were being unnecessarily restrained.

The opposing political faction favored exactly that type of restraint. The men of that faction wanted to make money just like the Dodge City Gang, but they also wanted to reduce the noise and dangerous gunfire and general mayhem that came with cattle season. Cowboys made a game out of getting wildly drunk and riding through the streets firing their guns. That act, along with the typical drinking, shouting, singing, and fighting, fell under the collective label of having a "hurrah." When the cowboys were out hurrahing, it was dangerous for everyone.

Dodge City was incorporated in November 1875, and Peter Beatty became the acting mayor. Beatty was a member of the Dodge City Gang, and for the next four months, he imposed very little restraint on the merriment. Granted, it was the winter of 1875/76—the off-season for cattle drives—but it still set a tone for the political infighting that plagued Dodge throughout the 1870s.

Dodge City held its first election in April 1876, and George Hoover, who opposed the Dodge City Gang, won the mayor's race. Hoover appointed Larry Deger to the post of town marshal. Deger appointed Jack Allen as a deputy marshal. Allen was known to have a fast draw, but early in his job as a deputy, his courage failed him. A particularly rowdy group of cowboys started firing their guns and causing trouble in town. Instead of confronting them, Allen hid in the railroad station. When the next train came through, he hopped on it and never came back. Dodge City needed a new deputy, and as luck would have it, Mayor Hoover heard of an assistant marshal in Wichita who was recently out of a job.

Hoover made Wyatt Earp the new assistant marshal in Dodge City and gave him the power to hire the rest of the police force. Joe Mason had been on the force with Deger, and Wyatt kept him on the team. Wyatt's first new hire was Bat Masterson's younger brother, Jim, who was an inexperienced twenty-year-old at the time. Wyatt liked and respected Bat and probably assumed Jim would be cut from the same mold. That left one more opening on the force, and Wyatt offered the job to Bat. Bat accepted and moved to Dodge to wear a badge for the first time.

As the cattle season picked up steam and spring rushed toward summer, Dodge City sported an all-star team of young lawmen. In the town marshal's office were Wyatt Earp, Bat Masterson, and Jim Masterson. And in the county sheriff's office were Charlie Bassett and a deputy named Bill Tilghman, who would become a legend in his own right many years in the future.

As the summer of 1876 approached, Dodge City was stocked with lawmen for the first time. Wyatt instructed his men to wear two guns. He stashed loaded shotguns in secret hiding places around town. The deputies were the only men who knew the locations, and they could grab the weapons when needed. Wyatt, Joe, Jim, and Bat—even with his cane and his pronounced limp—patrolled the streets of Dodge while Marshal Deger manned the office. The early cattle herds were already arriving, and the new lawmen were ready to test their mettle against a swarm of thirsty cowboys.

As Wyatt and Bat and the others walked the streets of Dodge, a different, yet similar, scene played out five hundred miles to the north. In Deadwood, miners swarmed the crude saloons on the single muddy street that ran through the gulch. They were dirty and wild, like many of the cowboys in Dodge, but a major difference between the two scenes was that there was no law in Deadwood. And there were many who planned to take full advantage of the lack of authority.

When Al Swearingen arrived in Deadwood with his wife, Nettie, in the spring of 1876, he was already a well-known saloon operator and purveyor of all things sordid and intoxicating. He grew up outside Oskaloosa, Iowa, and seems to have headed west in his late teens. In 1866, at the age of twenty or twenty-one, he was arrested for the vague crime of "breach of peace" in Virginia City, Montana Territory. He likely bounced from one rough mining camp to another until the gold rush in the Black Hills began in earnest in 1875. In the fall of 1875, he loaded up some wagons in Cheyenne and journeyed to the new town of Custer City.

A couple of months earlier, in the summer of 1875, General Crook led an expedition through the Black Hills, and he forced many of the miners in the area to leave. They moved about forty miles south and established a camp that was alternately known as Custer and Custer City. Less than a month after the camp's establishment, Swearingen arrived and built a saloon on the outskirts of town. He stocked it with dance hall girls, gamblers, and plenty of cheap whiskey. In no time at all, the saloon was one of the hottest joints in town. But six months later, in the early spring of 1876, the exodus to Deadwood began.

The army had kept at least some of the miners out of the Black Hills throughout the spring, but with the impending launch of the campaign on the northern plains, the army abandoned its effort to stop the influx of fortune seekers. With no one left to stand in their way, the miners hurried back to Deadwood Gulch.

Swearingen followed his customers north and arrived in the fast-rising town of Deadwood in May. In less than a week, he bought a lot in town and constructed his new venture, the Cricket Saloon. Like most buildings, it had a wood frame and a canvas roof. It was long and narrow, and it was a crude version of his well-made saloon in Custer City. But it would certainly suffice for the next year. The miners poured in; the gold dust poured in; and Al Swearingen was well on the path toward becoming the most notorious operator in town.

Roughly six weeks later, he would learn about a great battle to the west that would be a short-term victory for the tribes of the northern plains, but would signal their downfall in the long run. The battle over the course of those two days in late June would do more to assure that the Black Hills, and Deadwood, and Al Swearingen's saloon would join the American union than anything else, though no one could have anticipated it in May when Swearingen opened his doors and General Sheridan's campaign finally began in earnest.

5

THE CAMPAIGN BEGINS

One week after President Grant opened the Centennial Exposition in Philadelphia, the Seventh Cavalry marched out of Fort Lincoln in Dakota Territory. The campaign was roughly three months behind schedule. General Sheridan wanted it to begin in the winter when the tribes that refused to go to reservations were scattered in small camps. Now it was mid-May, the weather was warming, and warriors and their families streamed into Sitting Bull's growing village, though no one in the army knew it. The advantage of a surprise attack in the winter was lost, but the campaign moved forward anyway.

Lieutenant Colonel Custer, for one, could not have cared less about the lost advantage. He was thrilled to be part of the campaign at all. A little more than two weeks earlier, Custer had been at his lowest point when President Grant removed him from command and sidelined him for the campaign. One week later, Custer was elated to learn that he had been reinstated. And now, Custer was at his high point. The long-awaited moment was finally here.

On May 17, 1876, while thousands flocked to the Centennial Exposition and Wyatt and Bat patrolled the streets of Dodge City, Custer led the Dakota Column out of Fort Lincoln. Libbie Custer rode beside her husband at the head of the column, and the regimental band played "Garry Owen" and other songs at full volume. The only thing that dampened the mood was the weather. It had rained for several days, and a thick gray mist hung in the air as 1,200 men and 1,600 horses and mules tramped westward through the muck of the soggy ground. General Alfred Terry wanted to leave on May 15, but a torrential downpour forced a delay.

Before the column departed at 7:00 a.m. on the seventeenth, Custer divided the Seventh Cavalry into two wings. His second-in-command, Major Marcus Reno, led one wing, and the regiment's senior captain, Frederick Benteen, led the other. General Terry still maintained overall command of the column, but it was clear that Custer would do more than simply accompany the regiment.

May 17 marked a big moment for the regiment. It was the first time since the Battle of the Washita eight years earlier that all twelve companies were together in one place. But the makeup of the Seventh Cavalry was a far cry from the group that had earned the nickname the "Fighting Seventh" after Washita. The nickname was rooted in the sole experience of the Washita, and since that battle in 1868, the regiment had fought in only two skirmishes: the engagements against Sitting Bull and Crazy Horse along the Yellowstone River in 1873. Since then, the soldiers hadn't seen action of any kind. And four of the twelve companies had not been present for the 1873 engagements. They had no combat experience whatsoever. Of the force of 1,200 men, fewer than 200 could claim experience against Native American warriors. Many of the soldiers were raw recruits with minimal, if any, training. Most of the battle-hardened veterans from the Civil War were gone, and that included the cavalry's horses. Many of the men rode young horses that were untrained and unprepared for the ear-shattering volume of battle and the terror of their riders during intense periods of chaos.

The officer corps of the Dakota Column suffered, as well. Even though the regiment was back at full strength in terms of total numbers, fifteen regular officers were missing from the campaign. Custer was forced to shuffle the lineup to fill the gaps. As a result, several officers now led men whom they didn't know. And time also took its toll on the regiment. More than a few of the officers who were veterans of the Civil War became disillusioned. They hardened into shells of their former selves and drank heavily, even though Custer, their regimental commander, abstained. A nucleus of good officers and soldiers still existed at the center of the Seventh Cavalry, and the regiment was at full strength, but its abilities were not ideal.

Other new additions included Custer's youngest brother, Boston, as a civilian guide. Custer stayed true to his word and brought along his eighteen-year-old nephew, Autie Reed, as well as Dick Roberts, the brother of one of Libbie's closest friends. Mark Kellogg extended his stay with the Seventh Cavalry and agreed to join the expedition as a newspaper correspondent. Kellogg had met Custer and Libbie two months earlier when the couple returned to the fort from their extended furlough in New York City. Kellogg had been on his way to the Black Hills to find his fortune when he got stuck on a train with Custer and Libbie during a severe blizzard.

Kellogg was in his early forties and had fallen on hard times since his wife passed away in 1867 or 1868. His two young daughters lived with his wife's parents while he hurried to the Black Hills to find the gold that he hoped would pull him out of his financial troubles. After meeting the Custers and learning about the up-coming campaign, he postponed his trip to the Hills. He stayed with the Seventh Cavalry and became a newspaper correspon-dent for the mission. He was contracted for the job by Clement Lounsberry, the publisher of *The Bismarck Tribune*. Lounsberry was supposed to ride with the expedition and cover it firsthand, but his wife fell ill shortly before the date of departure. He made the fateful decision to hire Kellogg to take his place.

On May 17, 1876, Mark Kellogg rode out with the rest of the Dakota Column on the greatest adventure of his life. That night, the full group camped together for the final time. The next morn-ing, Libbie Custer kissed her husband goodbye and then joined a small group to return to Fort Lincoln. The column resumed its march to the west. With any luck, the soldiers would find the Lakota and Cheyenne before they reached the western border of Dakota Territory—or, at the worst, in eastern Montana.

But Sitting Bull had led his people farther west, deeper into south-central Montana. In the second half of May, they were much closer to the other columns of the army expedition. That fact was already known to the Montana Column, but it wouldn't reach the Dakota Column for three crucial weeks.

Colonel John Gibbon's Montana Column spent more than six months on the march in 1876. It wasn't the first to begin the great campaign, but it stayed in the field longer than the other columns. In February, when General Sheridan had pushed his departmen-tal commanders to send units into the field, travel was impossible for the Dakota Column. It wasn't much better for the Wyoming and Montana Columns, but General Crook was able to launch the expedition on March 1. He led the Wyoming Column out of

Fort Fetterman and struck Cheyenne chief Old Bear's village on March 17. After the brief engagement, Crook decided to take his tired, hungry men back to Wyoming to regroup. He was the first to begin the expedition, but he couldn't sustain it.

Colonel Gibbon led the Montana Column out of Fort Ellis near Bozeman, Montana, on March 28, the day before Custer testified for Congressman Clymer's committee for the first time. Gibbon was another career military man. He graduated West Point as a second lieutenant and saw his first action in the Mexican-American War. He was a captain when the Civil War began, and he rose to the rank of brevet major general during four years of heavy fighting. He held the same rank as the much younger George Armstrong Custer and, like Custer, found his rank reduced after the war. He returned to his captaincy but quickly earned promotions up to the rank of colonel. He stayed a colonel for the next twenty years until he received his final promotion to brigadier general in 1885.

In the campaign of 1876, his 480 soldiers and scouts began by traveling east along the Yellowstone River. They followed the old Bozeman Trail that had been so hotly contested ten years earlier during Red Cloud's War. After several days of marching, the column reached a proverbial fork in the road. The Bozeman Trail turned southeast toward Wyoming, and the Yellowstone River angled northeast toward Dakota Territory. The column stayed with the Yellowstone and rode northeast.

General Sheridan didn't give the columns specific instructions, but he hoped one of two things would happen: either an individual army would find and crush the hostiles, or the armies would coordinate a large-scale, multipronged attack that would crush the hostiles. None of the commanders, from Sheridan down to Custer, were deeply worried about a battle. All assumed the army would prevail in virtually any scenario. With three columns moving toward the presumed area of operation from three directions, it increased the likelihood that the armies could work together.

But the hope for a coordinated attack suffered its first setback when Crook returned to Wyoming after the assault on the Cheyenne village in mid-March. Just as Gibbon's column was marching into the field, Crook's column was leaving it. And with Crook out of the area, no one knew the locations of the other villages. The winter camps of the Lakota and Cheyenne were usually near the Little Missouri River in the extreme western portion of Dakota Territory or near the Powder River in southeastern Montana. That knowledge had been confirmed by Crook when he struck Old Bear's village on the Powder River.

Two months later, in mid-May, General Terry still hoped to find the tribes in the vicinity of their traditional winter camps. It would make the expedition relatively short, and Terry could wrap it up quickly and be back home in St. Paul to enjoy the rest of the summer. But the Dakota Column would soon learn the situation had changed, though it received that information only after a long march and a series of costly delays.

The Montana Column trekked through the Yellowstone valley for six weeks without spotting a single sign of the tribes. During the exhausting march through frigid temperatures and blinding snowstorms, Lieutenant James Bradley proudly earned the right to lead a detachment of scouts. He kept a daily journal of the column's experiences, and he noted, with frustration, the struggle to find the Lakota. Day after day, week after week, the men trudged through mud and snow and marveled at the ghostly quality of their quarry. This was the heart of the Lakota's territory, yet the Lakota seemed to have vanished.

Bradley's men and other units scouted streams, creeks, and small rivers in the area and found nothing. They discovered herds of buffalo but saw no sign of hunters . . . until May 3. Bradley's entry for that day said, "We have found the Sioux, or rather, they have found us." After reveille that morning, the company discovered that a horse and a mule were missing. As the soldiers and Crow scouts raced around the camp to inspect their belongings, the Crow learned that every one of their horses had been stolen during the night. More than thirty animals disappeared, and no one in the camp heard a thing. It was clearly the work of a Lakota raiding party, but an attempt to track the group failed.

The column continued to march through the Yellowstone valley but was forced to halt on May 14 when a savage hailstorm ripped through the camp. Two days later, Lieutenant Bradley and his scouts made their important discovery. On May 16, the day before Custer and the Dakota Column began the expedition, Bradley and the scouts spotted an enormous Native American village. They had followed the trail of a group of Lakota down the Tongue River, one of the major rivers in southern Montana that joined the Yellowstone. The scouts quietly crawled up to the top of a bluff and looked out over about eight miles. They were rewarded with their first look at the village they had hunted for nearly two months. They were the first men to see the village of Sitting Bull, Crazy Horse, and a force of nearly one thousand warriors. The problem for the U.S. Army was that Lieutenant Bradley and his scouts were the *only* men to see the village for another five weeks.

The scouts quietly retreated from the bluff and jumped on their horses. They galloped back to the Montana Column's camp on the Yellowstone. They told Colonel Gibbon about the village. Gibbon was excited—it was only a day's march from their position. But there was a problem, and it was one of those problems that seems unbelievable from today's perspective, but it was a serious issue in 1876.

The Montana Column was stationed on the north bank of the Yellowstone River. To get to the village, the column needed to cross to the south bank. In mid-May, the water was high and moving fast, as it was fed by melting snow in the mountains. The column had small boats, but after an hour of trying to cross the river, only a few men and ten horses made it successfully. Four horses drowned in the attempt, and Gibbon stopped the crossing. And as the column experienced its first major setback, it realized it had an even bigger problem than the Yellowstone River: a group of Lakota warriors watched the soldiers flounder in their effort to cross. The warriors sat on their horses high on the bluffs on the south side of the river. The element of surprise—if it had been there at all—was gone.

Over the next few days, the warriors occasionally swam across the river and stole army horses, and they killed and scalped three soldiers. Then, eleven days after the scouts first saw the village, Lieutenant Bradley and his team returned to the same lookout spot. They saw the village again, but this time it was closer and larger. It had moved from the Tongue River to Rosebud Creek, a smaller waterway that also flowed into the Yellowstone. The scouts estimated the size of the village at approximately five hundred lodges. That could mean there were a thousand warriors in the camp, more than double the number of soldiers in the Montana Column. The scouts raced back to Colonel Gibbon with another report.

After hearing the numbers, and factoring in the fast-flowing river and the harassment from the Lakota raiding party, Gibbon chose not to attempt an attack. Instead, he sent a report to General

Terry with the Dakota Column, which was almost two hundred miles away. The report was odd. It lacked the urgency that seemed logical, given the importance of the information.

There were two goals for the expedition: number one, locate the native village or villages; number two, attack as soon as possible. The goals sounded simple on paper, but in reality, they were far more complicated and difficult to achieve. Gibbon had finally accomplished the first goal—he found a village. He likely decided an attack would be suicidal, so he chose to coordinate with the Dakota Column. But instead of shouting the news of the discovery of the village in big, bold letters at the beginning of his message, Gibbon added it at the bottom, almost as an afterthought. And that was the strange part of his report. By adding the information about the discovery in a brief addendum at the bottom of the note, Gibbon seemed to reduce its importance. He wrote: "P.S. A camp some distance up the Rosebud was reported this morning by our scouts. If this proves true, I may not start down the Yellowstone so soon."

In the last days of May, Gibbon's couriers set off in the direction of General Terry and the Dakota Column. It would take a week for the riders to find Terry. And during that time, the village continued to grow and strengthen. Its leaders, like Sitting Bull and Crazy Horse, knew soldiers were in the region. The younger warriors were eager to fight, and the chiefs wouldn't be able to hold them back much longer . . . and General George Crook chose *that* time to lead his Wyoming Column back into the field. He didn't know it, but he was about to march headlong into the first major battle of the campaign.

Two days after Colonel Gibbon's scouts spied the village for the second time, Crook marched north from Wyoming Territory with roughly thirteen hundred men. They rode up the old Bozeman Trail, replicating their advance from two months earlier. As they drew closer to southern Montana, they were within the realm of Sitting Bull's scouts. The Lakota had already harassed Gibbon's column to the west, and now they spotted Crook's column to the south. The tribes would tolerate Crook's encroachment for only so long before they acted, and the time for action was rapidly drawing near.

For the Lakota, it was fueled by more than just the love of battle and the defense of the village. By the time the warrior army met Crook's force in the first real engagement of the campaign, Sitting Bull had experienced two powerful visions that were interpreted as prophecies. Both foretold Lakota victories over white soldiers, and Sitting Bull had received the first vision earlier that spring.

The exact date isn't known, but sometime late in the spring of 1876, Sitting Bull sat on a butte near Rosebud Creek. He looked out over the hills and valleys of southern Montana. Below him, a village that had grown to more than four hundred lodges stretched out for almost a mile. He settled into a good spot high on the butte and began to pray. After a while, he drifted off to sleep and had a dream. In the dream, he saw a village shaped like a cloud. The cloud hovered over the ground as a threatening dust storm rolled in from the east. The dust storm slammed into the cloud, and the collision caused bursts of lightning and rain. Then the cloud smashed the dust storm and forced it away.

When Sitting Bull awoke, he believed he had seen a vision of the future. He believed the dust storm was created by white soldiers, and the village, represented by the cloud, successfully repelled it. Before he had scaled the butte to pray for guidance, his scouts told him that soldiers were moving in from the west, and maybe the south, as well. After the dream, Sitting Bull was confident that an attack would come from the east—from soldiers he didn't even know were there. He had dreamed of a fight with the Seventh Cavalry, but as it turned out, that battle would be the second of the two that were fought in June of 1876.

In the waning days of May, Colonel Gibbon's Montana Column was on the banks of the Yellowstone River about thirty-five miles north of the Native American village. General Terry's Dakota Column, with Custer at the helm, was slogging through hellish weather far to the west of the village. And General Crook's Wyoming Column was well south of the village, but moving closer by the day. Crook's column—the last to begin the main thrust of the expedition—would be the first to see action. But that wouldn't happen for another two weeks.

During the interval, the village grew to an unprecedented size, and Sitting Bull had the most powerful vision of his life during the most sacred ritual of the Lakota people. It showed him a bloody clash between his warriors and white soldiers. It showed him many dead on both sides. And it showed him a great victory for his people. As far as the Lakota were concerned, the U.S. Army was essentially walking into a trap.

6

THE BATTLE OF THE ROSEBUD

Wyatt Earp and Bat Masterson walked the streets of Dodge City with no idea of the forces that were converging in Montana Territory. The warlike conditions that were brewing six hundred miles northwest of Kansas were unknown to nearly everyone as spring turned to summer in 1876. General Sheridan, who was at the Centennial Exposition in Philadelphia, received updates through his headquarters in Chicago. But communications were intermittent and lacked substance because, quite simply, there was little substance to report.

Libbie Custer and the other wives at Fort Lincoln received letters from their husbands in the Dakota Column, but the intelligence could only be about the weather or musings about the journey. The column was still a month away from spotting a hostile Indian. The reporters with the Dakota and Wyoming Columns filed dispatches with their various news outlets, but the drudgery of marching for hours each day didn't provide the juicy details that would thrill readers and sell newspapers.

In Dodge, Wyatt and Bat and the rest of the lawmen were far more concerned with corralling the rowdy activities of the cowboys who entertained themselves south of the "Dead Line." Front Street was the main thoroughfare of Dodge City, and the town found itself in a situation that was much like Deadwood's. In Deadwood, the upper end of Main Street was the more civilized, respectable area. The lower end was known as "the Badlands." That area was home to most of the saloons and brothels. In Dodge, the north end of Front Street was the respectable area and the south end was the entertainment district. The dividing line between north and south was the tracks of the Santa Fe railroad, and the division became known as the "Front Street Dead Line." In the summer of 1876, Wyatt, Bat, Jim Masterson, and the others tried to confine the worst of the shenanigans to the south end of Front Street.

That summer, the lawmen of Dodge City were tasked with enforcing some new laws, two of which were that it was now illegal to take a horse or any other animal into a saloon, and it was illegal to carry a gun north of the Dead Line. When cowboys tried to trespass with a weapon or carry their excessive celebrations above the Dead Line, they quickly learned two things: Wyatt was an above-average boxer, and he was an enthusiastic practitioner of the art of buffaloing.

If there was one overarching mandate in Dodge City in 1876, it was to reduce the number of killings. The lawmen were wholeheartedly on board with the policy. They didn't join the force to become hired gunmen. In short order, and probably led by Wyatt, the deputies in Dodge ended altercations and prevented potential gunfights by bashing the offenders on the head with the butt of a pistol. The swift, skull-cracking blows usually knocked the recipient out or dropped him to his knees while draining him of the desire and ability to continue his prior behavior. Either way, the buffaloed offender was hauled off to jail to spend a painful night sobering up. But headaches were better than murders, so it was hard to argue too forcefully against the tactic.

In the instances when Wyatt couldn't get the drop on a trouble-maker and whack him over the head, he stepped into a straight-up street fight. Two examples typically rise to the top of the list for noted authors and historians. In the first, a group of cowboys arrived in town at the end of a long, dusty trip from Texas. As always, they were primed to spend their wages in the most exuberant ways possible. This particular group wanted to begin its night north of the Dead Line. New assistant marshal Wyatt Earp stopped them at the line and informed them of their options: they could stay south of the line and keep their guns, or they could go north of the line but give up their guns. The cowboys bristled at restrictions of any kind, and the biggest man in the group stepped forward to demonstrate to the lawman that they would keep their guns *and* go where they pleased.

Wyatt wasted no time. He swung a fist at the man's mouth. He drove a punch into the man's gut. Then he hit the man in the mouth a second time and sent him sprawling into the dirt of Front Street. The cowboy was out cold, and the fight was over before the Texan knew it began. The cowboy's friends dragged him out of the street, and the group prudently decided to spent its time south of the Dead Line.

The second incident ended with a similar result, but it took a much greater toll on Wyatt. A group of Texas cowboys confronted Bat and Wyatt and loudly voiced their protests about the new laws in Dodge City. The biggest cowboy in the group stepped forward to challenge the lawmen. Wyatt unbuckled his gun belt and handed it to Bat. Wyatt and the cowboy launched into their fight, and Wyatt eventually knocked the Texan out, but not before the Texan battered, bruised, and bloodied the assistant marshal.

With the first cowboy down, Wyatt glared at the others and asked if anyone else wanted to fight. Somewhat surprisingly, another member of the group stepped forward. Wyatt made quick work of him, and then waited to see if there were any more challengers. The others decided two knockouts were enough, and they dragged their friends out of the street without any further conflict.

Wyatt and Bat continued their rounds and settled into a routine in the early days of summer. So far, so good. There was plenty of raucous behavior south of the Dead Line, but it didn't venture north nearly often as it had in the past. And there were no murders, thus far. Bat, Wyatt, Jim Masterson, and the full host of lawmen aimed to keep it that way. And while they firmly established a new law in Dodge, events on the northern plains rapidly moved toward the first explosive collision.

General Terry's hope for a swift campaign was dashed at the end of May, and he resigned himself to the long haul in early June. The Dakota Column had marched west out of Fort Lincoln for twelve days until it reached the Little Missouri River at the edge of Dakota Territory. The initial stage of the march crossed a flat, grassy prairie. But when the column reached the valley around the Little Missouri, the landscape changed. The prairie was replaced by rocky canyons and craggy ravines that made the next few days agonizing for men and animals alike. The soldiers, horses, mules, and cattle in the column tentatively descended each jagged cut in the earth and then trudged up the other side, and then repeated the process at the next obstacle.

The column traversed the canyons for three days before bless-edly reaching the banks of the Little Missouri. At that point, Custer led a brief scout south along the river until the waterway made a sharp turn to the west. At the turn, he circled back and reported to Terry. He confirmed the news that many already sus-pected: there were no hostile Indians near the Little Missouri. The tribes that may have been there during the winter months—when General Sheridan wanted the expedition to begin—had moved. The most likely destination was the fertile hunting ground around the Powder River to the southwest, which meant the expedition had just been extended indefinitely.

As if to emphasize the coming misery, the weather dealt the col-umn a painful gut punch. A freak snowstorm engulfed the soldiers and animals between May 31 and June 1. Blizzards in the late spring were rare but not unheard of. The storm dumped six inches of snow on the Dakota Column and forced it to stay in camp for two days.

When the sun blissfully returned and melted the snow, the column readied itself to continue its march to the west. But then three riders appeared in the distance. They were clearly soldiers, but their identities were unknown. They turned out to be the cou-riers from Colonel Gibbon's column with news of the first sighting of a Native American village. When Terry read the message, he learned about the village, but also that Gibbon was now marching *away* from it.

Technically, Gibbon was doing what he was supposed to do. Ter-ry's original orders to Gibbon were to lead the Montana Column along the Yellowstone River toward a rendezvous with Terry. But now that Gibbon had spotted a village, and Terry knew there were no signs of camps on the Little Missouri, Terry sent the couriers back to Gibbon with orders to turn around. Gibbon should march back to the junction of the Yellowstone and the Rosebud and re-establish the camp from which he had discovered the village. Terry would meet him there, and that would be the new rendezvous point.

For the next week, the Dakota Column moved on a steady course to the southwest, along a parallel track to the Yellowstone River. The Yellowstone was still many miles north of the column, but the territory between the regiment and the river was so desolate that the column skirted south to avoid it. Terry's initial plan was to set up a supply depot next to the Yellowstone near the modern-day town of Glendive. But after reading Gibbon's news, Terry wanted to shift the location farther west to the junction of the Yellowstone and the Powder.

Now the column trekked through some of the harshest land-scape of the campaign. Even with a jog to the south, the regiment couldn't fully avoid the badlands of eastern Montana. Rugged ra-vines and ridges continued to plague the regiment. The grasslands of central Dakota were now a distant memory. They were replaced by bare rock and clumps of prickly pear cactus. And the sun was relentless. The column received the full treatment of life on the northern plains: the expedition began with a miserable combina-tion of rain and fog; that gave way to warm spring weather; then a blizzard pounded the column at a time when the rest of the coun-try was celebrating summer; and now the sun blazed in a clear blue sky that seemed so vast and all-encompassing that it threatened to swallow the soldiers. There were few specimens worthy of being called trees, and the confusing geographical features were enough to disorient even the most seasoned guides in the column.

On June 7, with significant help from Custer as an advance scout, the column reached the Powder River. The heart of the tribal hunting grounds was to the south, but it was immediately clear why the Lakota and Cheyenne valued the area so fiercely. The barren, near-alien landscape of the past few days transformed into rolling, grassy hills with wooded areas along the watercourses. The region certainly held promise as a hunter's paradise.

Terry instructed Custer to remain on the Powder River and prep the men for the next leg of the journey. Rosebud Creek, the last known position of the village, was still seventy miles to the west. While Custer and most of the regiment rested and hunted, Terry led two companies north to the confluence of the Yellowstone and the Powder. There, for the first time in three weeks, General Terry gazed upon a welcomed sight: a paddle steamer called the *Far West*.

The U.S. government chartered two paddle steamers to support the expedition, the *Far West* and the *Josephine*, and the *Far West* now waited with its crew of thirty for Terry's arrival. The boats had established a supply depot, as ordered, at a crude fort called Stanley's Stockade at the confluence of Glendive Creek and the Yellowstone River. The rough outpost had been built during Custer's Yellowstone expedition in 1873, and now it acted as a warehouse for supplies that had been shuttled from Fort Lincoln. The *Far West* had moved farther upriver to the Yellowstone's junction with the Powder, and now it sat in the water like a floating sanctuary for General Terry.

Captain Grant Marsh piloted the steamer, and by 1876, he was known as the best riverboat captain in the region. He had spent thirty years navigating the waterways of the upper Midwest and the northern plains, and he knew the Yellowstone better than anyone. And though the site of Marsh and the *Far West* was inviting, Terry received frustrating news when he stepped on board. The expedition had been nothing but aggravating thus far, and here was one more layer: his message to Colonel Gibbon had not been delivered. Gibbon and the Montana Column were still leisurely marching down the Yellowstone instead of retracing their steps to the Rosebud so that they would be within striking distance of the village. Terry immediately sent couriers to Gibbon's command to tell him to stop.

Early the next morning, June 9, Terry instructed Marsh to steam upriver to meet Gibbon. It was time for a conference and an updated planning session. They spotted Gibbon five miles downriver from the Montana Column's camp and ushered him on board. Gibbon and Terry huddled for two hours as they both relayed the events of the past three weeks. To add to Terry's frustration, Gibbon had not left a surveillance team to maintain visual contact with the village. The last sighting, on May 27, was now twelve days old. Given the frequent travel habits of the tribes, the village could now be near any of a dozen rivers or creeks in the area.

Terry reiterated his order: Gibbon needed to turn around and march approximately fifty-five miles back to his former station at the junction of the Rosebud and the Yellowstone. With any luck, the village hadn't strayed too far from Rosebud Creek. Neither commander had heard a word from General Crook, but they believed the combined force of the Montana Column and the Dakota Column—more than sixteen hundred soldiers—should be enough to whip a Native American army of any size.

Terry returned to the Dakota Column's camp on the Powder River on the evening of June 9, and he met with his officers on the morning of June 10. There was a new plan: the Montana Column would hustle back to the Rosebud and set up camp. The Dakota Column would split into its two wings and move in separate directions for a few days. The right wing, led by Major Marcus Reno, would scout south along the Powder River and then head west to the Tongue River to search for any sign of a village. The left wing, led by Custer, would essentially do a mirror-image maneuver. It would march north along the Powder until it reached the Yellowstone and then turn west until it reached the junction of the Tongue and the Yellowstone. At that spot, the two wings would reunite and, if no hostiles had been sighted, continue up the Yellowstone until they connected with the Montana Column.

The plan thrilled Reno, disgusted Custer, and surprised everyone else. The entire regiment—and particularly Custer—was accustomed to Custer leading scouting missions. But Custer's insatiable need to freelance had tested Terry's patience one too many times on the march. Now, Terry gave command of the reconnaissance patrol to Reno, and the major could not have been more excited to finally break away from the column and prove himself in the field. Terry's order was designed more to put Custer in his place than to reward Reno with an opportunity, and Terry probably had an ulterior motive, as well. It was highly unlikely that a village would be anywhere around Reno's scout, so it cost Terry nothing to let Reno traipse around the region and confirm that the enemy was, in fact, not there.

That afternoon, Reno and three hundred soldiers rode south along the Powder River to begin a scout that was expected to last six or seven days. The next morning, June 11, Custer and the left wing began their casual march north toward the Yellowstone River.

While the two wings of the Dakota Column trotted through the Powder River country of southeastern Montana, they had no idea that General Crook's Wyoming Column had crossed into south-central Montana. Less than one hundred miles from the

Dakota Column, the Wyoming Column was about to find itself in a fight for its life. Crook's men would need desperate maneuvers to stave off total disaster.

The same day Custer's left wing started its march toward the Yellowstone, General George Crook's column established Camp Cloud Peak on Goose Creek in northern Wyoming Territory. The base camp was near the present-day city of Sheridan, Wyoming, and just a few miles short of the Montana border. At the time, Crook was approximately 150 miles southwest of the other columns, but he made no attempt to communicate his position to Terry or Gibbon.

The Wyoming Column had been on the move for thirteen days and had followed the same route it took in mid-March. The column set up its camp on Goose Creek, which was a tributary of the Tongue River, and planned to follow the creek up to the Tongue River and into southern Montana. During the previous expedition, the unit had marched nearly halfway to the junction of the Tongue and the Yellowstone before turning back and then ultimately striking the Cheyenne village on the Powder River. Exactly three months later, the column wouldn't make it nearly that far.

On the morning of June 16, Crook left his supply wagons and pack train at the base camp and ventured north with roughly thirteen hundred men. Crook's Crow scouts believed the Lakota and Cheyenne were somewhere on the Tongue River. But one of Crook's civilian guides, Frank Grouard, examined the signs and said the tribes were camped farther west on the Rosebud. Crook angled the column toward Rosebud Creek and pushed the troops through a hard thirty-three-mile march before they stopped for the night just a few miles from the mouth of the Rosebud.

Frank Grouard was right. The Wyoming Column wouldn't know it for sure until the next day, but Sitting Bull's enormous village was about fifty miles away on the banks of the Rosebud.

Two Cheyenne hunting parties spotted the immense column on the afternoon of the sixteenth and raced back to the village with the news. By mid-June, the population of the village qualified it as a good-size town. Nearly every nontreaty band on the northern plains had joined the group. Hundreds had streamed in from the agencies. And with soldiers just fifty miles from the women and children, there was no way Sitting Bull or any of the other old-man chiefs could hold back the tidal wave of warriors that burst from the village.

Sitting Bull wouldn't fight—for good reason—but it was time to fight, nonetheless. For months, the village had moved and stayed away from the soldiers while it grew in strength and size. But the time for cautious avoidance was done. And after Sitting Bull's recent vision, he knew battle was inevitable.

Sitting Bull elicited nearly unprecedented levels of respect from the tribes of the northern plains. He was a powerful medicine man, a fearless warrior, and a proven battlefield commander. His legend truly began about twenty years earlier when he was twenty-five years old. He and a group of Lakota warriors went on a horse-stealing raid against their hated enemies, the Crow. Oftentimes, the raids turned into battles, and this one looked like it might be headed in that direction, but then the two sides settled into a tense standoff.

Sitting Bull stepped forward from the line of Lakota warriors. He held a musket in one hand and a buffalo-hide shield in the other. He shouted across the gap to the Crow and challenged their chief to one-on-one combat. The chief stepped forward and accepted the challenge. The chief and the young warrior charged at each other. As Sitting Bull ran, he sang a song about bravery in battle.

The Crow dropped to one knee. He flipped his musket up to his shoulder and fired at Sitting Bull. The ball slammed into Sitting Bull's shield and ricocheted down toward his left foot. It tore into his foot behind his big toe and exited below his heel.

But now it was Sitting Bull's turn to shoot. He dropped to one knee, raised his musket, and fired. Through the cloud of black powder smoke, the battle lines of Crow and Lakota warriors watched the Crow chief topple to the ground. Sitting Bull limped over to the fallen man, took out his knife, and stabbed the chief in the heart. After the frightening display, the Crow turned and ran, and Sitting Bull was a warrior of unquestioned courage.

In the twenty years since the killing of the Crow chief, Sitting Bull had led his people in clashes against other tribes, white travelers, and white soldiers. In the 1860s, while Red Cloud conducted his war in Wyoming, Sitting Bull fought a four-year campaign in Minnesota and Dakota. When Red Cloud essentially retired in the wake of the Fort Laramie Treaty of 1868, Sitting Bull became one of the most prominent members of the Lakota tribe and arguably *the* most prominent member. He led his band of Hunkpapa west from Dakota into Montana and joined with other bands like Crazy Horse's Oglala and the northern Cheyenne.

The combined force of warriors who refused to submit to the U.S. fought back the railroad survey crews and their army escorts in 1872 and 1873. They kept largely to themselves in 1874 and 1875 while the army focused its expeditions on confirming the existence of gold in the Black Hills. But in early 1876, the American government issued its ultimatum, and the prospect of war grew stronger each day.

By the first week of June, the signs were undeniable. Small groups of warriors had been harassing soldiers to the west for two weeks. Sitting Bull's vision earlier in the spring foretold soldiers encroaching from the east. And now there was news of an American army moving up from the south. When the village set up a new camp along the Rosebud from June 4 through June 7, Sitting Bull decreed it was time for his Hunkpapa band to hold its most sacred ceremony: the Sun Dance.

On a patch of land selected for the ritual, Sitting Bull sat at the base of a tall lodge pole and impassively endured a sacrifice to the Great Spirit, Wakan Tanka, that was called a *scarlet blanket*. Sitting Bull's adopted brother, Jumping Bull, used an awl to pierce one of Sitting Bull's arms and remove fifty small pieces of flesh that were the size of match heads. When Jumping Bull finished with one arm, he gave the same treatment to the other.

After about a half an hour, blood streamed down Sitting Bull's arms from his shoulders to his fingertips. The pain must have been searing, but Sitting Bull rose to his feet and began to dance. He raised his face to the sky and danced around the lodge pole. For hours, he defied hunger and thirst and pain until he stopped suddenly and stared up at the heavens. As he stood motionless, he received his second vision about the coming conflict with the white soldiers.

When Sitting Bull's strength finally gave out, members of his band helped him to the ground. He whispered his vision to those around him. He had seen a multitude of soldiers and horses falling upside down into a village. A voice told him the soldiers had no ears. He saw warriors falling upside down into the village, as well, but their numbers were few. The assembled Lakota and Cheyenne interpreted the vision to mean the tribes would have a great victory over the white soldiers. They rejoiced over the vision, and less than two weeks later, they put it to the test.

The village continued to move south along the Rosebud until it shifted west to a small creek that flowed into the Greasy Grass River, a waterway that the white population called the Little Bighorn. Buffalo had been spotted near the creek, and the tribes changed direction to follow the herd. The village was there along the creek when two Cheyenne hunting parties galloped into camp with news of a large force of soldiers to the south. It was June 16, less than two weeks after Sitting Bull's Sun Dance.

The chiefs met in a tribal council and continued to advise a course of patient avoidance, but the younger warriors were having none of it. With no hope of restraining the warriors, the chiefs relented, and nearly every male of fighting age prepared himself for battle. They donned their finest war clothes. They loaded rifles and cartridge belts. They secured their medicine pouches full of charms that would protect them in combat. And some, like Sitting Bull's nephew White Bull, fastened majestic bonnets of red and white eagle feathers to their heads.

When the warriors were outfitted, they climbed onto their ponies and rode all night to meet the Wyoming Column near the mouth of Rosebud Creek. Sitting Bull and Crazy Horse rode with them. Sitting Bull was too weak to fight, and as an old-man chief, he wasn't expected to. But he could certainly motivate.

On the morning of June 17, the soldiers of the Wyoming Column broke camp and resumed their march to Rosebud Creek with no idea that roughly seven hundred warriors were bearing down on them. After about an hour, the column spotted the Rosebud, which was only a thin stream in the grass in that part of southern Montana.

Crook paused the march to take a break. The stream flowed into a canyon, and Crook thought the Lakota camp was at the other end of the canyon about eight miles away. The soldiers unsaddled their horses and started to relax. Some put up tents to block the sun. Crook and some of his officers played a game to pass the time. Some of the Crow and Shoshone scouts raced their ponies, as if they were out on the plains with no one around for miles.

Less than an hour later, they heard gunshots. The advance scouts galloped back into camp and yelled the warning: the Lakota were coming. In fact, the Lakota and Cheyenne were right behind them. The scouts led the warriors straight into Crook's position. Seven hundred screaming warriors rushed toward the camp. The Crow and Shoshone rushed to the front to meet their hated enemies. More than a few soldiers credited the bravery of the Crow and Shoshone with keeping the battle from becoming a rout.

There was no coordinated plan. The Lakota and Cheyenne simply swarmed the area. It was a maelstrom of roaring guns, thundering hooves, and shrieking men and animals. The Battle of the Rosebud surged back and forth. It flowed in waves over meadows, hills, and ravines. The warriors charged and retreated, then regrouped and swept in from different directions. The Wyoming Column fought the same way: soldiers and scouts attacked, retreated, pivoted to new positions, and attacked again. The battle raged back and forth for six hours, which was nearly unheard of in that part of the country.

Typically, a Native American attack focused on one big assault, and if that didn't get the job done right away, the warriors retreated and lived to fight another day. But this was different. The Lakota warriors under Sitting Bull and Crazy Horse, and the Cheyenne warriors like the fabled Dog Soldiers, stayed in constant contact with their enemy. The battle was a seemingly endless series of small engagements that were spread over a wide area, many of which were conducted at the speed of galloping horses. The native ponies were smaller and faster than the army horses, and they swerved through the soldiers with incredible agility.

The superior horsemanship and the advantage of the faster ponies were on display during the highlight that gave the battle its name for the Cheyenne. A Cheyenne warrior named Chief Comes in Sight charged the soldiers and made bravery runs in front of their lines. As he dashed back and forth, a soldier shot the warrior's horse, and Chief Comes in Sight crashed to the ground. At the sight of the fallen warrior, a young woman called Buffalo Calf Road Woman raced out from the Cheyenne lines. She galloped toward Chief Comes in Sight while army rifle fire slammed into the ground all around her. She scooped him up, pulled him onto the back of her pony, and rushed back to the relative safety of the Cheyenne lines.

In the Cheyenne tradition, the supreme act of bravery was said to have inspired the rest of the warriors to renew their fight when the engagement seemed to have turned against them. Buffalo Calf Road Woman had rescued her brother, Chief Comes in Sight, from certain death. Later, when the Cheyenne sang of the battle, they referred to it as "Where the Girl Saved Her Brother."

While the fighting was still hot, General Crook set up a command post on a nearby hill and tried to bring some organization to the battle. After several hours of combat, he believed his larger force was gaining control of the struggle. He rightly assumed the village was close—that was why the warriors were fighting so ferociously without retreating.

Crook ordered half his cavalry to disengage and rush up the Rosebud to find the village, but that made them an easy target. Warriors shifted their focus to the cavalry and moved in. At the same time as they attacked the cavalry unit, they took aim at Crook's hilltop headquarters. Crook's position appeared to be in jeopardy, but the Shoshone scouts hurried to the rescue and turned back the warriors.

After six hours of furious fighting, the warriors had halted all attempts by the soldiers to penetrate the canyon that led to the village. During the all-night ride to engage the U.S. Army, the warriors had stopped only once—at dawn—to rest and water their ponies. The men and their mounts were now exhausted. They broke off the attack and melted back into the landscape. They began the long ride back to the village, and although they were tired and hungry, they already composed songs of their great victory.

Crook wanted to pursue the warriors, but his scouts said no. If the village was back in the canyon, as Crook suspected, then the entrance to the canyon would be the perfect place for an ambush. The Crow scouts said they wouldn't ride into a trap. Reluctantly, Crook agreed to stay where they were for the night.

As the soldiers made camp, they buried their dead. Crook officially reported ten killed and twenty wounded. He estimated about one hundred casualties on the Native American side, but he also estimated that his men fired 25,000 rounds to inflict those hundred casualties. He then deduced that he couldn't continue his march. If the marksmanship of his troops was so poor that the ratio was going to be 250 bullets for every killed or injured warrior, his men needed more ammo. His wagon train with the bulk of the food and ammunition was more than thirty miles behind him at yesterday's camp on Goose Creek.

The next day, June 18, the Wyoming Column trudged back to its base camp. A few days later, Crook lost most of his Crow and Shoshone scouts. They fought bravely and tenaciously, but they were disgusted by the army's performance at the Battle of the Rosebud, and they went home. The soldiers settled into camp and stayed there for six weeks, during which time they completely missed the Battle of the Little Bighorn.

7

FAILURE TO COMMUNICATE

General Crook sent his first report about the Battle of the Rosebud to General Sheridan's headquarters in Chicago on June 19. Crook claimed victory, though he inflicted minimal casualties, captured no prisoners, retreated from the battlefield, and failed to damage Sitting Bull's plans in any meaningful way. Crook could call it a win if he wanted to, but Sheridan's official report stated that the battle was "barren of results."

In the crucial days after the battle, Crook's attempts to protect his reputation weren't the biggest problem. Crook had no trouble sending a stream of messages to Sheridan to say that his men needed supplies and reinforcements before they could even *consider* continuing the campaign. And he went so far as to suggest that the army should construct forts in the area before moving any further with the expedition. But Crook made no attempt to communicate with the other commanders in the field.

Crook believed he knew the location of the village. At a minimum, he had a sense of the size and strength of the warrior army.

He saw their tactics and their weaponry. He witnessed the longest sustained battle between soldiers and warriors on the northern plains, but he sent none of the intelligence to General Terry or Colonel Gibbon. As a result, when Custer led a few hundred men into battle along the banks of the Little Bighorn one week later, he was unaware that he was facing the largest Native American army in recorded history.

On the morning of the Battle of the Rosebud, Major Reno's reconnaissance patrol awoke on the banks of Rosebud Creek about fifty miles north of the impending engagement. For the past two days, Reno had been in breach of General Terry's orders. Ironically, and unknowingly, his detachment was closer to the hostiles than any member of the Seventh Cavalry had been since they left Fort Lincoln a month earlier.

But to this point, Reno and the right wing had seen very little sign of a village. They spent five days scouting parts of the Powder River, the Tongue River, and the smaller creeks between the two larger waterways. There were no signs on the Powder. Reno didn't know it, but Sitting Bull's village hadn't been in that area for nearly two months.

The detachment continued west to Mizpah Creek and then Pumpkin Creek before striking the Tongue River. When the soldiers reached the Tongue on June 15, they finally saw their first significant signs of a village. They found the torn-up patch of ground that had been home to the village exactly one month earlier when Lieutenant Bradley from the Montana Column spotted it. Reno's scouts and guides estimated the size of the village at four hundred lodges, but that count was now thirty days old. No one knew the current size of the village, but the patrol received a wake-up call two days later.

When Reno made it to the Tongue River, his mission should have been complete. His orders were to turn north and lead his scouting party to the junction of the Tongue and the Yellowstone to rendezvous with Terry and Custer. Instead, Reno continued west to the forbidden zone of Rosebud Creek. Terry expressly ordered Reno to stay away from the Rosebud. That was the last known position of the village, and Terry wanted Custer to handle a scout of the area. But Reno was determined to prove himself. He led his troops west for another day and a half, and as they neared the Rosebud, Reno sent a unit of scouts south along the creek.

The men returned with new information: they'd spotted the remnants of two old campsites and a wide trail of churned-up earth that led farther south. The command continued its westward trek and traveled deeper into the valley of the Rosebud. By that time, the trail of the village was impossible to miss. More than three thousand people, and an animal herd that probably tripled that number, trampled the grass as they moved south along to the creek. Private Peter Thompson said later that it was hard to find a place to camp because the ground was so thoroughly scoured.

On the morning of June 17, while Sitting Bull, Crazy Horse, and seven hundred warriors screamed toward General Crook's Wyoming Column about fifty miles to the south, Reno's men performed one final scout of Rosebud Creek. Reno's civilian guide, Mitch Boyer, led a group of Arikara about twenty miles south along the creek. They concluded their scout near Deer Medicine Rocks, the site of the Lakota Sun Dance ceremony two weeks earlier, though none of the party knew about the ceremony at the time. Boyer and the scouts found a larger, fresher campsite and clear evidence of smaller groups that streamed toward the main body. The village was immense and growing by the hour, and it was somewhere farther south.

The scouts couldn't pinpoint the exact location, but they estimated it was no more than a two-day ride away.

Reno needed to decide how far he wanted to push this scouting expedition. He had already disobeyed orders and was overdue to meet Terry and Custer up on the Yellowstone. His rations were low and his horses were tired, but there was a chance for glory. Custer certainly would have taken it, despite the warning that Reno received from his senior Arikara scout. The man, called Forked Horn, said: "If the Dakotas see us, the sun will not move very far before we are all killed." That sealed the decision. Reno and the right wing of the Seventh Cavalry pointed their horses north and began the ride to the rendezvous.

At the junction of the Tongue River and the Yellowstone River, Custer and the left wing of the Seventh Cavalry fished and drank and gambled to pass the time while they waited for Reno and the right wing. It was June 17, and the left wing expected Reno to arrive any moment. When the columns split seven days earlier, Reno led the right wing south along the Powder River, and Custer led the left wing north. Custer's men paused at a supply depot that had been established by the crew of the *Far West* at the junction of the Powder and the Yellowstone. For four days, the men relaxed and reoutfitted themselves for the next leg of the journey, and they gulped beer and whiskey at a makeshift bar that was constructed by an enterprising sutler named John Smith.

The merriment ended on June 15, and they resumed their march to the appointed rendezvous spot at the confluence of the Tongue and the Yellowstone. When the column rode away from the depot, it was stripped down and ready for action. The column left most of the herders at the Powder River depot. It left behind boxes of sabers that were cumbersome and would slow the progress of the march. It left behind any soldier who didn't have a horse, and, to Custer's chagrin, the regimental band. The left wing was now a swift fighting force in search of an opponent.

The men marched for two days until they reached the junction of the Tongue and the Yellowstone. They set up camp on a site that was used by a Lakota village earlier in the winter. On the same day the Wyoming Column battled the Lakota and Cheyenne far to the south, and Reno's right wing concluded its scouting trip, Custer and some of the men of the left wing desecrated burials at the old Lakota village.

The bodies of the Lakota dead lay on scaffoldings around the campsite. Members of the cavalry wasted little time before looting the bodies. Lieutenant Edward Godfrey, who would play a significant role in the battle to come, kept a diary about the campaign. In it, he noted with disgust: "Several persons rode about exhibiting trinkets with as much gusto as if they were trophies of valor, and showed no more concern for their desecration than if they had won them at a raffle."

Custer instructed an African American interpreter named Isaiah Dorman to pull down a corpse that smelled particularly bad and throw it in the Yellowstone River. Dorman carried out his order, though it probably made him feel conflicted because he was married to a Dakota woman. Dorman was a former slave from New Orleans who had been an interpreter and courier at Fort Rice before signing on to the 1876 expedition. He wasn't a young man, but he wanted one more chance to see the untamed country of the West. His choice had provided him with a month of relatively uneventful travel up to this point, highlighted only by the typical hazards of rough terrain and nasty weather. Whether or not Dorman could feel it coming, the streak of uneventful days would end one week later.

Many of the officers in the Seventh Cavalry were appalled at the disrespect and destruction. In most, if not all, Native American societies, such desecration brought bad luck to the perpetrators and a bad omen for the future. It's unlikely that the men of the Seventh knew it, but Custer was already living under the shroud of a dark omen. Custer himself probably didn't realize it, which was why his men were oblivious.

In the spring of 1869, a few months after the Battle of the Washita, Custer led the Seventh Cavalry on an expedition to persuade the remaining Native Americans on the southern plains to move to reservations. Custer's superiors believed Custer had demonstrated the army's willingness and ability to fight anytime and anywhere. Now, Custer toured the area and hoped to use words instead of guns to herd the holdouts onto reservations. Along the way, he secured the release of two white women who were being held prisoner. The unintentional, yet successful, rescue of the captives helped cement his stature as America's number one Indian fighter. But toward the end of the trip, he accepted an invitation to a sit-down that ended with an ominous prophecy—or maybe *curse* is a better description.

The Seventh Cavalry arrived at a Cheyenne village, and Custer explained the purpose of their visit. The Cheyenne invited Custer into the Medicine Arrow Lodge. The name of the lodge was literal: it was the home of the sacred Medicine Arrows of that band of the southern Cheyenne. The name of the keeper of the arrows was Stone Forehead or Rock Forehead, depending on the translation. But the Americans referred to him as Medicine Arrow.

In the Cheyenne tradition, the story says that Custer entered the lodge alone and sat down with Stone Forehead and several others. Stone Forehead offered Custer a pipe and held it while Custer smoked. Custer famously abstained from alcohol and tobacco, but he respected the ritual.

As Custer smoked the pipe, Stone Forehead spoke the warning. Several versions of the specific words exist, but the point is the same in each variation. Stone Forehead told Custer that if Custer ever attacked the Cheyenne again, Custer and all his men would die. When Stone Forehead finished his warning, he dumped the ashes from the pipe onto the toes of Custer's boots and completed the curse.

Custer didn't have a translator. He didn't understand the words, nor did he understand the significance of Stone Forehead's final action. When Custer reported his own version of the experience, he made no mention of the ashes and almost certainly did not comprehend the gravity of the moment. Now, in June of 1876, a little more than seven years after Stone Forehead's warning, Custer participated in, and to some extent supervised, the desecration of a burial site. Custer was one week away from his first serious conflict with the Cheyenne since he'd smoked a pipe in the Medicine Arrow Lodge, and he was blissfully ignorant that he was bringing yet more bad luck upon himself and his men.

The left wing sat at the junction of the Tongue and the Yellowstone for another two days while it waited for word from Reno. General Terry had stayed on board the *Far West* as it paddled upstream and mirrored the march of the cavalry. On June 19, two couriers arrived and informed Terry and Custer of Reno's new position on the Rosebud.

Terry was understandably angry about Reno's disobedience. Terry could barely tolerate Custer's tendencies to freelance, and now he was seeing it from Reno, too. Reno was now in the vicinity of Colonel Gibbon's column, so Terry sent his aide-de-camp to order Reno to halt and wait for the left wing to join him. Terry would get all his commanders in one room and organize a new plan, but first, he needed a full report from Reno. The major's written message was brief and short on detail but promised more information when they met in person.

Terry, on board the *Far West*, and Custer, with the cavalry, traveled up the Yellowstone and connected with Reno the following day, June 20. Reno's full report provoked two different kinds of fury: continued anger from Terry about Reno's disobedience, and outrage from Custer about Reno's decision to abandon a potential attack on the hostiles.

An unspoken understanding evolved in the U.S. Army during the years of fighting Native American tribes after the Civil War. If a commander disobeyed orders so that he could seize an opportunity to attack, the disobedience could be forgiven . . . as long as the attack was successful. If the commander disobeyed orders and failed in the attack, it signaled disaster for the commander. The unspoken understanding was essentially Custer's guiding principle in the army. He followed orders only up to the point when his own judgment told him otherwise. He had a proven record of disobeying orders when he believed an opportunity arose, and now, when Reno did the same thing, Custer criticized him for it.

Two days after the rendezvous with Reno, Custer wrote an anonymous letter to *The New York Herald* in which, to use a modern expression, he said the quiet part out loud.

In one passage, Custer wrote:

Reno, after an absence of ten days, returned, when it was found, to the disgust and disappointment of every member of the

*expedition, from the commanding General down to the lowest
private, that Reno, instead of simply failing to accomplish any
good results, has so misconducted his force as to embarrass, if not
seriously and permanently mar, all hopes of future success of the
expedition. He had not only deliberately and without a shadow of
excuse failed to obey his written orders issued by General Terry's
personal directions, but he acted in positive disobedience to the
strict injunctions of the department commander.*

That section alone was dripping with irony. Another passage
took it even further:

*Had Reno, after first violating his orders, pursued and overtaken
the Indians, his original disobedience of orders would have been
overlooked, but his determination forsook him at that point, and
instead of continuing his pursuit, and at least bringing the Indians at bay, he gave the order to countermarch and faced his
command to the rear.*

Custer plainly stated the unspoken understanding. If he had
been leading the scout, he would have disobeyed orders and attacked the village without knowing—or *despite* knowing—the size
and strength of the opposing force. In less than a week, he would
do exactly that. But after hearing Reno's report, Custer excoriated
Reno in the press for taking the prudent course of action. Reno
wisely led his company back to the main body of troops to coordinate a large-scale assault. And despite Custer's words to the newspaper, Reno's disobedience did produce positive results.

After one month in the field, the Dakota Column now had its
best information about the location of the Native American vil-

lage. And, on top of all the other ironies with Custer's letter, there was one more: Custer would be the beneficiary of Reno's disobedience and new intelligence. Custer already knew he would lead a team up the Rosebud in search of the village, and he now found himself in the unique position to do three things at the same time. He could condemn Reno for disobeying orders; he could accuse Reno of cowardice for failing to attack when he had the chance; and he could capitalize on the intelligence that was gained from Reno's disobedience.

Terry spent the evening of June 20 devising a new strategy on board the *Far West*. The next day, he proudly outlined his plan for Colonel Gibbon, Lieutenant Colonel Custer, and Major James Brisbin, the cavalry commander of Gibbon's Montana Column. Based on Reno's patrol and new intelligence from Terry's Crow scouts, Terry believed the hostiles were near one of three waterways: Rosebud Creek, the Little Bighorn River, or the Bighorn River.

No one knew the exact location of the village, but Terry's plan called for Custer to lead the entire Seventh Cavalry south along Rosebud Creek, nearly to the Wyoming border. If Custer spotted a trail of the village that led west toward the Bighorn or the Little Bighorn, he should send a message to the Montana Column and then continue south before looping back to the north. At the same time, Gibbon and the Montana Column would march west along the Yellowstone until the river met the Bighorn. At that point, the column would follow the Bighorn south until it split with the Little Bighorn. The column would continue into the valley of the Little Bighorn and, with any luck, reunite with Custer's column.

Custer's Seventh Cavalry was the larger, yet faster, of the two forces. His regiment was comprised entirely of cavalry, whereas the Montana Column was a mix of cavalry and infantry. Terry knew the

Montana Column would move more slowly than Custer's column, which was part of the reason why he wanted Custer to extend his ride to the south even if he spotted the trail of the village. The goal was for Custer to ensure that the Indians had not escaped to the south or the east. Then, he could drive hard against them and push them toward the Montana Column. Gibbon's slower force would block escape routes to the north and west. If the plan worked, the hostiles would be caught between Custer's strike force and Gibbon's blocking force.

Terry anticipated the Montana Column would be in place by June 26. If Custer followed instructions, he would arrive at about the same time, and they would coordinate a multipronged attack. But that was a major *if.*

To reuse and paraphrase Custer's words from his anonymous letter that criticized Reno, every member of the expedition, from General Terry to the lowest private, knew Custer would attack the village if he thought he had a good opportunity. And in Custer's mind, every opportunity was a good opportunity. He was supremely confident in his own ability and the ability of his regiment, no matter the size of the opposing force. Terry's orders, both written and verbal, seemed to give Custer approval to act on his own authority.

Terry's written instructions told Custer to perform his maneuver, send a message to the Montana Column if he found a fresh trail of the village, and then wait to coordinate an attack. But Terry also added an out clause that would allow him to cover himself in the future. With so many unknowns—chiefly the size and specific location of the village—Terry stated that it was impossible to give Custer definitive orders that he should follow to the letter. If Custer was "nearly in contact with the enemy," as Terry phrased it, then Custer should rely on his own judgment regarding an attack.

The orders were another masterful example of double-talk from the man who had helped write the Fort Laramie Treaty. If Custer stuck to the plan, he would find the village and organize an attack with Terry, and they would all share a glorious victory. If Custer attacked by himself and succeeded, Terry could claim he gave authorization. If Custer attacked and failed, Terry could claim Custer disobeyed orders. And on top of the written orders with their qualifiers, there were multiple reports after the planning session that said Terry gave Custer verbal authorization to attack if he thought he could win.

Lieutenant James Bradley, the chief of scouts for the Montana Column who first spotted the village a month earlier, wrote in his diary at the time: "It is understood that if Custer arrives first he is at liberty to attack if he deems prudent. We have little hope of being in at the death, as Custer will undoubtedly exert himself to the utmost to get there first and win all the laurels for himself and his regiment."

Interpreter Fred Gerard testified later that he overheard Terry say, "I told [Custer] if he found the Indians not to do as Reno did, but if he thought he could whip them to do so."

That night, Custer relayed the plan to his officers. The briefing was terse and light on detail, as usual. Custer wasn't long-winded or comprehensive when distributing orders. He gave his men the bare minimum. In this case, he told them to pack supplies and ammunition for fifteen days on assignment. But at the same time, he instructed them to carry only the essentials. He wanted his fighting force to be lean and fast. Lastly, he restructured the regiment's organizational chart. He merged the two wings back into a single unit that would be solely under his command. Each company commander would report directly to Custer. The column would move out the next day, June 22. With that, Custer sent his officers to inform their troopers.

The soldiers, civilians, and scouts spent the night making final preparations for the next phase of the expedition. They all felt it. The long days of monotonous riding were done. They were close to the enemy, and there would be a battle soon. Many soldiers spent the evening writing letters to family or scribbling their last wills on scraps of paper and passing them to comrades for safe-keeping. The Arikara scouts sang their death songs in their camp some distance from the soldiers' camp. Major Marcus Reno, now removed from command of a wing of the regiment, started drink-ing. He and several others swayed on the decks of the *Far West* and belted out old inspirational tunes.

Later in the evening, Custer and Benteen renewed their mutual hatred with a heated argument during a discussion among several officers. Custer then spent a good portion of the rest of the night writing his final letter to his wife. He eventually fell asleep with the pen still in his hand.

Mark Kellogg, the reporter who was contracted by *The Bismarck Tribune* to be a correspondent for *The New York Herald*, wrote his final dispatches for the press. During the expedition, his horse had given out, and he was now riding a mule. Despite the possible limitation in mode of travel, he had just changed his mind about the next phase of the campaign. Instead of staying with General Terry aboard the *Far West* and then accompanying the Montana Column, he was going to ride with Custer. If there was going to be a fight, or action of any kind, Custer was most likely to find it. Kellogg wanted to be there to see it.

The next day, the men of the Dakota Column finished their letters, their wills, and their dispatches. The scouts finished singing their death songs. The soldiers strapped rations and ammunition to their horses and loaded the rest onto a train of pack mules, the same exhausted animals that had recently completed a week of hard riding in support of Reno's scout.

General Terry saluted the men as they formed up and prepared to ride. He planned to avail himself of the comforts of the *Far West* as long as possible and would spend the next few days on the Yellowstone River while the rest of the troopers marched under the blazing sun.

The Seventh Cavalry marched out under the gaze of Custer, Terry, and Colonel Gibbon. The main body of troops led the way, followed by the pack train and then the rear guard. When the entire column had passed, Custer shook hands with the other commanders. As he began to gallop toward his men, Gibbon called out, "Now, Custer, don't be greedy, but wait for us." Custer laughed, waved, and shouted back, "No, I will not."

The regiment was packed for a trip of fifteen days. Nearly half would be dead in three.

8

THE CROW'S NEST

On Thursday, June 22, the day the Seventh Cavalry began its march up the Rosebud toward Sitting Bull's village, the National League was about one-third of the way through its inaugural season. The Chicago White Stockings led the league with twenty-two wins after beating the New York Mutuals 6–4. The White Stockings were the powerhouse of the league, thanks in large part to two of the early legends of the game. Pitcher Al Spalding started twenty-five of Chicago's twenty-six games up to that point and was on the mound for twenty-one of its twenty-two wins. His counterpart at the plate and in the field was Adrian Anson. He would be known in later years as "Cap" Anson for his longtime captaincy of the team. The 1876 season was his first of twenty-two seasons with Chicago, and he was well on his way to becoming the first superstar of baseball.

The Hartford Dark Blues held steady in second place with nineteen wins after a 3–0 victory over the struggling Louisville Grays. Tommy Bond was in the first half of thirty-two straight starts as the pitcher for Hartford. He started forty-five of the first forty-seven games for the Dark Blues, with his streak broken only by two starts by Candy Cummings, the man who was credited with inventing the curveball. In late June of 1876, Bond dueled Jim Devlin of the Louisville Grays. Louisville lost five of the seven games in the series, and Devlin started just two more games in the rest of the season. He started every game of the 1877 season—all sixty-one—but that was his final year of professional baseball. After the season, he was one of the first four men banned from pro baseball for life as part of the sport's first major gambling scandal.

In Cheyenne on June 22, the time of departure for Charlie Utter and Wild Bill Hickok was down to less than a week. The gold mines of Deadwood were calling, and the two men were eager to begin the trip. In Missouri, wannabe outlaw Hobbs Kerry continued to wait anxiously for his chance to pitch a robbery idea to Jesse James. Kerry's new acquaintances, Charlie Pitts and Bill Chadwell, were still trying to wrangle a meeting with the James brothers and the Younger brothers. In Dodge City, Wyatt Earp, Bat Masterson, and the rest of the new force of lawmen were well on their way to racking up an average of three hundred arrests per month. A seemingly endless parade of cattle trudged toward Dodge from Texas. By the end of the cattle season, an estimated 250,000 head made the trek.

On the northern plains, the space between hunters and hunted grew smaller by the hour. The Seventh Cavalry was just two days away from discovering the trail of Sitting Bull's village, and just three days away from sending a small portion of its number on one of the most ill-fated cavalry charges in American history.

All spring, Native American warriors and their families flowed into Sitting Bull's camp. Many spent the winter starving at the

Red Cloud Agency or the Spotted Tail Agency. They learned of the U.S. Army's attack on the Cheyenne village in mid-March and answered Sitting Bull's call to fight back against the American government. Warriors typically left the agencies in the spring and early summer to go hunting, but now the yearly hunt turned into a wholesale move as they took their families to join an effort that could lead to war.

During the week between the end of Reno's scout and the first day of the Battle of the Little Bighorn, Sitting Bull's village doubled in size from roughly four thousand people to eight thousand people. Two of the most prominent new arrivals were warriors of great renown from Sitting Bull's band of Hunkpapa: Crow King and Gall, a childhood friend of Sitting Bull's. Every major chief and warrior who still had the drive to fight led his people to the village, and they all recognized Sitting Bull as the spiritual leader of the largest gathering on the northern plains.

The village moved from the banks of a small creek into the valley of the Greasy Grass River, a waterway that was known to whites as the Little Bighorn. The growing camp spent six days at its first site and then shifted north in search of fresh grass. The Lakota and Cheyenne found a spot that was protected by a severe loop of the river. Tribal leaders tucked the village in behind the loop so that it was mostly hidden from riders who approached from the south.

A line of bluffs rose above the village on the other side of the river and sheltered it from view, though those same bluffs could be a hazard if an enemy captured the high ground and fired down into the village. But the likelihood was low that an enemy—especially the U.S. Army, which was not known for its stealth—could sneak up on the village and gain complete control of the bluffs. Sitting Bull had heard reports of soldiers to the northeast, which would be a different group from the army the warriors had fought a week earlier. The chiefs sat around council fires in the evening and decided not to launch an attack like they had against Crook's column. This time, they would wait and see the intent of the new soldiers. If the soldiers wanted peace, the chiefs would talk. If the soldiers wanted war, like the declaration of the U.S. government had stated six months earlier, the chiefs would accommodate.

Sitting Bull's vision of a battle and soldiers falling upside down into his camp hadn't been fulfilled, so he likely believed that the chance for peace was remote. But from the beginning, he had advised a strategy of avoidance first and battle second, and he remained consistent now.

And while the village made its final move north before the great battle, Custer led the Seventh Cavalry south along Rosebud Creek.

After the first full day's ride since leaving the Yellowstone River, the Seventh awoke on the banks of the Rosebud on June 23, and Custer made another change in the order of march. Each of the twelve companies in the cavalry was responsible for driving its own group of mules in the pack train. The companies sent small groups of unlucky soldiers back to the mule train to wrangle the animals. Custer ordered the lieutenant who supervised the pack mules to report the three companies whose animals caused the most problems. Those three companies would be relegated to the rear of the column to guard the mule train.

Senior Captain Frederick Benteen's company was one of the three with a failing grade, and Custer instructed him to take his company to the rear, which probably delighted Custer to no end. Custer, who was clad in his now-famous white buckskin suit, led approximately 660 men on a day of march that proved to be the first significant advance since the column left the Yellowstone.

The cavalry approached the area where Reno ended his scout several days earlier. Now Custer and the rest of the Seventh saw the signs of the village that Reno reported from his patrol. Numerous small campsites dotted the landscape. The column camped along the Rosebud again on June 23, and when it departed the next day at 5:00 a.m., every man plainly saw the trail of a massive village.

At about 7:30 a.m., the column found the site of Sitting Bull's Sun Dance. The remnants of the original camp were now seventeen days old, but the trail that led away from the site showed clear evidence of the groups that were riding toward the village from the agencies. Custer admitted to his officers that he expected to find an army that could number as many as fifteen hundred warriors. He emphasized caution and vigilance and the importance of following orders without question, but he still said nothing about General Terry's overall strategy to coordinate an attack with the Montana Column.

As far as the officers of the Seventh Cavalry knew, they were out there on their own with raw recruits and limited rations and ammunition. They could be outnumbered more than two to one, and they could be expected to launch an assault with little warning or preparation. And when they reached the site of Sitting Bull's Sun Dance on the morning of June 24, they were greeted with a grisly display: the bloody scalp of a white man dangled from one of the Sun Dance lodge poles.

The Arikara scouts examined the area and determined that the Lakota knew an enemy was approaching and they were confident of victory in battle. The alarming omens were starting to stack up, but Custer remained unconcerned. All day, the column rode south through one campsite after another. Some were so recent that embers still smoldered in their campfires. The entire width of the valley around Rosebud Creek was torn up by thousands of animals and people who were on the road to Sitting Bull's village.

At 4:00 p.m. on June 24, Custer halted the march to allow some of the scouts to range farther ahead. They reported a fresh campsite twelve miles up the trail, at a spot where a smaller creek branched off from the Rosebud and led to the west. It looked like the main village was in that direction and might be no more than thirty miles away. An hour later, Custer resumed the march and made the first of several decisions that helped determine the fate of the Seventh Cavalry over the next twenty-four hours. The column had reached the point at which Custer was supposed to send a messenger to meet General Terry and the Montana Column.

Terry's orders required Custer to send a civilian frontiersman named George Herendeen to report the movements of the Dakota Column and relay any intelligence that had been gathered. Herendeen rode up to Custer and reminded the commander that they were at the appointed spot. Custer simply stared at Herendeen and said nothing. When Custer looked away and still didn't speak, Herendeen returned to the main body of the column and fell in with the rest of the men. The only real opportunity to coordinate an attack with both columns was gone.

Of all of Custer's decisions that could be questioned with the benefit of hindsight, this was possibly the most damning. A full day before the Battle of the Little Bighorn, Custer knew he was outnumbered. If he had sent Herendeen to link up with the Montana Column and then continued to march south according to General Terry's orders, there was likely a good chance that the Montana Column and the Dakota Column could have coordinated an attack on the village. The soldiers still would have been outnumbered, but the ratio would have been much closer to even.

In that scenario, the battle that was now about thirty-six hours away would have been very different. But Custer's thirst for glory, his zeal for battle, and his belief in his own invincibility overruled his orders from Terry. And by the end of the day on June 24, he would be out of options. Regardless of the lopsided numbers, and everything else, there would be just one course of action available.

Along the banks of the Bighorn River, General Terry and the Montana Column knew nothing of Custer's decision to chase the village alone. Since the separation of the two columns on June 21, the Montana Column had marched west along the Yellowstone River. Terry stayed on the *Far West* as it chugged upriver next to the column. On June 23, as the Dakota Column began seeing the accumulating signs of Native American activity along Rosebud Creek, the Montana Column reached the junction of the Yellowstone and the Bighorn River. At that point, the Yellowstone continued west and the Bighorn led south. The *Far West* spent much of the day ferrying soldiers across the junction. With the column now on the east bank of the Bighorn River, it had access to the whole region between itself and the Dakota Column. Terry had every reason to believe his plan was cruising along nicely.

The Montana Column was in place to block escape routes to the north and the west as it began its march south along the Bighorn on June 24. It was in a good position to link up with the Dakota Column when the time was right. Terry didn't know the exact location of the Native American village or the Seventh Cavalry, but the area of operation was finally shrinking. The village was probably no more than a couple of days' march to the south, and Custer was no more than fifty miles to the west. And with two days remaining until the intended rendezvous of the two columns, Terry expected to see George Herendeen arrive at any time with news from Custer. But as daylight dwindled with the coming evening, there were no sightings of Herendeen and no word from Custer.

Custer halted the Dakota Column along the banks of the Rosebud at 7:45 p.m. on June 24. The men and animals were exhausted. They'd traveled twenty-eight miles that day, and only a lucky few didn't spend the entire time choking on dust. Custer sent his scouts forward, and they returned at 9:00 p.m. with news that the expanding trail of the village led west toward the valley of the Little Bighorn River. Custer was now at the critical crossroads of the expedition. His orders told him to continue south toward the headwaters of the Tongue River, even if he saw that the trail of the village turned away from the Rosebud. He was supposed to ensure that the tribes had not scattered and run to the south. When he had confirmation, then he should turn north and west toward the rendezvous with the Montana Column.

But his orders also told him to meet the Montana Column on June 26. If he followed Terry's instructions to the letter and continued another thirty miles south toward the headwaters of the Tongue River, he would be a day late for the meeting. And there was now a more urgent consideration: the Seventh was so close to the village that there was virtually no chance the column hadn't been spotted. If the column had somehow remained undetected, its presence wouldn't be a secret for long. A force of 660 men with a mule train was impossible to hide. The dust alone could be seen for miles.

Custer had to assume the column had been seen, or would be soon. His scouts judged the village to be no more than a day away.

And Terry had given him the freedom to deviate from his orders if he felt there was "sufficient reason" to do so. Despite knowing he could face a force that might double his own, Custer believed he had sufficient reason. His enemy was within striking distance, and if he, Custer, didn't strike first, he ran the risk of giving the advantage to the enemy. And, of course, there was the opportunity for unprecedented glory.

Custer's scouts believed the village lay in a valley beyond a ridge of small mountains to the west. Custer gathered his officers and informed them of the new plan. They would not continue south toward the Tongue River as ordered. Instead, they would march through the night and follow the trail of the village to the west. They would set up camp at the base of the mountains in the predawn and scout the village during the daylight hours of June 25. Then they would attack at dawn on June 26.

Custer allowed the main column to rest for two hours. He scheduled the departure for 11:00 p.m., but he wanted his scouts back out in the field immediately. The Crow scouts told him about the perfect reconnaissance spot in the ridge of mountains to the west. There was a high hill with a hollow that was hidden from view. The Crow used it as the launch point for horse-stealing raids against the Lakota. From that spot, observers had a clear line of sight toward the valley of the Little Bighorn. If the Crow were right and the village was there, the scouts should be able to see the smoke from cook fires and other signs.

Custer's chief of scouts, Second Lieutenant Charles Varnum, was thoroughly exhausted after ranging across sixty miles that day. But he accepted the mission to go to the lookout post with the Crow scouts. They needed to be there before dawn so they could sneak in undetected and confirm—hopefully—the location of the village.

Varnum wolfed down a hasty supper and wearily climbed back into the saddle. The scouting party began its ride as night settled in.

The main body of the Dakota Column rested for another two hours and then started its night march. It was a black night; the thin crescent moon did nothing to illuminate the terrain; and torches were forbidden. Each man could only follow the dust trail of the man in front of him.

As six hundred troopers picked their way through the darkness, Varnum and the scouts reached the observation post in the Wolf Mountains. They were a party of fourteen men: Varnum, civilian guide Mitch Boyer, interpreter Charley Reynolds, six Arikara riders to act as couriers, and five Crow scouts to act as observers. This was Crow territory, and they knew it better than anyone.

At roughly 3:00 a.m. on June 25, the group reached the steepest point of the trail up the mountains to the hollow that would act as their hideout. The horses couldn't go any farther, and Varnum dismounted and collapsed on the spot. He had been in the saddle for nearly twenty-four hours, and now he fell asleep almost instantly. The Arikara couriers and two of the Crow scouts followed his lead. While they slept, the other three scouts, plus Reynolds and Boyer, finished the climb to the hidden hollow and waited for the first glow of sunrise. About an hour later, Boyer shook Varnum awake. The Crow scouts wanted the leader of the party to see something.

Varnum scrambled up through the juniper trees and buffalo grass to the concealed lookout spot. The Crow pointed west and used sign language to communicate that they could see a Sioux camp. Charley Reynolds studied the scene through his field glass and concurred. The youngest Arikara courier, Red Star, nodded his agreement and added that he could see wisps of smoke from early-morning cook fires. But Second Lieutenant Charles Varnum could see nothing.

In the faintest light of dawn, he saw only the outlines of the landscape. His eyes weren't trained to look for the signs that were readily spotted by the Crow and the Arikara. And even if he'd had years of experience in circumstances like these, his eyes were bloodshot and weary and inflamed from a long day of riding in the heat and the dust. The scouts said they could see the telltale signs of an immense herd of horses. But again, Varnum had to take their word for it. He couldn't see horses or smoke, but now there was a consensus that the great Sioux village was no more than twenty miles away in the valley of the Little Bighorn.

Varnum trusted the scouts, and he scribbled a note on a piece of paper for Custer. He gave the note to the eldest Arikara courier, Crooked Horn, who passed it to two younger riders, Red Star and Bull. They would have the honor of carrying the vital intelligence to the general. And the general wouldn't be hard to find. When the scouting party turned and looked east, they could clearly see the smoke from the cook fires of the Seventh Cavalry.

The Crow scouts were furious. If there had been any hope of retaining the element of surprise, it was gone now. There was no way the smoke would go unnoticed. But at least it would help Red Star and Bull reach the column as fast as possible. The two young men mounted up and rode toward the smoke.

Custer had pushed the column until about 2:00 a.m., roughly the time that the scouting party reached its destination. As the soldiers straggled into camp, most crawled down from their horses, dropped to the ground, and passed out. At about 3:00 a.m., as the Crow scouts saw the earliest signs of the village, some of the soldiers made fires and cooked breakfast. Two hours later, those fires enraged the Crow scouts. The smoke was clearly visible against the morning sky. Unless every member of the village had been struck blind overnight, the Lakota and Cheyenne would soon know the location of the Seventh Cavalry.

Red Star and Bull began the four-mile ride to the column's camp. Bull's pony struggled, and he fell farther and farther behind. Red Star claimed most of the glory when he made it to camp at about 7:30 a.m. on the morning of June 25. Interpreter Isaiah Dorman escorted Red Star to Custer's bivouac, and the courier communicated with the lieutenant colonel through sign language. Red Star confirmed he had seen the village, and he passed Varnum's note to Custer.

Custer now had trustworthy intelligence. He leaped onto his horse and rode bareback through camp. He told the men to be ready to ride by 8:00 a.m. Then he grabbed interpreter Fred Gerard and a group of Arikara couriers and galloped toward the observation post. He wanted to see the village for himself.

9

THE VALLEY OF THE LITTLE BIGHORN

Custer couldn't see the herd of ponies. He couldn't see anything that *resembled* the herd of ponies. But his scouts and interpreters assured him it was there. He had reached the observation post in the hidden hollow a little after 9:00 a.m. Lieutenant Varnum led him up to the lookout spot, which was now called the Crow's Nest, and Custer scanned the horizon to the west. Custer saw nothing with his naked eyes. He said to his men, "I've been on the prairie for many years. I've got mighty good eyes, and I can't see anything that looks like Indian ponies."

Mitch Boyer, the civilian guide, repeated a sentiment he'd been voicing for the past four days, but now with some emphasis at the end: "If you don't find more Indians in that valley than you've ever seen before, you can hang me." Boyer and several others had been warning the officers of the Seventh Cavalry that the Lakota and Cheyenne were not scattering, as the officers feared. The village was growing. Bands were uniting, not running and hiding.

Interpreter Charley Reynolds offered Custer a pair of field

glasses. Now Custer could make out a dark mass in the distance and a rising dust cloud that was the hallmark of a herd of horses. He agreed that they had finally found the village, but he needed to handle the immediate matter of timing. The scouts told Custer of two sightings that had happened before he'd arrived.

First, shortly after Red Star and Bull began their ride toward the column with news of the village, the scouts in the Crow's Nest saw two riders heading east in the direction of the cavalry. They guessed the riders were a Lakota man and boy. The pair looked like they had retrieved a pony from somewhere in the area and were leading it straight toward the column. The scouts had been preparing to kill the riders to keep them from discovering the soldiers, but then the man and the boy changed their course and disappeared behind some hills.

Next, a line of seven riders appeared on a ridge that ran parallel to the column's line of march. Dust from the column was clearly visible, and it was a near certainty that the riders saw it. The riders promptly vanished behind the ridge, but then a single dark shape reappeared and stayed steady. He was likely an observer who was stationed on the ridge to maintain a visual on the column.

Custer's scouts had initially agreed with his plan to spend the day scouting the camp in preparation for a dawn attack on June 26. But now they argued fervently against the delay of a day. They were positive that the column had been detected. If the entire village didn't know by now, it would soon.

At first, Custer refused to acknowledge that his command had been compromised. But the scouts were emphatic, and Custer eventually relented. There was no time to do a proper scout. They would have to strike as soon as possible. But even at this stage of the campaign, Custer's urgency to attack was still driven by his belief that the villagers would scatter and run when they learned of the presence of the cavalry. Even though he knew there could be fifteen hundred warriors in the camp, he couldn't envision a scenario where the warriors united into a single army and attacked his column. Custer was afraid of losing the enemy, not of being overwhelmed by him. And, of course, he knew nothing of the sustained combat between the Native American force and General Crook's Wyoming Column a week earlier. Even with the need for a fast decision rising, the group stayed in the Crow's Nest for an hour and studied the terrain. Then Custer led everyone back to the main body of the column.

The Seventh had begun its march at about 8:30 a.m. and was now within a mile of the Crow's Nest. As Custer and the scouts approached the regiment, Tom Custer rode forward to meet his brother. His news echoed the alarms of the scouts: there were multiple reports of Indian sightings near the column. At this point, the amount of time before the village knew about the cavalry depended entirely on how fast a rider could gallop back to camp. It could be a matter of minutes, but certainly no more than a matter of hours.

Custer gathered his officers and explained the situation: the village was about fifteen miles to the west in the valley of the Little Bighorn River; the regiment had obviously been discovered; and unfortunately, a day of valuable reconnaissance wasn't possible. Nor was it possible for the soldiers and animals to rest and gather their strength before battle. The Dakota Column was the attack force, and it must attack *now*.

Custer told his company commanders to assign 5 or 6 men from each unit to fall back and guard the pack train that carried the extra food and ammo. Roughly 130 men, out of a total of about 660, trudged to the rear to guard the mules. Custer was preparing to go into battle with a little more than 500 soldiers.

The main body formed up and moved out. George Herendeen reiterated his assignment to Custer and said that he could still link up with General Terry and the Montana Column. But Custer knew that the ride would now be fifty miles. Unless Herendeen's horse magically sprouted wings and flew, there was no way he could reach the Montana Column in time for it to help the attack. Civilian guides Charley Reynolds and Mitch Boyer continued to say that the village was the largest they had ever seen. Those statements filtered back through the ranks, and the soldiers rode forward in solemn silence. The regiment followed a stream—Sun Dance Creek—that ran toward the Little Bighorn.

Less than two hours later, at about noon, Custer halted the march and handed out assignments. To some extent, he knew he was entering a scenario that was similar to the Battle of the Washita eight years earlier. At the Washita, he had spotted a lone village and attacked immediately. He hadn't fully reconnoitered the area and didn't know that larger villages with hundreds of warriors were tucked into a loop of the river a few miles upstream. The warriors had surprised and wiped out the scouting party that was led by Major Elliott, and they could have overrun Custer's command if he hadn't retreated back over the Washita River.

Now, as he approached the Little Bighorn, he envisioned the same possibility. If the village was as big as his scouts believed, it could easily be a sprawling network of separate camps that could be strung out over miles of territory. He needed to ensure that he wouldn't be surprised again. But to do that, he needed to stretch his force to a dangerously thin level.

One squad would have to perform a rapid scout of the area and drive any outlying Indians toward the main village. Two squads would then have to attack simultaneously from different directions to reduce the chance of escape. And at the same time, Custer needed to ensure the security of the pack train. His men carried limited ammunition on their horses, but there were twenty-six thousand rounds of extra ammo on the pack mules. He had nearly lost his supply of extra ammo during the Battle of the Washita, and he couldn't afford to let that happen here.

Custer split the assault force of the regiment into three battalions: five companies would ride with him, three companies would follow Major Reno, and three companies would follow Captain Benteen. The rest would stay with the pack mules. Custer planned to lead his battalion and Reno's battalion along the creek toward the village until it was time to separate for the attack. Custer assigned Benteen's battalion to scout a line of bluffs to the southwest. If there were no camps beyond the bluffs, Benteen would circle back and rejoin the other two battalions as they rode toward the valley of the Little Bighorn.

Benteen didn't like the assignment. He considered it a needless detour that was designed to deprive him of the glory of leading part of the attack. But when it was all over, the scouting mission probably saved his life.

The night of June 24 had been cool, but the morning dawned bright and hazy and signaled a hot day ahead. In the village, which now boasted a population that was equal to a good-size town in the West, the day of June 25 began like the previous days along the Greasy Grass River. Boys swam in the water, or rode horses, or played games. Women and old men bustled about the camp completing endless sets of chores. Several women, including the two wives of Sitting Bull's friend Gall, dug turnips near the water. A contingent of warriors rode out to go hunting. A village of that size required a constant supply of fresh meat, which was one of the reasons why villages moved so often. Feeding eight thousand people quickly wiped out the resources around each new campsite.

Early that morning, a Hunkpapa man named Crawler and his ten-year-old son, Deeds, rode out to retrieve a pony that Deeds had been forced to abandon when the village moved. The animal was too exhausted to keep pace with the moving civilization, but now that the new camp was established, Crawler and Deeds retraced their path to find the horse. They were the two riders whom Custer's scouts were preparing to kill before Custer arrived at the Crow's Nest to see the village for himself. The man and his son were among the first Lakota to see signs of intruders beyond the Wolf Mountains.

Next came the group led by Black Bear. His party of six men and one woman lived at the Red Cloud Agency in northwestern Nebraska, but they left the reservation to track horse thieves. The group followed the thieves all the way to Sitting Bull's village and recaptured the horses. As the group rode back to the reservation, it climbed a ridge of hills and rode single file along the spine. The riders spotted a column of soldiers in the valley below and quickly hid themselves from view. While they waited and watched, a third group discovered the soldiers.

Technically, the third group discovered the soldiers the previous day and trailed them throughout the night. The group was a band of Cheyenne led by Chief Little Wolf. The small party was on its way to join Sitting Bull's village when it stumbled upon the soldiers. In the early-morning hours of June 25, three members of the band were rummaging through a box of hardtack that had fallen from a pack mule when some soldiers saw them and fired a few shots. The brief encounter was part of the report that Tom Custer delivered to his brother. It went a long way toward reinforcing the urgent need for an attack on the village.

At about 1:00 p.m., while the village was still unaware of the encroaching soldiers, the three battalions of the Dakota Column resumed their march. Benteen led his battalion southwest toward the bluffs to scout for additional camps. Custer's battalion of five companies rode along the north bank of Sun Dance Creek. Reno's battalion of three companies rode along the south bank. The creek meandered in a northwesterly direction toward the Little Bighorn River and joined the larger waterway a couple of miles below the village.

From the Crow's Nest lookout spot, Custer believed the landscape around the Little Bighorn Valley was a series of rolling hills that would eventually reveal a good view of the village. But as the columns trotted along the creek, he realized the landscape was a series of jagged ravines. They might not be able to see the extent and layout of the village until they were right on top of it.

The battalions rode for about an hour, pausing only once so that Custer could survey the land ahead with his field glasses. He still couldn't see the village, so they continued forward at a fast walk. The scouts ranged ahead, and the couriers galloped back and forth between the scouts and the command. The heat of the day pressed down on the men and animals. Dust choked the air, and the combined factors caused the mule train to fall farther and farther behind. Before long, it was completely out of sight.

A little before 2:00 p.m., when the battalions were about ten miles beyond the Crow's Nest, the scouts discovered a fresh campsite along Sun Dance Creek. The Crow found it first and climbed to the top of a nearby bluff to watch the warriors who had stayed there the previous night. When a second group of scouts, including George Herendeen and Lieutenant Varnum, made it to the campsite, they hurried up to the bluff.

The Crow pointed to a cloud of dust two or three miles in the distance. Fifty warriors kicked up the dust as they raced toward the village. The warriors had probably been warned about the soldiers by one of the three groups who had spotted the column earlier in the morning. The ashes of the campfires were still smoldering. The scouts had missed the warriors by just a few minutes. But if the observers from the morning hadn't already alerted the village to the presence of the U.S. Army, the warriors were about to frantically raise the alarm.

A few minutes later, Custer led the eight companies of the two assault battalions into the campground. He saw the clouds of dust from the warriors who rushed toward the village and knew there was no time to lose. When the warriors reached the village, Custer assumed the villagers would scatter in all directions. If he had any hope of catching them before they escaped, he would have to strike immediately.

Custer ordered the Arikara couriers to hurry to the village and capture the pony herd, but they refused to move unless they were supported by soldiers. After a heated argument, Custer turned to one of his aides and told him to take a message to Major Reno. Custer ordered Reno to chase the fifty warriors and attack the villagers whenever and wherever he found them. As Reno relayed the orders to his men and pushed them forward, they passed Custer on the other side of the creek. Custer shouted, "Take your battalion and try and overtake and bring them to battle and I will support you!"

At the moment, that was the extent of the plan: Reno would attack as he saw fit, and Custer would support him in some way that wasn't specified. And none of that information was communicated to Benteen or the men who rode with the pack train. Benteen had been out of sight for two hours and hadn't sent any updates to Custer. Benteen was somewhere in the hills to the southwest, and Custer had expected him to rejoin the command by now. But it was largely due to Custer's own orders that Benteen was mired in no-man's-land.

When Benteen's battalion split from the regiment, it moved at a fast walk into the hills southwest of the creek that led to the Little Bighorn River. If an overhead view of the regiment had been available, it would have shown Custer's battalion walking along the right side of the creek, Reno's battalion walking along the left side, and Benteen's battalion moving to the extreme left of the area of operation.

As Benteen's battalion entered a landscape of hills and bluffs and ravines, Benteen sent six men forward as advance scouts. The six men did the hard riding up and down the bluffs and hills and used field glasses to scan the landscape. As they crested each new ridge, they signaled back to Benteen: there were no Indians in sight. With each update, Benteen became increasingly convinced that his mission was a fool's errand. But twice, messengers arrived from Custer with orders to continue the scout, so Benteen continued. Custer's original orders stated that Benteen should only send a messenger back to the command if he found Indian camps. Benteen hadn't found any camps, so he didn't send any news.

As the day progressed into midafternoon, Benteen's advance scouts rode to the top of the highest hill they had found during their trek. They surveyed the scene and, once again, saw no Indians or signs of camps. At that point, Benteen decided the exercise was complete. He had marched farther than expected, he had been gone longer than expected, and he had seen no sign of activity. He recalled his advance scouts and turned the battalion to the right to head back to the creek. Benteen was now several miles southwest of Reno and Custer, and several miles behind them. And he had no idea an attack was imminent.

Along the banks of Sun Dance Creek, Reno's battalion began its march toward battle. Custer sent all the Arikara couriers and all but four of the Crow scouts with Reno, which gave Reno roughly 140 troopers and 35 scouts for a total of about 175 men. Custer now commanded about 220 soldiers and scouts, plus his eighteen-year-old nephew, Autie Reed, and newspaper correspondent Mark Kellogg.

Reno's battalion led the way, and at about 3:00 p.m., it reached the junction of Sun Dance Creek and the Little Bighorn River. The men found a natural ford and splashed across the river. A few stopped to water their horses, and a couple observed Reno swigging whiskey from a flask. It would be a common sight over the next twenty-four hours.

As the men crossed the river, they saw their first real signs of the village: herds of ponies grazed up ahead on both sides of the river. Several Arikara raced away from the battalion to capture the herds. The rest of the men rode out of the water and into the trees that lined the Little Bighorn. They pushed through the timber, and then a few dismounted to adjust their saddles before the assault. When the troopers were ready, Reno re-formed them into a single column of four men across. But before they moved forward, Reno received some jarring news.

Two Crow scouts rode ahead of the column and spotted something in the distance. They turned and shouted their news to civilian

guide George Herendeen. Herendeen passed the message to interpreter Fred Gerard. Gerard rode over to Reno and announced that
the Crow saw dust clouds up ahead, and the clouds weren't from
villagers who were scattering in terror. They were from riders who
were galloping *toward* the soldiers. According to the scouts, the
Sioux weren't fleeing. They were attacking.

10

RENO'S CHARGE

s Reno readied his men for a charge on the west side of the Little Bighorn, Custer led his men into the bluffs on the east side. Custer's scouts told him about the warriors who were riding out to meet Reno's battalion, but Custer believed the warriors were executing a defensive maneuver. He thought it was a blocking tactic that was designed to allow the women and children to flee to safety. Following that logic, the camp should be vulnerable to an attack from a different direction.

While Reno occupied the warriors south of the village, Custer intended to swoop in from the north or the east. He led his five companies through the bluffs and allowed them to briefly water their horses in a creek. During the pause, a sergeant informed Custer of a group of fifty to seventy-five warriors on a hill to the north. Custer rallied his men and pushed them forward at a trot. Below Custer and to his left, Reno's soldiers rode across an open plain toward a village and a swarm of warriors whom they still couldn't see.

Reno knew that an enemy force of undetermined size was riding toward him. As his battalion rode at a northwest angle up the valley of the Little Bighorn, the village was still hidden by the switchback loops of the river and the timber that lined the water. That same geography concealed the warriors who were rushing forward. The soldiers knew they were getting close: they were following the small group of warriors who had fled the campsite on Sun Dance Creek, and the pony herds of the village were visible in the hills to the left. The main village had to be somewhere in front of them, but it was impossible to know the distance to it.

Reno sent messengers with updates to Custer, but Reno and his men could see Custer's companies riding higher into the bluffs on the other side of the river. If Reno wondered how Custer planned to support him by disappearing into the hills, he didn't have long to ponder the question. Reno's battalion picked up its pace. It moved from a fast walk to a trot to a slow gallop. As the horses increased their speed to a full gallop, Reno shouted, "Charge!"

For a few moments, it looked like an epic scene from a Hollywood movie was about to play out on the plain next to the Little Bighorn. A cavalry unit of 150 soldiers galloped straight at a force of hundreds of screaming warriors. In the movie, they would have slammed into each other in a melee of flying bullets, arrows, and lances. The crash would have been bone-crunching. The viewers would have felt it in their guts. Many would have asked: Is that what it was like in real life?

In real life, it didn't happen. Reno began the ride with about 175 men, but the number dwindled as they moved deeper into the valley. Groups of Arikara split off to chase the pony herds, as they had been instructed to do by Custer. Others, both troopers and scouts, had trouble crossing the river and were stuck back at the ford. As a result, the charging battalion was down to about 150 men, and new obstacles began to develop.

The Little Bighorn, with its thick blanket of timber, was generally on the battalion's right. It still blocked the view of most of the village. But the troopers began to see part of a village in the distance on their left, and it contained roughly four hundred lodges. If that was only part of the village, then the size of the full camp must be truly enormous. And that meant the estimates about the number of warriors could actually be true: there could be 1,500 to 2,000 fighters in the village . . . and Reno was charging with 150 inexperienced troopers.

Straight ahead, a ditch loomed in the path of the cavalrymen. It had once been part of the Little Bighorn, but the river had changed course over a period of years, and now the dried-up streambed was an impediment. The cavalry's horses would have to leap over the ravine at a full gallop to continue the charge—*if* they made it that far. Warriors were swarming up out of the streambed and riding toward the soldiers. Hundreds more followed them in a shrieking, roiling mass. The original fifty warriors from the camp on Sun Dance Creek—the ones who were the specific focus of Reno's charge—were now engulfed by an army of reinforcements. Custer's orders were to catch the fleeing warriors and stop them before they reached the village. Clearly, it was too late for that, and Reno aborted the charge.

He shouted for the men to halt and dismount. He ordered them to form skirmish lines and fight on foot. But for some, that was easier said than done. Several troopers couldn't control their horses. The terrified animals galloped straight into the horde of warriors, and at least two of their riders were never seen again. The rest of the soldiers executed Reno's orders, but as they did, the fighting force dwindled again. Teams of men led the horses into the timber to picket them away from the fight. When the remaining soldiers stepped into their lines of battle, there were fewer than one hundred men arrayed against hundreds of warriors.

But Reno's inexperienced troopers possessed one advantage: their breech-loading Springfield rifles. The soldiers opened fire when the warriors were still five hundred yards away, and an odd calm before the storm settled over the scene. As the rounds found their marks, and warriors and horses crashed to the ground, the survivors broke off the charge. Reno's scant force was holding its own, and his men gained confidence. Some smiled and laughed. They were out on a wide-open plain, cut off from the rest of their command, less than half a mile from the largest village in recorded history, with a warrior army bearing down on them, and they were winning—for about fifteen minutes.

Sometime after 3:30 p.m., the volume of warriors increased significantly. The soldiers never knew what drove the increase. And even if they had been right in the middle of the village and had heard the shouting, they wouldn't have understood the words. The frightened people were cheering, and their cheers translated to this: "Crazy Horse is coming!"

The village was a hive of frantic activity. Despite the three groups who had seen the bluecoats, and the delays by the cavalry, the village didn't learn of the oncoming soldiers until the fifty Cheyenne warriors from the camp on Sun Dance Creek shouted the alarm. At that point, the village erupted into panic.

Women hurried to collect family members. Warriors raced for

their horses. Their numbers were depleted because many were out hunting. And many of those who were still in camp had spent the night dancing and singing in celebration of their victory on the Rosebud a week earlier. They were asleep, or relaxing in the shade, or cooling off in the Greasy Grass when screams of warning filtered through the camp. Men and boys ran through camp gathering ponies and quickly dressing in their battle gear. Old men sang death songs, and women trilled encouragement. The camp was a maelstrom of chaos and excitement.

The first fifty warriors who found their horses and were closest to the bluecoats galloped down the valley and dashed back and forth to raise a dust cloud that acted as a screen. Waves of warriors followed, but it was a frenzied, unorganized effort. There were reports of soldiers who were charging up the valley. More soldiers appeared on the bluffs on the other side of the river. The size of the bluecoat army couldn't have been known, but it was closing in from multiple directions. Crow and Arikara scouts were infiltrating the edges of the village. They stole horses and attacked vulnerable villagers, including women and children.

Custer's favorite scout was a man named Bloody Knife. His mother was Arikara, and his father was from Sitting Bull's Hunkpapa band of the Lakota. Bloody Knife grew up in a Hunkpapa village and was tormented throughout his childhood by Gall, one of Sitting Bull's good friends and a prominent warrior who had joined the village with his family.

Eight years earlier, Bloody Knife stabbed Gall three times, trying to get revenge, but Gall survived. When the Battle of the Little Bighorn began, a group of Arikara scouts slipped into the trees by the river and ambushed some women and children. Gall's two wives and three children were killed. Conflicting reports make it impossible to know who, exactly, killed the women and children, but Bloody Knife is the likeliest candidate.

Gall rushed to the last known location of his wives and children and discovered their bodies. He threw down his rifle and grabbed his hatchet. He would ride out for revenge, but he would do it in the old way: hand-to-hand combat.

Sitting Bull was among the warriors who made it to the shallow ditch that had been the first big obstacle for the advancing soldiers. The soldiers had stopped, dismounted, and formed lines of battle. Sitting Bull and others traded furious fire with the soldiers as a wave of warriors swept over the ditch and continued toward the bluecoats. The warriors closed to within about five hundred yards of the soldiers before they started falling from rifle fire. After the first major volley from Reno's skirmish lines, the warriors made a hard turn to the west and rode out of range to regroup. While they gathered their force for another advance, reinforcements assembled in the village behind a warrior who was a legend in his own time: Crazy Horse.

The Oglala war chief was deeper in the village when Reno's charge began, and he was taking a bath when he heard the first gunshots. He calmly painted his face and meticulously prepared himself for battle, which tested the patience of other warriors. But when he was ready, he jumped on his horse and galloped through the camp. Hundreds of warriors fell in behind him, and villagers waved and cheered the rushing army. And as Crazy Horse and several companies of warriors rode toward the front line, the front line started to change.

After about fifteen minutes, Major Reno realized his position was untenable. New legions of warriors arrived in front of him. More warriors rode around his left flank. On his right flank was the Little

Bighorn River and the dense timber that lined its banks. His battalion's horses were stationed in the trees while most of his men were arrayed in skirmish lines on an open plain.

The men knelt or lay on the ground in a line that was about 250 yards long. The cavalry's old Springfield rifles had performed reasonably well as long-range weapons, but they weren't the modern rapid-fire weapons of the day. After firing eight to ten rounds, the weapons became so hot that the cartridge extractors tore the soft metal shells instead of ejecting them. Troopers were forced to dig out the spent shells with knives. The process of loading and firing, which was already slower than with the repeating rifles of companies like Winchester or Henry, became dangerously slow and laborious.

The initial jubilation of stopping the oncoming warriors quickly faded. The warrior army was growing, and Reno's battalion was not. The Springfield rifles were overheating, and the rate of fire was dropping. Reno ordered the troopers to fall back to the timber to retrieve their horses, but it wasn't an orderly retreat. Some soldiers turned and hustled toward the trees, which prompted some of Reno's junior officers to scream at the soldiers to face the enemy and keep firing as they retreated.

As the soldiers ran for the tree line, the fight intensified. Constant gunfire went back and forth. Warriors screamed their battle cries and blew bone whistles that produced earsplitting shrieks. One trooper remembered it simply as one long, continuous roar. The attack was the work of Crazy Horse. He rallied many of the warriors who had been in the first wave of defense, and added hundreds more from the village, and swooped in from Reno's left.

The soldiers, scouts, and guides who were already in the timber with the horses heard the approaching battle. Lieutenant Varnum, the chief of Custer's scouts, glanced up and saw Custer's battalion riding along the bluffs on the other side of the river. Varnum assumed Custer was leading his men in an attack from a different direction. But Reno didn't know what to think.

At the beginning of the fight, Reno had seen Custer up on the bluffs, and Custer had waved his hat enthusiastically. Reno didn't know how to interpret the gesture. Did it mean Custer was coming down to support the charge? If so, why was he on the opposite side of the river and moving away from Reno's battalion? Did it mean, as Varnum assumed, that Custer was going to attack from a different direction now that Reno had drawn the attention of the warriors? Or did it simply mean that Custer was excited about the battle?

Reno knew nothing of Custer's intent or strategy beyond the idea that he, Reno, was supposed to try to stop the warriors who had fled the camp on Sun Dance Creek earlier in the day. Now Reno's tiny force was fully engaged with hundreds of warriors and in serious danger of being overwhelmed. The priority was no longer overtaking a small group of warriors. Now, it was survival.

On the bluffs above the river, Custer watched Reno's men break their skirmish lines and scurry toward the timber. In terms of casualties, they were in relatively good shape. They had sustained minimal damage from the warriors, but now they were in danger of being overrun and they retreated to a position with better cover. And, as far as Custer could tell, the warriors were entirely focused on Reno, which meant the women and children could be vulnerable to capture. If Custer could seize a good number of women and children, he could end the battle and win the day. But from his position on the bluffs, he could see that it would be a larger chore than he'd expected. The village was colossal. There were more than a thousand lodges arranged in giant circles. As Custer's scouts suspected, it was the largest village anyone had heard of.

In the valley below, the most intense action was concentrated south of the village, where the warriors were engaging Reno's battalion, and west of the village, where pony herds were grazing. But Custer also saw dust clouds north of the village. He assumed the women, children, and old men were fleeing in that direction. They were now his objective. Custer turned his battalion away from the river and led it east into a landscape of hills and ravines.

It was mayhem in the timber near the river. Most of Reno's men made it to the cottonwood trees along the water, but they began to take casualties, and the warriors became more aggressive. The warriors surged toward the retreating soldiers. They dove into the river and slipped into the trees where Reno's men were hiding and trying to regroup. In addition to the constant roar of gunfire, hundreds or maybe thousands of arrows sliced through the trees toward the soldiers. Some troopers and scouts found defensive positions in ditches and in the thick underbrush between the trees. Others hurried toward the small clearing where most of the horses were stationed.

As the troopers recovered their horses, a volley of gunfire ripped through the bushes behind them, and Major Reno felt the first visceral shock of the battle. One of the shots hit Custer's favorite scout, Bloody Knife. The bullet struck him in the back of the head and showered Reno with blood and bits of bone.

Reno reeled at the splatter of gore and issued conflicting orders. He had told his men to retreat to their horses so they could escape. Now he told them to dismount and return fire. He quickly followed that order with new instructions that weren't really instructions. In essence, he told the men that if they wanted to escape, they should grab their guns, get on their horses, and follow him. He climbed into the saddle, spurred his horse, and galloped toward the river crossing, leaving his confused men to decide if they should stay and fight or mount up and follow their commander.

They did both. Many who had found good cover thought it was better to hide and wait for the battle to pass by. Those who made it to their horses followed Reno. They charged out of the timber and attempted to ride back to the natural ford in the Little Bighorn. But the ford was two and a half miles away, and it quickly became apparent that they would never make it to their original river crossing. They veered to their left and rushed toward the river in a desperate attempt to find the first available place to cross. And it was during that run for the river that the battle turned into a slaughter.

Soldiers died in ones and twos from arrows and bullets, and then they fell in whole groups. A unit of twenty splashed into the river together, but only five made it to the other side alive. Another fifteen were killed in quick succession. A surviving soldier described the warrior army as "a whooping, howling mass of the best horsemen, the most cruel and fiercest fighters in all our country, or any other."

When the troopers made it to the water, the killing became worse. Reno and the soldiers on horseback plunged into the Little Bighorn River. The drop from the riverbank to the water was at least five feet, and men and horses thundered off the edge of the cliff and dove into the river. As they waded through the water, they discovered that the only place to exit was through a narrow V-shaped cut in the cliff on the far side of the river. It was barely wide enough for one horse, which forced the horses to scramble out of the river in a single-file line.

Almost instantly, the waterway was clogged with men and animals. They were easy targets for the warriors, and the warriors pounced from all angles. Some stood on the riverbank and fired down at the soldiers. Others rode into the river and engaged the soldiers in hand-to-hand combat. According to a warrior who told his story later in life, Crazy Horse was at the forefront of the hand-to-hand fighters.

The Oglala chief dragged soldiers from their horses and killed them in the river. In a matter of seconds, the river became a horror show. Blood ran in the water. The bodies of men and horses littered the riverbanks and floated downstream. The warriors set fire to the grass, and now smoke choked the air around the scene. But despite the carnage, soldiers managed to escape into the ravines on the other side of the Little Bighorn.

Panicked horses trampled the riverbank on the far side and opened a wider exit spot than the original narrow V-cut. Soldiers and horses who survived the melee faced the challenge of climbing a steep ravine to reach a bluff that overlooked the river. As they clawed their way to the top, they continued to weather volleys of gunfire, and many didn't make it. One of the first who *did* make it was Major Marcus Reno.

When the luckiest soldiers made it to the top of the bluff, some said later that they found Reno pacing excitedly. His three companies were spread out over more than a mile of territory. Some were still hiding in the timber back near the place where the soldiers first engaged the warriors. Some were hiding in spots along the river and waiting for a safe chance to rejoin the command. And many more were dead on the ground in the timber and the river and everywhere in between. All told, about half of Reno's men made it to the bluff in the first attempt.

It was around 4:00 p.m., and it had been a little more than half an hour since the fight began. In the woods near the site of the skirmish lines, civilian guide George Herendeen and about a dozen soldiers hid in the thick underbrush. Some hadn't heard Reno's call to mount up and run. Others, like Herendeen, tried to ride away but lost their horses. Herendeen's horse had stepped in a prairie dog hole and thrown him from the saddle. Now he was stranded in the timber with a ragtag collection of miscellaneous soldiers. But as the battle surged past them, their fate was better than those of many out on the plain.

Charley Reynolds, an interpreter and civilian guide, was shot and killed as he rode toward the river. Isaiah Dorman, the aging Black interpreter, suffered a worse fate. When he galloped out of the timber, he was surrounded by warriors. He shot and killed one of his attackers, but the rest killed his horse. The animal collapsed, and Dorman knelt beside it and continued to fire with his sporting rifle until a bullet struck him in the chest near his heart. The wound was fatal, and he slumped into a sitting position.

As warriors closed in to finish him off, Sitting Bull rode up to the group. He told the warriors to leave the dying man alone. Dorman had given Sitting Bull food several years earlier when Sitting Bull was in need. Now, the Hunkpapa chief repaid the favor by giving Dorman some water and allowing him to peacefully expire. But when Sitting Bull continued to the river, Dorman's situation changed.

A Lakota woman named Eagle Robe rode up to Dorman. Dorman asked her to let him die on his own. It would be over soon anyway. She retorted by saying that if he didn't want to be killed, he shouldn't have attacked their village. Eagle Robe's ten-year-old brother had been killed by Arikara scouts early in the battle, and she had no pity for Isaiah Dorman. She shot him in the head with a revolver and then hurried to the river to join other women and children who were killing injured soldiers. Behind her, more women arrived and mutilated Isaiah Dorman's body.

On the bluff that would become known as Reno Hill, some soldiers collapsed to the ground. Others, like Lieutenant Varnum and Private Luther Hare, shouted for the men to stand and fight. Their calls of encouragement seemed to reinvigorate Reno. He ordered some soldiers to form a skirmish line along the edge of the bluff.

In the valley below, thirty two soldiers lay dead between the timber and the bluff. Their bodies formed a grisly trail up to the hill that would be the home of the survivors for the next twenty-four hours or so. At least twenty men were missing, including the civilian guides and the Native American scouts. The remnants of Reno's battalion were trapped on a hill with very little food, water, and ammunition, and they were surrounded by as many as a thousand warriors. But the warriors were not scaling the ravines to continue the attack. In fact, it looked like their attention was shifting.

Lakota warriors to the north shouted and waved blankets at their comrades at the base of Reno Hill. The warriors signaled the presence of soldiers in the bluffs near the other end of the village. The warriors in the river whipped around and galloped downstream to defend against another attack.

At nearly the same time, the soldiers on the hill looked in the opposite direction and felt their spirits surge. A column of troopers rode up from the south, following the same trail Reno and Custer had used an hour earlier. Captain Frederick Benteen and his battalion had arrived at the Battle of the Little Bighorn.

11

THE LAST CHANCE FOR VICTORY

Benteen's battalion returned to the trail along Sun Dance Creek at roughly the same time Reno's battalion began its charge. Benteen's men were about five miles behind those of Reno and Custer, and when they rejoined the trail that led into the valley of the Little Bighorn, they came upon a morass that held a sizable puddle of water.

The battalion stopped to water its horses, and Benteen didn't seem to be in a rush to move forward. As the pause dragged out, several officers grew frustrated. One of Benteen's company commanders, Captain Thomas Weir, risked Benteen's wrath by taking his own initiative and resuming the march without orders. His company was in the lead, and when it began to move, Benteen issued the order for the entire battalion to continue the march. The rear of the column had just left the morass when the first mules of the pack train came into sight and hurried toward the water.

The battalion reached the campsite of the fifty Cheyenne warriors who had raced toward the village and forced Custer to make the decision to attack. Benteen's men heard gunfire in the distance. It was sporadic at first, but then the volume increased. Then they met the first messenger from Custer.

Sergeant Daniel Kanipe was riding back to the pack train with orders from Custer to hurry the animals to the battlefield. The troopers needed the twenty-six thousand rounds of extra ammo in the packs. Custer had dispatched Kanipe when he saw the enormous size of the village, and since Kanipe's message was for the pack train and not Benteen, Kanipe stopped only briefly to exchange words with the captain.

Kanipe told Benteen that the rest of the cavalry had struck a big camp and Benteen should quickly ride ahead. Then Kanipe continued down the trail toward the pack train. As he did, he shouted joyously to Benteen's men that the rest of the regiment was fighting the hostiles and winning. The battalion now believed that the battle was all but done and their chance for glory was lost. Seemingly to confirm their suspicions, the gunfire up ahead fell from a constant fury to a series of random pops and cracks.

The battalion resumed its march at a steady pace, and after another mile or so, Benteen met another messenger. Private John Martin carried a note with instructions for Benteen. The note had been dictated by Custer and hastily scribbled by First Lieutenant William Cooke. It read: "Benteen. Come on. Big village. Bring pack."

Benteen scrutinized the note. It seemed to say two different things at the same time. The first part told Benteen to hurry to the front lines, which made it sound like the fight was still going. If so, then the priority seemed to be to get Benteen's men into the fight as quickly as possible. But Custer also said to bring the pack animals that carried the extra ammo. To do that, Benteen would have to ride a mile back to the pack train and somehow force the slow-moving mules to pick up their pace. Benteen couldn't do both at the same time, and he asked Private Martin for more details. Martin said Custer was about three miles up ahead and was probably attacking the village by now. Reno had already charged and was currently in the fight.

Benteen now faced the first of three dilemmas that would present themselves in a short space of time. He couldn't rush his soldiers to the front line *and* bring up the pack train, so he split the difference. He sent Martin back to the pack train with orders to hurry forward, even though that was the same message that was about to be delivered by Sergeant Kanipe. Then Benteen urged his soldiers forward with greater speed and quickly came to his second dilemma.

He found the spot where Custer's column split from Reno's column. Kanipe hadn't said anything about the two battalions moving in different directions, and Benteen had no way of knowing which trail belonged to Reno and which belong to Custer. One led straight ahead and crossed the Little Bighorn, and the other led to the right and up onto the bluffs above the river. Captain Weir wanted to take the trail that led across the river, and Second Lieutenant Francis Gibson wanted to take the trail to the bluffs. Benteen settled for both: Weir's company followed Reno's trail across the river, and Benteen led the rest of the battalion up Custer's trail to the bluffs. When the men with Benteen climbed the bluffs, they received their first look at the valley of the Little Bighorn.

Two miles in the distance, smoke billowed from an area along the river. Hundreds of warriors—maybe as many as a thousand— swarmed the same area. A small group of soldiers battled the overwhelming number of warriors down by the river. Above the river, a group of men were clustered on a hill. But from this distance, it was hard to tell if they were friend or foe. Some of the mystery was solved when a few of Custer's Crow scouts arrived and pointed to the hill and said, "Soldiers."

Benteen led his men toward the hill. As they approached, Reno rode out to meet them. He implored Benteen to stop and help. Reno said he had lost half his men, and those on the hill were whipped. Benteen now faced his third dilemma: he had orders to advance to Custer's position, but Reno was a superior officer and was telling him to stop and help. Neither Benteen nor Reno knew the location of Custer's battalion, and Benteen suggested they combine their units and go find Custer. But Reno insisted that they wait for the pack train. His men had used at least half their ammo during the running fight to escape the warriors.

At that point, Benteen gave in. Reno's men were obviously in bad shape, and Benteen ordered his men to halt and fortify the hilltop. Captain Weir's company rejoined the battalion, and he deployed his men in a skirmish line against a group of sharpshooters on a ridge. More commanders formed lines to keep the warriors from swarming up through the ravines and overrunning the position. But as they set their lines, the situation changed again.

Somewhere to the north, gunfire erupted. The sounds of loud volleys rolled over the bluffs and reached Reno Hill. Suddenly, hundreds of warriors below the hill turned and galloped away from Reno's position. The sharpshooters on the ridge rode to the north. The warriors rode toward the gunfire, which was the opening salvo of the final charge of the Seventh Cavalry.

After Custer watched Reno's men retreat from their skirmish lines to the timber near the Little Bighorn, he led his battalion away from the river and deeper into the hills. He sent Sergeant Daniel Kanipe back to the pack train to tell its supervisor to hurry. He sent Private John Martin back to Benteen with the same message. Shortly thereafter, civilian guide Mitch Boyer hurried up to Custer.

Custer had released Boyer and the Crow scouts from service. They had done their jobs. They had found the village. While a few of the scouts rode away from the battle and eventually met Benteen on the trail south of Reno Hill, Boyer stayed on the bluffs and witnessed the second half of Reno's retreat. He watched the panicked flight out of the timber, the bloody battle to cross the river, and the mad scramble up the hill. Boyer saw hundreds of warriors decimate a good portion of Reno's command and trap the rest on the bluff. He rushed to Custer to inform him of the development.

When Custer heard Boyer's report, it added another complication to a rapidly devolving situation. At the Battle of the Washita eight years earlier, Custer had achieved an outcome that he could call a victory by capturing fifty-three women and children. But in the process, he failed to support his detachment of scouts led by Major Joel Elliott. The detachment was killed and butchered by an army of warriors that Custer didn't know was there. Benteen, for one, never forgave Custer for failing to make a stronger effort to save Elliott and the scouts.

Now, Custer faced a similar problem. He believed the noncombatants were running north from the village. But to his south, Reno's battalion was in danger of being destroyed. He couldn't capture the noncombatants and save Reno at the same time. As Custer deliberated, his youngest brother, Boston, rode up. Boston had ridden back to the pack train to exchange his horse for a fresh mount. Along the way, he passed Benteen's battalion, and now he told his brother that Benteen's men were on the trail to the battlefield and the pack train was only a mile behind them.

Custer decided he needed a better view of the landscape. He led his column farther north, across a wide ravine and up onto a high ridge. From there, he saw even more of the village and realized it was even larger than he'd previously believed. He also saw a dust cloud to the south that he thought was a sign of Benteen's battalion. If Benteen hurried as ordered, he could reunite with Custer in less than half an hour. That thought solidified the decision in Custer's mind, and Custer explained his plan to his senior officers.

Custer split his command into two wings. He told his old friend Captain George Yates to lead the smaller wing, with two of the five companies, over the hills and down a ravine toward the river. Yates would make a big show of acting like he was going to charge across the river and into the village, but in reality, he would secure a place to cross for the rest of the column.

Custer would stay with the larger wing—the three companies commanded by Captain Myles Keogh—and wait for Benteen. If Benteen arrived soon, his three companies would join with Keogh's three companies and rush down to Yates's position. Then all eight companies would cross the river together and storm the village. If Benteen was delayed, then Keogh's companies would fire a volley over the heads of Yates's men as a signal that Yates should lead his companies back up to high ground. The five companies would rendezvous on a ridge about a mile and a half to the northwest.

In the process, the movements would draw the warriors away from Reno's position and save him from destruction. The plan was a huge gamble, but Custer had gambled big at every stage of his career, and he had won nearly every time. Now, the only way to win was to stay on offense. If he retreated to Reno's position, there was no hope of victory. With that, Yates led his two companies over the hill to a ravine called Medicine Trail Coulee.

The two companies descended the coulee, which is a

French-Canadian word for *ravine*. As they neared the Little Bighorn River, they dismounted and found firing positions in the ravine. The well-used ford was below them, and they immediately took fire from the village on the other side of the river. The north end of the village was anchored by the Cheyenne camp, and warriors rushed to the riverbank to fight the soldiers. The two sides exchanged heavy fire across the water as Yates's companies waited for Custer's next move.

The soldiers down in Medicine Trail Coulee couldn't see what Custer was seeing: only one part of his plan was working, and it was the scariest part. Hundreds of warriors were leaving Reno's position and screaming north along the river toward Yates's seventy-six men. At the same time, a group of about fifty Lakota appeared on a hill north of the spot where Custer waited with Keogh's three companies. The troopers fired at the Lakota and scattered them easily, but the situation was growing more dangerous by the second.

Custer waited for Benteen for fifteen agonizing minutes, but he couldn't wait any longer. Custer ordered Keogh's three companies to fire volleys as the signal for Yates to abandon plan A and move to plan B. Then Custer led the companies toward the rendezvous point on the ridge to the northwest. As they rode, warriors closed in fast from the south and the east. These were the actions that Reno's men saw from their bluff but didn't understand—the sporadic gunfire from the north, followed by heavier gunfire, followed by the warriors below the hill turning and galloping to the north. Those warriors now converged on Custer's location.

Arrows rained down on Custer's companies, and his men began to fall from their horses. They returned fire as they rushed toward the ridge, and when they looked to their left, they saw Yates's companies dashing up the coulee with more warriors on their heels. During the run for the ridge, warriors moved in from three sides.

But the battalion made it to the ridge with enough time for Custer to quickly outline a new plan.

Captain Keogh's three companies would stay on the ridge and protect the upcoming movements of Captain Yates's companies. Custer would lead Yates's companies north to the end of the ridge, and then they would break west and try to find a place to cross the river. With any luck, they could capture a sizable number of non-combatants, which would force the warriors to stop their attack. Victory could still be achieved, but this was the only way.

Keogh's wing of the battalion took its position on the ridge. Custer led his wing—which now included his regimental staff; his brothers Tom and Boston; his eighteen-year-old nephew, Autie Reed; newspaper correspondent Mark Kellogg; and civilian guide Mitch Boyer—northwest along the ridge. A little more than eighty men galloped through the sagebrush and prairie grass, and they saw the size of their task in the valley below to their left. Thousands of people rushed into the hills north and west of the village. Custer assumed they were the women, children, and older men, and he was about to try to corral them with fewer than one hundred soldiers. The numbers weren't in his favor, but there was no choice now, so he continued forward.

Custer led the wing to the end of the ridge and then turned left and rode down to the Little Bighorn. He found a good place to cross, but he also found that it was heavily guarded. Warriors fired arrows and bullets from the brush on the other side of the river, and they stopped the progress of the soldiers at the riverbank. The troopers exchanged fire with the warriors for several moments while Custer tried to decide on his next move.

He quickly concluded that there was no way to cross the river. The resistance was too strong, and his outnumbered and exhausted men would never make it. He turned the wing and looped back toward the ridge. The soldiers charged up toward the high ground, but not without losses. Mark Kellogg was missing. He was last seen down by the river, frantically spurring his mule and trying to keep pace with the cavalry horses.

Before Custer reached the top of the ridge, he halted his companies on a rise. He grabbed his field glasses and looked back toward Keogh's position. Keogh's companies were about a mile to the southeast, but Custer could only see thick clouds of dust. The continuous roar of gunfire rolled over the ridges to Custer, and he must have known that Keogh's men were under attack. Whether or not Custer consciously realized it, his last chance for victory was gone. Now, the Battle of the Little Bighorn was about to become a desperate, brutal fight for survival.

12

CUSTER'S LAST STAND

While Custer led his men toward the river, Keogh deployed his men around the base of the ridge. His three companies split into smaller platoons and formed skirmish lines to defend the high ground. The men who were assigned to hold the horses moved the animals to the rear of the formation. As the soldiers shifted into their positions, the volume of enemy fire increased.

Warriors launched torrents of arrows and fired seemingly every type of rifle in existence, from old muzzleloaders to breechloaders to new repeaters. Warriors crawled up the gullies and ravines from the Little Bighorn. They crouched behind bushes and rocks and surrounded Keogh's position.

For roughly thirty minutes, the soldiers on the ridge held out against overwhelming odds. They fought back a group of warriors who charged on horseback. They extended their lines down the ridge toward the river to try to stop the flow of warriors who rushed up the ravines. The tactic worked for a moment, and the soldiers pushed the warriors away from the ridge. But the warriors soon regrouped with larger numbers and began an unstoppable assault.

On the ridge, every soldier needed to pick up a weapon and help in the defense. The companies could no longer afford to allow several troopers to stand in the rear and hold the horses. With every soldier in the fight, each man was now responsible for holding the reins of his horse with one hand and firing with the other. And as if that balancing act were not difficult enough, the relentless storm of incoming fire caused wounded horses to jump and buck and kick. Several horses broke free from their riders and ran down to the river. Warriors crept closer, and shouted and waved blankets to try to stampede the rest. And soldiers started to fall. Half the men of C Company died in a line next to one another.

Warriors from the village streamed up the ravines to the west of the ridge. Warriors from Reno's portion of the battle drove at the ridge from the south and swarmed the hills to the east. Crazy Horse was one of those who rushed up from Reno's fight to the south, but he took a circuitous route to the fight with Custer's companies. He rode through the village and stopped at his lodge to offer more prayers to the Great Spirit, Wakan Tanka. As always, he wouldn't be rushed, and a group of young warriors who had vowed to follow him in battle waited impatiently outside his lodge.

When he finished, he leaped on his pony and led his band north toward the river crossing near the Cheyenne camp. Crazy Horse led his group up a ravine on horseback until their mounts couldn't go any farther. They stashed their horses and crawled the rest of the way. From the top of the gully, Crazy Horse saw a group of soldiers to the south and fired his Winchester rifle as fast as possible.

All over the battlefield, prominent warriors and chiefs attacked the soldiers. Crow King, a celebrated Hunkpapa fighter with a fierce temper, led a band of warriors in a charge on horseback. Low Dog, a fearless Oglala warrior like Crazy Horse, led a similar assault. Lame White Man, a venerated Cheyenne chief who had raced to the river to fight Yates's companies, led a charge on foot up a hill from the west. As the warriors pressed in from three sides, the fighting turned savage and vicious.

Warriors ran into the cavalry's lines or jumped off their ponies to fight hand to hand. They sliced through the soldiers with tomahawks, knives, and lances. The soldiers pulled their pistols and fired at point-blank range or wielded their rifles like clubs and bashed their enemies. The sickening thud of breaking bones mixed with agonizing cries of pain, and screams of rage, and the wailing, thrashing stampede of wounded horses. And through it all, the deafening roar of gunfire remained constant.

The only avenue of escape for the dwindling number of soldiers who were still mobile was to the north. Panicked soldiers were already running in that direction. Captain Keogh understood that their survival rested on reconnecting with Custer's companies, and he spun his horse, Comanche, to the north. Comanche had already been wounded several times, but he stayed in the fight.

As the horse carried Keogh toward Custer's companies, a bullet slammed into Keogh's left knee and then burrowed into Comanche's side. After that wound, Comanche couldn't run any farther. Horse and rider crashed to the ground. The survivors of Keogh's troop, I Company, clustered around their captain as a wave of warriors rushed over them. The warriors killed every soldier in the group and then stripped their bodies of weapons and ammo and chased the handful of troopers who had escaped the engagement.

From Custer's position, he could see only dust and gun smoke through a set of field glasses. He could hear steady gunfire from Keogh's location, but he didn't know Keogh's status. Clearly, there was heavy fighting. And it was equally clear that there would be heavy fighting at Custer's position, too. The closest warriors were still more than two hundred yards away, but they moved steadily toward Custer's men.

The scene that played out at Keogh's end of the ridge was about to happen at Custer's end of the ridge. Warriors from the village crawled up every ditch, gully, and ravine. The warriors who had rushed in from Reno's fight and then overrun Keogh's companies kept moving toward Custer. They held the hills to the south and the east, and then they found positions to the north, as well.

Custer sent E Company south toward a ravine that was the main route to their location. Warriors boiled up from the ravine, and they needed to be stopped. E Company moved down the hill and engaged the warriors. At the same time, Custer led F Company and his regimental staff up to the top of the ridge. They commanded the high ground, but elevation was its only value. There was no cover and no way to keep themselves from being surrounded.

Custer ordered his men to shoot nearly all their horses and lay the bodies in a semicircle to act as makeshift breastworks. When the grim work was complete, troopers crouched behind the bodies of their horses and began defending their final position on the battlefield. In the center of the command post, where Custer and his staff stood, Sergeant Robert Hughes plunged Custer's personal guidon into the ground. Its red and yellow swallowtails fluttered in the light breeze, and it marked the spot that became the last stand.

In the ravine below the ridge, E Company collapsed. They had held their own for a few minutes and forced the warriors in the ravine to retreat, but then a group of twenty warriors made a bold charge on horseback that shattered the company's lines. The warriors killed several troopers and stampeded their horses. More warriors ran up to the edges of the ravine and poured fire down on the soldiers.

A few soldiers fought through the slaughter and scrambled up to Custer's command post, but they only delayed the inevitable. They were almost completely surrounded by more than a thousand warriors. And behind the warriors, crowds of women, children, and old men gathered to watch the end of the battle. They believed the outcome was secure, and they waited for their chance to mutilate the bodies of the dead soldiers.

On the ridge, the last moment of hope came and went. The handful of survivors from Keogh's companies straggled into Custer's position. Most were on their horses, but a few were on foot and had run about a mile down the ridge under the hot sun while being chased by the most terrifying enemy they had ever faced. When they crashed into Custer's station, Custer knew that Keogh's wing of the battalion was wiped out and Benteen had not arrived with reinforcements. Benteen might be on his way, but the prospect for survival hit its lowest point.

A legion of warriors followed the troopers from Keogh's wing, and Custer's men drove them back with a volley of rifle fire. As soon as Keogh's men arrived, they were forced to shoot the horses that had carried them to temporary safety and arrange their bodies in the line of barricades. There were now about fifty soldiers on the hill, and they absorbed relentless fire from warriors on all four sides. The soldiers popped up from behind their horses, fired at the warriors, and then ducked back down and moved to new positions. The warriors targeted the gun smoke from the rifles of the soldiers, so if a soldier didn't move after he fired, he would likely die with his next shot. But even if the strategy was successful, the end was near, and it was only a matter of time.

Custer began using his Remington sporting rifle with deadly effect, and the men who were solid marksmen made good use of their limited ammo. But it wasn't enough. Soldiers fell under showers of arrows and bullets, and they couldn't be replaced. At some point, as the death toll rose around Custer, he was shot in the chest. The shot knocked him back and caused him to drop his Remington rifle. He drew his English bulldog pistols and continued to make his stand until a bullet hit him in the left temple. The first wound could have been fatal if its effects had played out over a certain period of time. But the second wound brought a swift end.

Custer's brother Tom lay dead nearby, and there will always be speculation that Tom fired the fatal shot to save his brother from the hellish torture that awaited if he was still alive when the warriors overran the position. If Tom helped spare his brother from a grisly death, then he was killed shortly thereafter.

The death of Custer probably prompted the final charge of the last men on the hill. Mitch Boyer leaped to his feet and shouted at the ten or so men who could still move. They threw down their rifles, pulled their pistols, and ran down the hill toward the Little Bighorn.

Boston Custer and Autie Reed made it roughly one hundred yards before they were shot and killed. Boyer and several others made it halfway to the river before they were overwhelmed and killed. The remaining men made it deep into the ravine where the bodies of the men of E Company lay, and then they were killed next to their comrades. A few wounded soldiers took their own lives. It was a far better fate than to suffer the creative and exquisite agonies that were to come when the Lakota and Cheyenne took the hill.

When Mitch Boyer led the final run away from the hill, the warriors knew the battle was done. They swarmed the hill and killed the injured soldiers. Sitting Bull's friend Gall arrived in time to dispatch a few troopers. East of the hill, a soldier had dashed away on his own, and Crazy Horse galloped after him and killed him.

Warriors moved around the hill, firing into the bodies of the soldiers to make sure they were dead and then scalping them. They expected to find the famous soldier they called Long Hair, but none of the warriors on the hill at that moment had ever seen him, and none of the dead soldiers had long hair. Custer had cut his distinctive locks before the campaign, and now, in terms of hairstyles, he blended in with the other troopers.

The warriors made quick work of finishing the soldiers on the hill. This part of the battle was done, but there were still bluecoats on a hill to the south, the ones who had charged the village an hour earlier. The warriors began to regroup and turn their attention back to the soldiers who had started the battle.

On Reno Hill, south of Custer's last stand, Captain Thomas Weir paced anxiously along the rim of the bluff. The men of his company, D Troop, stood next to their horses and waited for orders. They all looked to the north and tried to understand what they were seeing. The hundreds of warriors who had surrounded their position suddenly turned and rushed in that direction. Weir and the others on the hill heard several booming volleys of gunfire that could only have come from soldiers. There was rising dust and swirling smoke and continuous gunfire near some ridges, but they were too far away for Weir to make out any detail. He and others were confident that they were watching Custer's battalion in action, and if that was the case, they needed to go help. But there were no orders to move from Major Reno or Senior Captain Benteen, and then the gunfire to the north stopped completely.

That was either a very good sign or a very bad sign. Considering the unparalleled number of warriors in the battle, it was probably bad. Weir didn't know it, but he had just witnessed the decimation of Captain Keogh's wing. Weir was about to lead a rescue mission that inadvertently placed his men in a similar situation to Custer's battalion, and they came very close to suffering Custer's fate.

13

THE SIEGE OF RENO HILL

Captain Weir marched up to Major Reno and requested permission to ride north. Weir and Reno hated each other, and the request quickly spiraled into a heated argument. A few minutes later, Weir stalked back to his company, climbed onto his horse, and rode away without saying a word to his troop. His men assumed he'd received permission and quickly mounted up and followed their commander. Weir led them toward a series of three peaks about a mile to the north. The two peaks on the right were connected by what was called a sugarloaf ridge, and Weir angled in their direction.

When Weir's company reached the ridge, the men dismounted and formed skirmish lines. The action to the north resumed, but this time, it was centered on a different spot. The battle was more than three miles away, and Weir still couldn't see exactly what was happening. He saw hundreds of men on horseback, for sure, but the distance and the dust clouds made it difficult to understand the scene. Then he saw a few cavalry guidons and knew he was watching some of Custer's battalion. Initially, Weir thought he was seeing Custer's rear guard battling the warriors. That would mean Custer and the rest of his men were probably riding north to try to connect with General Terry and the Montana Column.

Weir was about to lead his men toward Custer's position when one of his sergeants stopped him. The sergeant handed Weir a set of field glasses and said that they were looking at warriors, not soldiers. When Weir raised the glasses, he saw that the sergeant was right. The figures who rode around the hill in the distance and fired at objects on the ground were Indians. Presumably, they were shooting wounded soldiers. And if a few of the objects that fluttered in the breeze were, in fact, the flags of the cavalry, then something tragic had happened.

Custer had never lost a flag, and a unit's colors were to be protected at all costs. Numerous soldiers were awarded the Congressional Medal of Honor during the Civil War for protecting or retrieving their unit's flags. Custer's younger brother Tom is one of nineteen men who have received two Medals of Honor, and both of Tom's awards were earned by capturing an enemy's flag.

If Custer's flags were in the hands of the Lakota, then the situation to the north was worse than Weir had previously thought. And as if to confirm the ominous suspicion, more than a thousand warriors turned and started to ride back to the south. They were no more than three miles away, and they were headed straight for Weir's lone company on the sugarloaf ridge.

There was confusion on Reno Hill. Major Reno was reportedly drunk and issuing conflicting or nonsensical orders. Many times, officers simply ignored him. But they all saw Weir's company ride to a ridge about a mile to the north. Benteen assumed they were all moving out. He had sent a man back to the pack train to retrieve extra ammo, and when the man returned, Benteen led three companies toward Weir's new position.

Captain Thomas French rallied his company and followed Benteen. French's company belonged to Reno's battalion, and French either assumed Reno had given the order to move or didn't care that he hadn't. When Reno saw Benteen and French lead four more companies away from his position, he ordered his trumpeter to sound the command to halt. No one listened, and Reno became the embodiment of a quote from the French Revolution.

It is attributed to Alexandre Auguste Ledru-Rollin, one of the leaders of the revolution. The quote is probably apocryphal and has several variations, but the one that fits Reno is: "There go my people. I must find out where they are going so I can lead them."

With more than half his men already in motion, Reno ordered the rest of his men, including the wounded, to pack up and move to Weir's ridge. The beleaguered mule train with the extra food and ammunition had finally arrived at Reno Hill, and now it was instructed to continue marching for another mile toward a different ridge. Reno rode away from the hill, and the able-bodied soldiers, the wounded, and the pack train followed in his wake.

When Benteen's companies reached the sugarloaf ridge, the men deployed in skirmish lines to support Weir's troop. It didn't take long to realize they were in trouble. The gunfire to the north had died down, and the mass of horsemen who were riding toward them were warriors. Benteen looked around at their location and said, "This is a hell of a place to fight Indians." He told his men to mount up and follow him back to Reno Hill. Benteen, Weir, and Benteen's companies descended the ridge and started to retrace their steps. But Weir's company and Captain French's company remained on the ridge.

Benteen's group met Reno about halfway between the two positions. Benteen advised Reno that they should turn around. Reno Hill was a better defensive position, and warriors were already moving in their direction. At that moment, the two companies on the ridge began firing. The warriors who had been three miles away were closing fast. The first wave was less than a thousand yards away, and they returned fire.

The column of men who followed Reno turned around and hurried back to the hill that had been their refuge for the past hour. In the confusion of movements, no one told the two companies on the ridge to retreat. As the warriors drew closer, the companies figured it out for themselves and raced to withdraw to Reno Hill. By that time, the first few warriors were nearly on top of them. Warriors and soldiers traded gunfire, and then the warriors swarmed the sugarloaf ridge and chased the soldiers toward Reno Hill.

A savvy lieutenant, Edward Godfrey, recognized a new problem. If some soldiers didn't form a rear guard to delay the momentum of the warriors, the warriors would follow the soldiers straight onto the hill and wipe them out. Godfrey organized twenty-two men of his K Company to act as the rear guard that probably saved the rest of the Seventh Cavalry.

The troopers dismounted, split into two squads, and knelt in firing positions. The first squad fired at the oncoming warriors and then fell back. The second squad fired and then fell back. Godfrey supervised the methodical retreat, and it went well in the early stages. But as the number of warriors grew, and as they found positions on higher ground around Godfrey's men, the rear guard's retreat became more perilous.

When a trumpeter rode out to Godfrey with orders from Reno to return to the hill as quickly as possible, Godfrey's men were more than happy to comply. Godfrey shouted orders to run for the hill, and his men did exactly that: they turned and sprinted toward their old position.

Benteen had organized the troopers on the hill into defensive lines along the perimeter, and Godfrey's men crashed through the lines without a moment to spare. Behind them, more than a thousand warriors galloped over the ridge and surrounded Reno Hill.

The seven companies of soldiers on Reno Hill—three from Reno's battalion, three from Benteen's battalion, and the company that guarded the pack train—formed a shape that looked like a frying pan. Most were arranged in a loose circle on the rim, but a few extended out onto a thin ridge on one end of the formation. The soldiers herded horses and mules into the center with the wounded. Dr. Henry Porter, the lone surviving surgeon, set up a crude hospital in a shallow depression in the middle of the hill. It was no fault of Dr. Porter, but the hospital became a place of special misery for the next twenty hours.

On the perimeter, the soldiers threw themselves on the ground and laid as flat as possible. There was no natural cover on the hill—no trees, no large rocks, and no earthworks. The men used saddles or boxes of food as shields. In very short order, they were surrounded by an army of warriors, and the siege tactics began.

Warriors stationed themselves on hills at all points of the compass. Several hills were higher than Reno Hill, and warriors sniped the soldiers with rifle fire. Volleys of arrows arced down onto the soldiers' position at random intervals. Few arrows hit human targets, but they devastated the horses and mules in the center of the hill. Soldiers dragged the dead animals into a protective circle around Dr. Porter's field hospital.

Occasionally, groups of warriors crawled up to the skirmish lines and fired at close range. Others settled into a routine to try to break the cavalry's lines. They poured heavy fire onto the hill and then galloped toward the position in a direct charge. Each time, the soldiers massed their fire and repelled the charge. The assaults came from different directions as the warriors attempted to end the stalemate before sunset. But as late afternoon faded into evening, and evening paled into night, the soldiers still held the hill. Possession, though, came with a cost.

One man died when a bullet punched through a box of hardtack and hit him in the head. Another soldier was shot through the bowels. Due to his position on the line, his comrades couldn't drag him back to the hospital right away. As his pain grew worse, he yelled in agony. Each time he yelled, warriors targeted his spot and poured gunfire on it. Captain Weir urged the man to stay quiet, and eventually, the man complied. But when the soldiers were finally able to carry him to the field hospital, they found out why he had fallen silent: he was dead.

In the hours before darkness descended on the valley of the Little Bighorn, twelve soldiers died on Reno Hill and twenty-one were wounded. Counting those who were injured before the siege, Dr. Porter treated thirty wounded men in his crude hospital by the time the sun set on June 25. The goal of the daylight hours was to survive until sundown. The goal of the nighttime hours was to fortify the hilltop to the best of the soldiers' abilities.

With darkness as a mask, the troopers felt confident to move around more freely, and they started their work. They dug rifle pits with anything they could find: tin cups, plates, spoons, forks, knives, and pieces of wood. They reinforced the barricades around the perimeter with anything that might slow down a bullet.

Oddly, the only troop that didn't spend at least part of its night building defenses was Benteen's company. By all accounts, Benteen was great during those first hours on the hill. He patrolled the lines, shouted orders and encouragement, and seemed oblivious to danger. But for some reason, he thought the warriors would simply leave during the night, so he didn't tell his men to build fortifications. That decision would jeopardize everyone the following day.

While most of the men fortified the hill, a few discussed the possibility of breaking out under the cover of darkness. Lieutenant Charles Varnum, Custer's chief of scouts, tried to convince Reno to let him go find Custer. Reno refused, but he eventually allowed Varnum to send a couple of Arikara scouts out into the night. The Arikara slipped through the army formation and barely made it beyond the lines before they hurried back. Their report was simple: the Sioux were everywhere.

When the soldiers finished their work, many collapsed into much-needed sleep. Some scrounged food from the packs that were scattered around the hill. A few discussed theories about Custer. The scenes witnessed by Captain Weir and others were disturbing and dismaying. But it was virtually impossible to believe that Custer's command had been dealt a mortal blow.

The prevailing theory was that Custer had retreated up the Bighorn River and connected with General Terry and the Montana Column. The worst-case scenario was that Custer was trapped on a hill at the other end of the valley. When the soldiers heard a trumpet in the night, they thought it was proof that Custer was alive and coming to the rescue. But it was just a warrior having fun with a souvenir.

As the night grew cool, troopers brought out their overcoats. Major Reno spent a good portion of the night drinking from a flask of whiskey. He had settled into a rifle pit near the hospital during the fighting of the afternoon and evening. He shared it with Captain Weir, and he spent most of his time lying in the little depression and drinking from his flask while Benteen organized the defense of their position.

Now, protected by the darkness, Reno walked a few circuits around the perimeter before returning to his spot and the small keg that was stashed in his belongings.

Throughout the night, the soldiers listened to scenes of celebration and mourning in the village below the hill. Drumbeats echoed in the night. The villagers sang and danced and fired an occasional rifle in celebration. But there was also wailing for the dead. Many had lost loved ones, and those loved ones weren't just warriors who had died in battle. Women and children had been killed, too.

At dawn on June 26, Benteen ordered his trumpeter to play reveille. He intended it to be a show of strength and defiance, but all it did was provoke immediate gunfire from all directions. The gunfire started as a sporadic response, but then it came on heavily.

As the sun rose and the morning grew hotter, the warriors tried new tactics to draw fire from the soldiers. They stood in plain sight and dared the troopers to shoot. They held up articles of clothing on the barrels of rifles. At one point, they manufactured a dummy and strapped it to a horse and sent it riding in front of the soldiers' lines. The tricks worked initially and drew heavy, though ineffective, fire from the soldiers. But as the morning wore on, officers told the men to stop wasting their ammo. The best marksmen were the only soldiers who were allowed to fire, and they eventually put a stop to the tricks. And the sneaky tactics weren't as effective as simple bombardments. The warriors possessed superior numbers and superior firepower, and they used both to their advantage.

Benteen's company suffered the most during the escalating onslaught. His company was out on a narrow ridge at the end of the formation—the handle of the frying pan—and it was the only company that did not fortify its position overnight. And worse yet, Benteen had been up all night. It was helpful at the time, but now he was exhausted, and he lay down to take a nap just as the fighting ramped up again.

His company started losing men, and the survivors were running out of ammo. His men ran to him with urgent needs, and despite his exhaustion, he jumped up and became a commander again. Benteen finally told them to build barricades with whatever was available. He marched across the hill and found Reno in the rifle pit from which he had barely moved for hours. Benteen said his company was in danger of being overrun. If his company fell, the whole position would fall. He asked for reinforcements, and Reno eventually sent a few men who were not happy about going to the deadliest spot on the hill.

Benteen's company was such an inviting target that the warriors moved dangerously close to his position. They crawled up the ravines and were so close to his lines that they could throw rocks at his men. Unknowingly, Benteen was in a situation like Custer's the previous day: defense wasn't an option, and offense was the only chance for victory.

So Benteen ordered a bold move. He told his men to get up and charge down the hill, and he led the charge himself. Benteen and his men ran down into the gullies and ravines, firing as they went and screaming as loudly as they could. The sudden advance shocked the warriors and pushed them back. Benteen's company lost two men in the charge, but it stopped an assault by the warriors.

A couple of hours later, Benteen repeated the feat on the other end of the hill. Warriors were massing a few hundred yards away from Major Reno's position on the line. Reno was still in his rifle pit as Benteen boldly walked around the hill and surveyed the situation. Benteen organized a charge and shouted encouragement to the men. And just before the men jumped over their barriers, Reno stood up and helped lead the charge.

All but one of the men in the four companies on the north end of the bluff marched out from the hill and fired steadily at the warriors. The soldiers advanced just fifty yards beyond their lines, but it was enough. The warriors retreated, and all the soldiers made it back alive. The troopers resumed their positions on the hill, and then they settled in to battle an enemy that was even more suffocating than the legions of warriors: the heat.

It was only 10:00 a.m., and the soldiers had been fighting steadily for at least four hours. The heat was already stifling. There was no shade on the hill, and the sun brought new levels of misery. Conditions in the makeshift hospital were especially bad. Troopers rigged their tents to provide shade for their injured comrades, but the most urgent need was water. Water had been a problem for hours, and as the sun grew harsher and brighter, something had to be done. The next phase of the day revolved around missions down to the river.

The first group of soldiers tried to make a water run at about 11:00 a.m., and it didn't go well. They scurried down the hill to the Little Bighorn, but warriors lined the brush on the opposite side of the river and opened fire. The troopers rushed back to the hill and decided that that avenue was closed. The only other option was to send troopers from the location of Benteen's company out on the frying-pan-handle ridge.

Benteen formed a detail of twelve men. Their orders were to run down the ravine at the base of the ridge, break into smaller groups, fill canteens and cook pots in the river, and then race back up to the ridge. From above, Benteen's four best riflemen would provide cover fire.

This was the same ravine the men had charged down a couple of hours earlier, and now they started the first run. The riflemen stood and started shooting despite their exposure to enemy fire. The twelve men jumped down into the ravine. It was steep and full of thick underbrush and scrub trees, and it was five hundred yards long. This wasn't going to be a quick sprint to the river. It was going to be a life-threatening journey.

As the men worked their way down the ravine, the riflemen up top took heavy fire from the backside of the ridge. They scrambled over to the front side and then took heavy fire from that direction. For the next twenty minutes, the scene looked like a crazy, deadly children's game. The four riflemen ran back and forth across the ridge, dodging enemy fire on both sides while they tried to provide cover for the men below.

Down at the river, the troopers threw themselves onto the bank and dipped their jugs in the water. They took fire from across the river, but eleven of the twelve made it back up to the hill unharmed. The twelfth man took a bullet to the leg that broke a bone. He was stranded in the ravine until a rescue party scrambled down and carried him out. He was the newest patient in Dr. Porter's field hospital, where most of the water was delivered.

With the success of the first run from Benteen's position, the troopers kept going. Eventually, over the course of the early afternoon of June 26, they collected enough water to stave off crisis and probably madness. The temperature was pushing one hundred degrees Fahrenheit, and most men had consumed very little, if any, water in the past two days of riding and fighting and building barricades. And for the wounded, it was worse.

The condition is called *volumetric thirst*. The loss of blood heightens the thirst for water. The missions down to the river helped calm the cravings of the wounded, but now the men in the hospital fought the urge to become sick from the overwhelming smell of rotting corpses. The hospital was ringed by dead horses that were being used as barricades, and the carcasses began to cook in the hot summer sun.

By midafternoon, it must have seemed like the day would never end. The heat, the smell, the water shortage, the food shortage, the ammunition shortage, and the constant gunfire from warriors in the surrounding hills were creating an unbearable combination.

But then there was a change. At about 2:00 p.m., the warriors unleashed a huge volley of gunfire. After that, the gunfire tapered off. By 3:00 p.m., it was noticeably less. By 4:00 p.m., it had stopped altogether. The soldiers were understandably confused. The reduction of gunfire could easily be a pause before an assault. Or it could be some other trick that was designed to lull the soldiers into a false sense of security before the warriors surprised them with a new tactic.

It took time for the soldiers to understand what was happening, and when they did, it was not what they had expected. Warriors had vacated their positions on the surrounding hills and moved down to the village. This was definitely something new, and it might signal the slightest glimmer of hope for the men on Reno Hill.

Around 5:00 p.m., thick clouds of smoke billowed up from the river. It was a literal smoke screen to hide the movements of eight thousand people and twenty thousand horses. The Lakota and Cheyenne were leaving the valley of the Little Bighorn.

Soldiers watched from Reno Hill as the procession continued south for hours. A lieutenant estimated that the column of people stretched for three miles and was nearly a mile wide. It was almost dark by the time the last people moved out of the largest Native American campsite in recorded history. A contingent of warriors remained by the river as a rearguard unit. But with the last rays of light, the warriors climbed onto their horses and followed their families.

On Reno Hill, the soldiers stood up from their defensive positions and stared at the migration of the village. They shared mixed feelings. There was a flood of relief, but also trepidation. There was no way to know if the battle was truly finished. The village could move away, and then the warriors could ride back during the night and ambush the soldiers. But for the moment, it looked like all the warriors were gone, and Reno didn't want to waste the opportunity. The men moved off the hill and down to a position closer to the river.

They dug new rifle pits and set up new barricades. They buried their dead friends and felt grateful to be away from the choking stench of the dead animals. During the hilltop siege, eighteen men were killed and fifty-two were wounded. The survivors settled into a new position and waited for what might come next. Around midnight, they received their first good news.

Interpreter Fred Gerard and another man hurried into the camp. A couple of hours later, two more missing soldiers appeared through the darkness. All four had been hiding in the timber near the original skirmish lines of Reno's charge. The charge, which had happened about thirty-six hours earlier, must have seemed like ancient history by that point. The soldiers set up picket lines for security around their new outpost. The cooks cobbled together a meal for the troopers. And when it felt like a measure of safety returned for the first time in two days, the men went to sleep.

When the sun rose the next day, the valley was quiet. There were no sounds of drums, or singing, or gunfire. The remaining men of Reno's battalion and Benteen's battalion looked across the river at the deserted village. Lodge poles and other items littered the ground. A few tepees still stood in place, but every living thing was gone. It looked like the siege was truly done, but then the men spotted dust clouds to the north.

The obvious first thought was that the battle was about to start all over again. The soldiers thought the warriors had moved their families to safety and then looped back around to finish the job of wiping out the cavalry. But as the troopers studied the dust clouds, they deciphered two columns of riders.

Warriors didn't ride in that type of distinctive formation. The dust was from reinforcements. And now, finally, there was genuine relief. The men near Reno Hill didn't know if the reinforcements were from Custer's battalion or the Montana Column, but they knew their ordeal was done. They had survived a battle that would soon enter the annals of American history.

George Armstrong Custer graduated near the bottom of his class at West Point but rose to the rank of brevet major general during the Civil War. (*Courtesy of the Library of Congress*)

Custer and his wife, Libbie, sat for this photograph in New York City. Custer cut his famous long hair during his extended leave in New York in the winter of 1876, and this is how he would have looked during the campaign in the summer. (*Courtesy of the Library of Congress*)

Sitting Bull and his adopted son, One Bull, sat for this photograph in 1884. One Bull fought in the Battle of the Rosebud and the Battle of the Little Bighorn in June of 1876. (*Courtesy of the Library of Congress*)

General George Crook's Wyoming Column fought in the Battle of the Rosebud in June of 1876 and the Battle of Slim Buttes in September of 1876. (*Courtesy of the Library of Congress*)

Brigadier General John Gibbon was a colonel during the campaign of 1876 and led the Montana Column from Fort Ellis near Bozeman, Montana. (*Courtesy of the Library of Congress*)

The earliest known photograph of Deadwood's Main Street was taken on June 15, 1876. Wild Bill Hickok and Calamity Jane arrived a short time later. (*Courtesy of Deadwood History Inc., Adams Museum Collection, Deadwood, SD*)

William F. Cody, better known as Buffalo Bill, was the chief scout for the Fifth Cavalry after the Battle of the Little Bighorn and fought a one-on-one battle with a Cheyenne leader named Yellow Hair in July of 1876. (*Courtesy of Old West Research and Publishing LLC*)

James Butler Hickok, better known as Wild Bill, was just thirty-nine years old when he arrived in Deadwood, but he was haunted by premonitions that it would be his final resting place. (*Courtesy of Old West Research and Publishing LLC*)

Martha Jane Canary, better known as Calamity Jane, lived a hard life and was one of the most colorful characters of the Old West. After Wild Bill's death, she spread rumors that she and Bill were in a romantic relationship. The people of Deadwood honored her wish by burying her next to Bill. (*Courtesy of the Library of Congress*)

Front Street in Dodge City was the site of frequent clashes between lawmen and cowboys during the cattle season. (*Courtesy of Old West Research and Publishing LLC*)

Wyatt Earp was forced out of the marshal's office in Wichita in the spring of 1876 and joined the overhauled police force in Dodge ahead of the town's first major cattle season. (*Courtesy of Old West Research and Publishing LLC*)

Wyatt recruited his friend Bat Masterson to join the marshal's office in Dodge City, though Bat was still recovering from the gunshot wound he'd suffered during the Sweetwater shootout in January of 1876. (*Courtesy of Old West Research and Publishing LLC*)

Jesse James and the James-Younger Gang made the fateful decision to travel out of their comfort zone and rob the First National Bank in Northfield, Minnesota, on September 7, 1876. (*Courtesy of the Library of Congress*)

This photo of Frank James was taken in 1898, more than twenty years after the disastrous Northfield Raid. Frank and Jesse suffered through two weeks on the run after the robbery and endured the breakup of the gang. (*Courtesy of the Library of Congress*)

The James-Younger Gang split into three groups and rode across Iron Bridge to begin the Northfield Raid. As the groups moved through the town square beyond the bridge, they were spotted by several citizens who viewed them with suspicion. (*Courtesy of the Northfield Historical Society*)

DAMPIER HOTEL

This photo is a composite of two photos that show Division Street as it looked in 1877, one year after the Northfield Raid. Note the outdoor staircase that runs up the side of the Lee & Hitchcock hardware store and the wooden box that sits on the sidewalk below the staircase. Bob Younger hid behind the box, and Anselm Manning hid behind the staircase during their short-range duel. Henry Wheeler, a twenty-two-year-old medical student, fired from a third-story window of the Dampier Hotel. (*Courtesy of the Northfield Historical Society*)

FIRST NATIONAL BANK

LEE HITCHCOCK

Cole (*right*), Jim (*middle*), and Bob Younger (*left*) were allowed to sit for a photo with their mother, Henrietta, during their time at Stillwater Prison in Minnesota. (*Courtesy of the Library of Congress*)

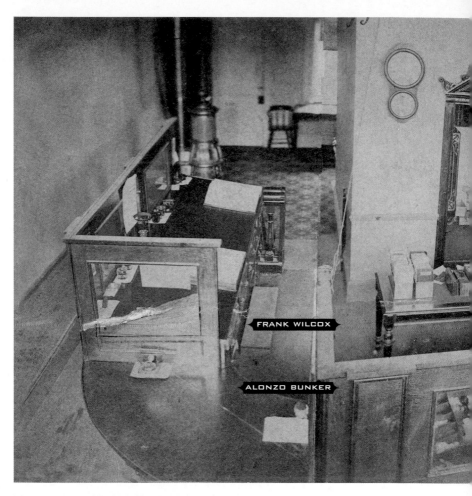

FRANK WILCOX

ALONZO BUNKER

The First National Bank in Northfield was a narrow building. Names have been added to the photo to show the positions of the three employees at the time of the robbery. Typically, Joseph Heywood would have been next to Frank Wilcox at the bookkeeper's desk, but Heywood was at the cashier's desk in front of the vault because he was filling in for George Phillips, who was in Philadelphia for the World's Fair. (*Courtesy of the Northfield Historical Society*)

JOSEPH HEYWOOD

Bookkeeper Joseph Heywood stood
up to the gang and refused to open
the safe during the Northfield Raid.
He was killed during the robbery and
was honored as a hero by the town.
(*Courtesy of the Library of Congress*)

Seven members of the posse that captured the Younger brothers and killed Charlie Pitts posed for a photo after they caught some of the most-wanted outlaws in America. LEFT TO RIGHT: George A. Bradford, James Glispin, William W. Murphy, Charles A. Pomeroy, Benjamin M. Rice, S. J. Severson, Thomas L. Vought. (*Courtesy of the Northfield Historical Society*)

William Arthur Cummings, better known as Candy Cummings, is credited with inventing the curveball. He brought his invention to the Hartford Dark Blues of the new National League in 1876. (*Public Domain*)

Albert Goodwill Spalding pitched for two seasons for the Chicago White Stockings before he retired as a player. He eventually became the club's owner and one of the most powerful men in baseball. (*Courtesy of the Library of Congress*)

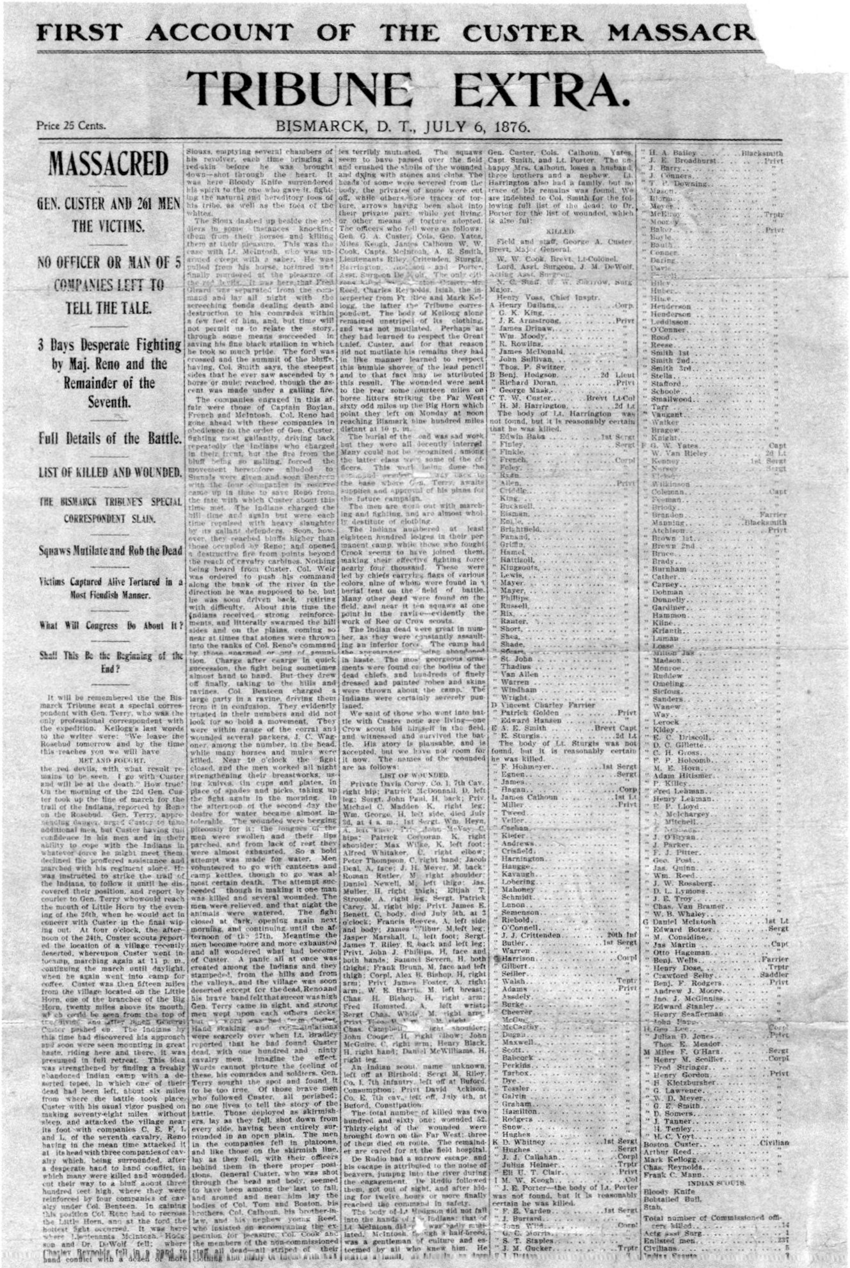

TRIBUNE EXTRA.

Price 25 Cents. BISMARCK, D. T., JULY 6, 1876.

MASSACRED

GEN. CUSTER AND 261 MEN THE VICTIMS.

NO OFFICER OR MAN OF 5 COMPANIES LEFT TO TELL THE TALE.

3 Days Desperate Fighting by Maj. Reno and the Remainder of the Seventh.

Full Details of the Battle.

LIST OF KILLED AND WOUNDED.

THE BISMARCK TRIBUNE'S SPECIAL CORRESPONDENT SLAIN.

Squaws Mutilate and Rob the Dead

Victims Captured Alive Tortured in a Most Fiendish Manner.

What Will Congress Do About It?

Shall This Be the Beginning of the End?

[Newspaper body text in multiple columns, largely illegible.]

Clement Lounsberry, the publisher of the *Bismarck Tribune,* produced a one-page extra edition of the newspaper on July 6, 1876, to explain the Battle of the Little Bighorn. (*Courtesy of the State Historical Society of North Dakota*)

⤙ 14 ⤚

THE AFTERMATH

On June 25, the day of Reno's charge, Custer's last stand, and the first half of the siege of Reno Hill, most Americans went about their business with no knowledge of the last major battle between Native Americans and white soldiers. It was a Sunday, and many Americans attended religious services and gathered with friends and family for a day of rest.

They did not attend the Centennial Exposition in Philadelphia. The World's Fair was closed on Sundays. They did not attend National League baseball games. Sunday baseball was prohibited until the early 1900s, when cities and clubs started to challenge antiquated laws. Chicago, St. Louis, and Cincinnati permitted Sunday baseball in 1902, but Philadelphia didn't see its first pro baseball game on a Sunday until 1926. Folks in Dodge City and Cheyenne and Deadwood knew nothing of the battles in a remote part of southern Montana Territory, but they would learn in less than a week.

Foremost among those who did not know about the battles were

General Alfred Terry and the 480 men of the Montana Column. On June 24, the column rode south next to the Bighorn River until it reached a stream called Tullock's Creek. That was the spot where Terry expected to meet civilian frontiersman George Herendeen. Herendeen was supposed to act as a conduit between Custer and Terry and deliver an update about Custer's movements and the location of the village. Terry paused the march and sent a group of Crow scouts to search for Herendeen. When they returned at around sunset with no news of the messenger or anything else related to Custer or the village, Terry grew nervous.

The soldiers who were camped near the creek on the night of June 24 steeled themselves for a long march the following day. They needed to cover forty miles of rugged territory in the next thirty-six hours to meet Custer at the confluence of the Bighorn and the Little Bighorn on the morning of June 26. That would have been no small feat even if the column had been made up entirely of cavalry. But the Montana Column was a mix of cavalry and infantry, and the infantrymen were about to suffer badly.

The column began its march at about 7:00 a.m. on June 25. At the same time, about fifty miles to the southeast, two Arikara couriers were riding from the Crow's Nest lookout spot to Custer's camp to tell the general that they had found the village. While the Montana Column marched through the rising heat of the early morning, Custer hurried to the Crow's Nest and learned the location of the village. He also became increasingly aware of the need for urgent action because his column had likely been discovered.

Throughout the day, the Dakota Column rode toward the valley of the Little Bighorn from the east, and the Montana Column rode toward the valley from the north. At about 3:00 p.m., while Benteen was wrapping up his fruitless scout, and Reno was leading his battalion across the Little Bighorn, and Custer was leading his battalion into the hills above the river, the infantrymen of the Montana Column collapsed from exhaustion. Under a blazing sun, they had trudged over barren hills and down into craggy ravines.

Terry halted the march for two hours to let the foot soldiers rest, and then they continued for another two hours before the infantry commander said his men could go no farther. At 7:00 p.m., the infantrymen dropped to the ground and camped for the night. They had covered more than twenty miles, and the infantry commander said later that it was the hardest march of his life.

Despite the valiant effort of the infantry, the column was still about twenty miles from the mouth of the Little Bighorn. If Terry wanted to keep his word to Custer and be there by the following morning, the cavalry would have to continue through the night. The horsemen ate a quick dinner and then climbed back into their saddles.

They picked their way through the darkening landscape for a couple of hours until they required the experience of an elderly Crow scout named Little Face. He guided them out of a potentially disastrous spot when they found themselves on a narrow ledge with chasms on each side and a canyon in front.

At midnight, when they finally stopped for the night, they were within a mile and a half of the Little Bighorn River. It would be a quick and easy trek for the scouts to reach the rendezvous point the following morning. If all went well, Terry would meet Custer, and Custer would have the necessary information to make a coordinated assault. There was still no sign of George Herendeen, who was supposed to act as a messenger from Custer, and that continued to make Terry nervous. But there could be any number of reasons why Herendeen didn't show. His absence didn't necessarily signal a problem. Terry held out some measure of hope that he would meet Custer in the morning and all would be well.

When the sun rose on June 26, Terry sent his Crow scouts forward while the cavalry waited at the campsite for the infantry to arrive. Time ticked by. The minutes turned to hours, and there was no sign of George Herendeen or Lieutenant Colonel Custer or any other member of the Dakota Column.

Terry's anxiety must have turned to a sick feeling in his gut. While he sat in camp and waited, his Crow scouts finally contacted someone who could tell them what was going on. When the scouts returned to Terry's camp, their news was too crazy to believe.

Terry's three Crow scouts, and their cavalry supervisor Lieutenant James Bradley, spent two hours riding around the landscape looking for any sign of the Seventh Cavalry. When they found it, it was in the form of three more Crow scouts. The three new scouts were from the Dakota Column. They had been at Reno Hill the previous day, and they were the first messengers to tell the story of the Battle of the Little Bighorn. They told the scouts of the Montana Column that the Sioux had killed all but a small group of Custer's men, and the survivors were trapped on a hill above the Little Bighorn River.

Lieutenant Bradley was willing to believe that Custer had run into trouble. But the Crow from the Dakota Column were saying the Fighting Seventh had been virtually wiped out. That had to be an exaggeration. It was inconceivable that Native American warriors had destroyed most of a regiment.

Nevertheless, Bradley and his scouts carried the news back to Terry and the rest of the Montana Column. By that point, the infantry had been able to march through the early-morning hours and rejoin the cavalry. Terry and the other officers listened to Bradley's report, and they all agreed that it couldn't be accurate. But as several officers argued about the authenticity of the information, Terry sat quietly, and his anxiety deepened and darkened. Whatever had happened to the Seventh Cavalry, the Montana Column needed to hurry forward.

The column resumed its march toward the valley of the Little Bighorn. Far to the south, heavy smoke drifted up from the horizon. It was the first clear sign that *something* had happened, but most troopers assumed Custer had attacked the village and was burning it to the ground. In reality, it was smoke from fires that had been set by the warriors along the Little Bighorn.

At that point, all the Crow scouts who had accompanied both columns split off from the command and rode home to their agency. They assured the commanders that they would return, but it was the last time the soldiers saw the Crow.

The Montana Column crossed the Little Bighorn and marched south into the valley. It paused at around noon to rest for a few hours. When the soldiers restarted the march, it was the middle of the afternoon on June 26. Custer and his battalion had been dead for about eighteen hours, and the combined battalions of Reno and Benteen had been trapped on Reno Hill for roughly the same amount of time. At that moment, the men on Reno Hill were watching thousands of villagers move south away from their campsite.

Ahead of the main column, Lieutenant Bradley and the advance scouts started to see disturbing and confusing images. In the distance, mounted warriors stood in a skirmish line that was the hallmark of the American army. Behind the skirmishers, there appeared to be three hundred or four hundred cavalrymen, one of whom appeared to carry a cavalry guidon. But there was no gunfire and no frantic action. The cavalrymen weren't chasing or attacking the warriors in the skirmish line, and the skirmishers just sat there watching Bradley's group.

As Bradley's men continued forward, they realized the hundreds of cavalrymen in the distance were not American soldiers. They were warriors wearing cavalry uniforms. That explained some of the confusion, but it prompted several questions. The most concerning was: How did the warriors acquire hundreds of cavalry uniforms and a regimental flag?

The advance column rushed back to the main column and reported the sighting. It was late in the day on June 26, and Terry ordered the battalion to stop and make camp. That night, rumors swirled through the ranks. Most of the infantry officers now believed the story from Custer's Crow scouts. The cavalry officers did not. The story was still too crazy to believe, despite the uniforms and the flag. There had to be another explanation.

Early the next morning, on June 27, the warriors dressed like cavalrymen were gone. The Montana Column continued its march south along the Little Bighorn and rounded a wooded bend in the river. The valley before them opened into a mile-wide expanse that had been occupied by thousands of people. The grass around the camp had been burned, and some of it still smoldered. Two lodges still stood, but now they were home to groups of dead Lakota. Personal items of every type and description littered the ground. They had been left behind in the haste to move, and a trail of items ran south for miles.

As the soldiers moved deeper into the camp, they found signs that intensified their worry. Cavalry saddles, uniforms, and boots were scattered around the grounds. Then the men made gruesome discoveries: the decapitated heads of three soldiers. And the sights only grew more horrifying from there. Farther into the village, the column found the dead bodies of white soldiers. All had been mutilated.

A short time later, Lieutenant Bradley and the advance unit returned from exploring the hills on the other side of the river, and they bore terrible news. Bradley told General Terry and the others that they had found the bodies of 197 soldiers. Most had been stripped, scalped, and mutilated. Bradley had never met Custer, but he said one of the bodies resembled a photo of the famous commander. It now seemed nearly certain that the Crow scouts had been right: Custer and a significant portion of the Seventh Cavalry had been killed. But before the information could be fully processed, two riders appeared in the distance.

The horsemen hurried toward the column, and when they drew rein, they turned out to be two lieutenants from Reno's battalion. The riders pointed upriver and told Terry that their position was near a bluff along the water. They said the last time they saw Custer, he'd waved his hat at them right before they charged the village. They didn't know where he was now. General Terry struggled to hold back tears as he informed the two men that they had found Custer.

At the base of Reno Hill, the survivors of the siege had watched the dust clouds in the distance. That morning, June 27, they thought the warriors were returning to finish the battle. But as they scrutinized the dust cloud, they recognized two columns of soldiers. That was when joy and relief spread through the men. Their long ordeal was finally done.

But now the question was: Who were the soldiers? The two

likeliest candidates were the Montana Column or Custer's battalion. But there was also speculation about General Crook and his Wyoming Column. Then two doctors rode into Reno's camp and reported that the dust in the distance was from the Montana Column.

The doctors had been sent ahead to help Dr. Porter with the wounded. And now that one question had been answered, the next one was: Where was Custer? The doctors reported the news that they'd heard from Lieutenant Bradley: 197 dead soldiers littered the hills and ravines a couple of miles to the north, and there was good reason to believe that Custer was among them. The men on Reno Hill reacted with the same disbelief as the men of the Montana Column when they had heard the news from the Crow scouts.

Shortly thereafter, the Montana Column made it to Reno Hill. The survivors gave several cheers even as they tried to grapple with the news about Custer. Some, like Captain Frederick Benteen, still didn't believe it. By that point, General Terry's nerves were raw, and he was short on patience. He ordered Benteen to take his company four miles into the hills and see for himself.

Benteen and his men climbed into the saddle and followed Lieutenant Bradley to the site of Custer's last stand. When they reached the area, the destruction was beyond anything they had seen on the plains. Dead bodies were strewn across the hillsides for more than a mile. Nearly all were stripped naked and violated in appalling ways. The body of Custer's brother Tom was so badly mangled that he could only be identified by a tattoo of his initials on his arm.

Custer escaped the worst of the mutilations. His body experienced minor disfigurement, but it was nothing when compared with Tom's. Custer had been stripped naked, and he leaned in a half-sitting position against two other soldiers. He had not been scalped, and there were clear bullet wounds in his chest and head. Benteen looked down and confirmed the identity. There could be no argument now, and the army and the nation would have to grapple with the reality.

America's number one Indian fighter, the dashing and courageous George Armstrong Custer, was dead. Half of his command was dead. The loss was magnitudes worse than the destruction of Captain William Fetterman's command ten years earlier during Red Cloud's War. That battle happened just seventy miles south of the Little Bighorn. In a few short days, the news of the tragedy at the Little Bighorn would send shock waves across the country. But until then, there was solemn work to be done on the northern plains.

The Montana Column set up a new camp near the timber that had been the site of the first stage of retreat after Reno's charge. The rest of the day on June 27 was dedicated to helping the wounded and burying the dead from Reno's command. The following day, detachments of the Seventh Cavalry rode to Custer's battlefield to bury their comrades.

Custer and his brother Tom were wrapped in sheets and buried in the same shallow grave. After hours of grim work, the troopers had buried 204 men. But an accurate count of the dead was impossible. Many bodies were dismembered, and others were caught in places that went unnoticed. For the next fifty years, the remains of the fallen soldiers of Custer's command were discovered on the battlefield.

During the experience, there were very few things that could be viewed as silver linings. Probably the only two involved Captain Myles Keogh. He was perhaps the only trooper who was not mutilated in any way. And his trusty horse, Comanche, was the only survivor of Custer's last stand.

Comanche was found wandering the battlefield. He had been wounded seven times, and three were very serious. But Comanche lived—in fact, he lived for another 14 years. When the storied warhorse finally passed away, a taxidermist preserved his body. Over the next 140 years, it was restored and refurbished, and it now stands in a museum at the University of Kansas.

While the Seventh Cavalry came to terms with the enormity and severity of the battles along the Little Bighorn, the Native American village moved south. Starting on the evening of June 26, and continuing for the next few days, nearly eight thousand people moved toward the Bighorn Mountains. Then, near a place where the Little Bighorn River split into three smaller creeks, the group split into two halves.

The Hunkpapa, Sans Arc, and Minneconjou bands of the Lakota followed their leader, Sitting Bull. The Oglala band followed their leader, Crazy Horse. Both groups headed east toward the Powder River, but Crazy Horse's group veered farther north toward the upper Powder. The villages followed their traditional patterns and moved around for the rest of the summer. The fighting wasn't done, but for now, the villages were once again free to roam Montana Territory and beyond.

On June 27, while the Montana Column discovered the horrors of Custer's battlefield and reunited with the survivors on Reno Hill, Wild Bill Hickok's wagon train finally departed Cheyenne. Hickok and his good friend Charlie Utter spent weeks assembling the seventy-or-so people and their wagons for the journey to

Deadwood. The caravan was prepared for a trek of about 230 miles, but the first major stop, Fort Laramie, was just 50 miles away. At the old fort, the group added another thirty people and one calamity.

Depending on the storyteller, Calamity Jane was at Fort Laramie because of a drunken buggy ride or a removal from the army. In the former version, which is far more fun, she was in Cheyenne and rented a horse and buggy for a day trip. She grabbed a bottle of whiskey and hit the trail. After a day and a half of drinking and traveling, she found herself at Fort Laramie. She parked the buggy in the corral, turned the horse out to graze, and headed for the saloons.

After her one-day joyride lengthened to several days, the owner of the horse and buggy went looking for his property. He found Jane at Fort Laramie and reclaimed the animal and the carriage. Jane thought she would be arrested. But when the man showed her mercy and declined to press charges for theft, she celebrated by getting extra drunk. And sometime during her celebration, a wagon train arrived from Cheyenne with a host of passengers, one of whom was Wild Bill Hickok. A new batch of people and wagons joined the caravan at Fort Laramie to make the trip to Deadwood, and Jane added herself to the group. It was the beginning of a rumored connection between her and Bill that will probably last forever, and Jane was the author and chief proponent of the rumor.

The second story of how she ended up at Fort Laramie before Hickok's wagon train arrived features tales of her adventures as an army scout, most of which can't be verified and are almost certainly creations of her own imagination. There seems to be enough evidence to say that she was part of the 1875 army expedition to the Black Hills that confirmed the existence of gold in the area. She was probably a teamster who drove one of the supply wagons, and she could have been acting as a prostitute, as well. She had been dressing like a man for quite a while, and she was reportedly a great driver, an impressive drinker, and a colorful storyteller who could make men blush with the quantity and quality of her vulgarities. And she was just nineteen years old.

By any standard, her childhood was brutal. She was born Martha Jane Canary in Missouri in 1850s, though the spelling of her last name and the year of her birth are still debated. In the twenty-first century, her last name is typically spelled Canary and her birth year is commonly accepted as 1856. Martha's family bounced around the rough mining camps of Montana during her early years. By the age of eight, she and two of her siblings were begging in the streets of Virginia City to survive. Her father was lazy and generally unfit, and a Montana newspaper described her mother as "a woman of the lowest grade." By the age of eleven, Martha was the head of the family and responsible for her five siblings. Her mother died in a mining camp in 1866, and her father died in Salt Lake City in 1867. The children were split up and taken in by different families.

In Martha's late adolescent years and early teenage years, she worked any type of menial job that was available: cooking, cleaning, and babysitting. By her middle teenage years, she was living in Cheyenne and likely working as a prostitute. Much later in life, she claimed that during those years, she somehow worked as an army scout. On one particular mission, she said she saved the life of a captain during a scrape with Indians, and the man proclaimed her "Calamity Jane, heroine of the plains!" It was a fun story that explained the nickname she was using by that time, and there is very little chance that it's true. But when she was nineteen, she found her way into the 1875 expedition to the Black Hills. At some point during the campaign, an officer learned she was a woman who had been disguising herself as a man, and he sent her back to Wyoming.

Later in life, again, she told stories of her time with the army during the 1876 campaign. She said she worked as a wagon driver for the Dakota Column for the first few weeks of the expedition and then briefly became a scout and messenger for General Crook's Wyoming Column after the Battle of the Rosebud. Through those adventures, she ended up at Fort Laramie at the end of June as the wagon train of Charlie Utter and Wild Bill Hickok rolled into town. Regardless of how much speculation or fabrication pervades the first twenty years of her life, she definitely joined the wagon train and began the journey to America's newest boomtown.

Calamity Jane, like the rest of the country, was within a few days of hearing the story that dwarfed all others that summer. As the wagon train pulled out of Fort Laramie, a rider was on his way to Fort Ellis, the home of the Montana Column near Bozeman, Montana, with the first official dispatches about the fights that would be collectively known as the Battle of the Little Bighorn. And the wounded from the battle were riding the *Far West* toward Bismarck along with the newspaperman who wrote the first draft of history.

Clement Lounsberry, the publisher of *The Bismarck Tribune*, was probably the first person outside of the army to learn the full scope of the Battle of the Little Bighorn. It would be his job to put into words the actions and results that were about to shock the nation.

Until the news of the battle broke in early July, the topic that dominated newspapers in the late spring and early summer was the upcoming presidential election. Current president Ulysses S. Grant had served two terms that were riddled with scandal, and now his party needed a new nominee. In mid-June, the Republicans nominated Rutherford B. Hayes, the governor of Ohio. One week later, the Democrats nominated Samuel J. Tilden, the governor of New York.

The Democratic Party held its convention in St. Louis on June 27–29, while the Seventh Cavalry buried its dead in southern Montana and Wild Bill Hickok's wagon train departed Cheyenne. The convention was touted as the first to be held west of the Mississippi River, but that was a bit of a comical technicality. St. Louis sits on the west bank of the Mississippi River, so the achievement of being "west of the Mississippi" was a matter of inches, not miles.

One week after the Democratic convention, the country would no longer be consumed by political discussion. Politics wouldn't completely go away, but newspapers were about to spend full pages analyzing every detail of an explosive new story. In late June and early July, as the papers debated the merits of the presidential candidates, the news of the Battle of the Little Bighorn was on its way to a telegraph to be distributed to the wider world.

⇥ 15 ⇤

THE ROCKY CUT TRAIN ROBBERY

The ten days between June 28 and July 7 were, in the words of J. R. R. Tolkien, "the deep breath before the plunge." The world did not yet know about the Battle of the Little Bighorn. Hobbs Kerry, the young outlaw in Missouri, had not yet met the James-Younger Gang. Wild Bill Hickok's wagon train was still more than two weeks away from Deadwood and his ultimate fate at a poker table in the No. 10 Saloon. The first partnership of Wyatt Earp and Bat Masterson was about to end in abrupt fashion, but neither man was aware of it.

On June 28, the country was holding a deep breath. It just didn't know it.

In the evening on Wednesday, June 28, the combined Montana-Dakota Column began its march away from the valley of the Little Bighorn. The soldiers marched north along the river toward a rendezvous with the paddle steamer *Far West*. It was slow going, as the troopers had to take special care of the severely wounded. As they trudged past the vacant village site for the final time, they spotted the body of Mark Kellogg on the other side of the river.

Kellogg had ridden a mule for five weeks as he followed Custer's command in search of a big story. He was a correspondent for *The New York Herald*, but he was contracted for the job through Clement Lounsberry, the publisher of *The Bismarck Tribune*. Lounsberry couldn't ride with the expedition himself, so he made a deal with Kellogg to take his place. Lounsberry was six days away from hearing about the Battle of the Little Bighorn and Kellogg's fate. Ironically, the publisher who stayed home would be the one to inform the world.

Early in the morning on June 30, the column spotted the *Far West*. The boat had carefully navigated down to the junction of the Bighorn and Little Bighorn Rivers. Soldiers moved the injured on board and took extra care to find a place for Captain Keogh's warhorse, Comanche. The troopers viewed the horse with reverence—he was the only surviving member of Custer's command. General Terry told Captain Grant Marsh to rush to Bismarck and Fort Lincoln as fast as possible, but the first stop needed to be the Montana Column's base camp at the junction of the Bighorn and the Yellowstone. Terry and Colonel Gibbon would march with the rest of the soldiers, and then the *Far West* would ferry them across the Yellowstone to the north side of the river. When all that was complete, Marsh would speed with all haste to Bismarck.

Marsh skillfully guided the boat 30 miles down the Bighorn River to the Yellowstone. The boat tied up at the Montana Column's base camp to wait for Terry and Gibbon to arrive with the bulk of the soldiers. At the same time, army scout Muggins Taylor began his ride. His mission was to ride 175 miles west to Fort Ellis, the headquarters of the Montana Column. He carried a bag of letters and telegrams that had been written by the soldiers, including two very short messages from General Terry to General Phil Sheridan in Chicago. The messages from Terry were the first official words about the Battle of the Little Bighorn. But by the time Taylor arrived at Fort Ellis, they were already outdated. Terry began rewriting his version of history as soon as he and the column arrived at the base camp on July 2.

In Terry's first long-form report about the final stage of the campaign, he told Sheridan that Custer had disobeyed orders by attacking the village. Terry listed Custer's numerous mistakes, but Terry was also careful to say that Custer's errors should not be held against him. Terry made sure to say that Custer paid the ultimate price, and that was a tragedy. But if Custer had just followed Terry's instructions, they surely would have been successful.

Terry left the report with Captain Marsh, and Marsh departed the camp on July 3 to begin a record-setting trip to Dakota Territory. The steamer navigated 710 miles of waterways in fifty-four hours to deliver the wounded and news of the battle to Bismarck. Meanwhile, Terry, Gibbon, and the rest of the column began a lengthy stay in camp. Before they could contemplate any further action, they needed to be resupplied.

While hundreds of troopers camped along the banks of the Yellowstone on the northern plains, a highly anticipated meeting happened in Missouri. The summer of 1876 was bookended by momentous events. On one end was the Battle of the Little Bighorn, which became infamous in military history. On the other was a bank robbery in Minnesota, which became infamous in criminal history. The robbery traced at least some of its roots back to the meeting that happened in early July along an isolated stretch of road in western Missouri.

Hobbs Kerry had been trying to wrangle a sit-down with the James-Younger Gang for two months, but the gang was cautious about meeting outsiders. At long last, Kerry's new friends Charlie Pitts and Bill Chadwell persuaded the gang to talk about Kerry's idea for a robbery.

Kerry dreamed up the idea during the winter of 1876. The twenty-three-year-old aspiring outlaw grew up in the town of Granby in the southwestern corner of Missouri. The heartbeat of the town was the Granby Mining and Smelting Company, and Kerry wanted to rob it. The company had been in business for twenty years, and a small town had slowly blossomed around the operation. Kerry eventually pitched the idea to Pitts and Chadwell, and they agreed to help him contact the gang.

Pitts, whose real name was Samuel Wells, and Chadwell, whose real name was William Stiles, were acquainted with members of the gang but had never participated in any robberies. Kerry was a friend of Bruce Younger, an uncle of the three Younger brothers who were still part of the core of the gang.

So, with Pitts and Chadwell as intermediaries, and a loose family connection in Bruce Younger, Kerry started asking for a meeting with the whole crew. He had heard that the gang was "red hot" to do a job, and he hoped he could persuade them to go to Granby. Currently, the persuasion was not going well.

Eight men stood along a road in western Missouri, and four of them argued about the robbery idea. Frank and Jesse James were in a heated debate with Cole and Bob Younger. Clell Miller, a longtime friend and gang member, hovered nearby. Some distance away, Kerry, Pitts, and Chadwell waited for the outcome. Eventually, Cole threw up his hands and said he would follow the James boys in whatever they wanted to do.

The debate was settled, and the gang broke the bad news to Hobbs Kerry: they were not going to do the Granby job. But there was a consolation prize. Kerry and his friends could ride with the gang on its next job. They were going to rob the Missouri Pacific Railroad in less than a week.

The *Far West* arrived at Bismarck at about 11:00 p.m. on July 5. It was a feat unmatched by any other paddle steamer anywhere on the Missouri River. As the boat approached the dock, its whistle shrieked its arrival. The unexpected wailing woke much of the town. People wandered down to the dock and learned the shocking news of the Seventh Cavalry. Word quickly spread through town, and for many, there was no more sleep that night.

Someone woke up Clement Lounsberry and J. M. Carnahan, the telegraph operator. Captain Marsh and several others accompanied the two men to the Northern Pacific Railroad freight office and told them the news. One of the officers dumped out a suitcase full of messages, reports, and dispatches from the field, including General Terry's long-form report to General Sheridan. The men from the boat also told Lounsberry about the tragic loss of Mark Kellogg. Lounsberry now had the somber and weighty task of organizing the mountain of information and writing the first major story about the battle. He worked all night, and by dawn, his story was ready. When the telegraph line opened early on the morning of July 6, Carnahan started transmitting the story to *The New York Herald*. He didn't stop tapping for twenty-two hours.

A little after 7:00 a.m., while the news of the battle buzzed across the telegraph line, two officers and a doctor stood in the parlor of the Custer house at Fort Lincoln three miles south of Bismarck. The piercing whistle of the *Far West* had awakened many in the fort, and now Captain William McCaskey, the fort's commander while the Dakota Column was in the field, had the terrible job of telling three women about the fate of their loved ones.

Libbie Custer, Maggie Calhoun, and Emma Reed listened to the news and then broke down in tears. Maggie was Custer's sister, and she had married one of Custer's favorite lieutenants, James Calhoun. Emma was Custer's niece and the younger sister of Henry Armstrong Reed, who was nicknamed "Autie" at a young age by his mother. Despite the heartbreaking loss, Libbie Custer felt it was her duty to accompany the three men as they informed the other wives in the fort.

While Libbie and the officers made the solemn rounds through the fort that morning, the news spread to other military units in the field. One of the most famous men in America was about to deliver it to his troop.

On July 6, the Fifth Cavalry was camped along the banks of Sage Creek in southeastern Wyoming Territory. William F. Cody, better known as Buffalo Bill, broke the news to a group of junior officers. He had come from the tent of the regiment's commanding officer, Colonel Wesley Merritt, and there was no mistake about the information. Merritt had received an official message from the army that notified him that Custer and a significant portion of the Seventh Cavalry had been wiped out.

Cody left the stages of the east a month earlier to rejoin the regiment for whom he was the chief scout in 1868. He felt a sense of loyalty to his old unit, but he likely viewed the expedition as a welcome distraction, as well. In late April of 1876, his only son, five-year-old Kit Carson Cody, passed away from scarlet fever. Buffalo Bill returned to the tour of his play, *Scouts of the Plains,* very soon after the death of his son. He tried to live up to the expression "The show must go on," but it was clear to everyone that Cody's heart wasn't in the performance.

Around the same time, he began receiving telegrams from the army asking him to return to service for the upcoming campaign against the tribes on the northern plains. He was originally scheduled to join General Crook's Wyoming Column, but by the time he traveled from the East Coast to Chicago, Crook was already on the move. Cody made it to Cheyenne on June 9 and reunited with the Fifth Cavalry. He was officially added to the payroll on June 10, one week before the Wyoming Column fought the Battle of the Rosebud and two weeks before the Dakota Column fought the Battle of the Little Bighorn.

The Fifth was still in southern Wyoming when it learned of Custer's fate. A few days later, the regiment was ordered to hurry north to join Crook's column in the retaliatory effort against the hostiles who'd killed Custer. But along the way, they were forced to detour because of a rumor that a thousand Cheyenne were about to leave the Red Cloud Agency. That detour led to Buffalo Bill's most famous, and controversial, fight: a shootout with a Cheyenne subchief named Yellow Hair.

In central Missouri, it was the day before the big day. On July 6, while people in Bismarck learned about the Battle of the Little Bighorn, and Buffalo Bill spread the news through the Fifth Cavalry, the James-Younger Gang split into two groups as a safety precaution before its next robbery. The groups reunited at about

2:00 p.m. on July 7 and rode to the chosen spot. It was called Rocky Cut, an excavation at an isolated stretch of the Missouri Pacific in a remote area outside the tiny hamlet of Otterville. Heavy timber crowded both sides of the tracks. A water tank stood next to the bridge over the Lamine River. A pump house sat near the water tank, and a single watchman manned the station. As the sun set behind the trees, the gang set the trap.

The eight men grabbed the watchman and blindfolded him. They moved some railroad ties onto the tracks to block the passage of the train. They positioned the watchman near the tracks and gave him a lantern. At about 10:00 p.m., they heard the chug of the locomotive, and the watchman waved the lantern as the signal to stop. The train's air brakes hissed, the metal screeched, and the engine cycled down. The cowcatcher on the front slightly crunched the railroad ties, but the train eased to a stop as planned.

The outlaws raced into action. Bill Chadwell ran onto the tracks and hauled a few railroad ties behind the last car to block any attempt to escape. The other men began a steady barrage of gunfire to scare the passengers. Most shots were fired in the air, but one slammed into the door of the baggage car that doubled as the express car.

There were two safes in the baggage car, one for the United States Express Company and one for the Adams Express Company. The man who guarded both safes—a position known as the express messenger—was J. B. Bushnell. As a messenger on the Missouri Pacific Railroad, this was not his first experience with the James-Younger Gang. But the robbery still caught him off guard.

When the train stopped suddenly, he peered outside the door of the baggage car. A bullet smacked the wood next to his head and forced him back inside. He ran through the three passenger cars and two sleeper cars until he found the brakeman at the back of the train. He persuaded the man to hide the key to the U.S. Express safe. The man slipped it into his shoe and sat down in a seat as if he were any other passenger. Bushnell started to walk back to the baggage car.

While Bushnell was gone, three outlaws jumped into the car and pointed their guns at the baggage master, Peter Conkling. Two of the bandits wore masks, but the third man, who appeared to be the leader, did not. Conkling swore later that that man was Jesse James, and he was probably right. Conkling described the man as tan and lean with straw-colored hair and blue eyes that blinked rapidly. That was Jesse. He had a condition that caused him to blink more than normal, and it was a telltale sign of the most famous outlaw in America. And now he leveled his pistol at Conkling's face and demanded the key to the safe. Conkling didn't have it, so Jesse turned him around and shoved him forward. They walked through the coaches, and Jesse told Conkling to point to the express messenger.

They found Bushnell, and Jesse told him to unlock the safe. Bushnell said he didn't have the key, and Jesse replied, "You want to find it damned quick, or I will kill you." After the threat, Bushnell's somewhat elaborate plan to thwart the bandits crumbled. He led Jesse and Conkling to the brakeman. The man handed over the key, and the trio marched back to the baggage car.

A moment later, the outlaws emptied the contents of the U.S. Express safe. Then they turned to the other safe in the car, and their angry cursing escalated. No one on the train had the key for the Adams Express safe. The brakeman explained that the Adams Express Company didn't have a full contract with the railroad. The Missouri Pacific had a contract only to transport a locked Adams Express safe from Sedalia, Missouri, to St. Louis. Adams employees in Sedalia or St. Louis might have a key, but J. B. Bushnell did not.

After another round of colorful profanity, and while some of the gang still fired their guns outside, the three outlaws found a heavy iron pick and smashed a hole in the side of the safe. They pulled out papers and envelopes, and considered the robbery complete. They abandoned the car, rejoined the men outside, and hustled to their horses.

Hobbs Kerry and Charlie Pitts had stayed with the animals, and Hobbs estimated later that the robbery took about an hour. They rode until dawn and then stopped and opened the packages and envelopes. The total haul was a little more than $18,000. They divided the loot, and Hobbs Kerry's share was $1,200. After that, they scattered.

Later that morning, the robbery made headlines in Missouri, right next to the continued headlines about the shocking news of Custer and the Seventh Cavalry. When the newspapers wrote about Custer, there were three descriptions that frequently rose to the top: massacre, slaughter, and disaster.

— 16 —

BREAKING NEWS

HEADLINE: THE CUSTER MASSACRE

Helena Weekly Herald—Helena, Montana—July 6, 1876

HEADLINE: THE INDIAN CAMPAIGN.

GENERAL CUSTER'S TERRIBLE FATE

Boston Evening Transcript—Boston, Massachusetts—July 6, 1876

HEADLINE: DEATH OF GENERAL A.G. CUSTER. REPORTS OF THE

INDIAN MASSACRE AT THE LITTLE BIGHORN CONFIRMED

Daily Record of the Times—Wilkes-Barre, Pennsylvania—July 7, 1876

HEADLINE: A TERRIBLE SLAUGHTER

The Daily Memphis Avalanche—

Memphis, Tennessee—July 7, 1876

HEADLINE: BRAVE CUSTER'S FATE.

HIS LAST ENGAGEMENT WITH THE SIOUX

San Francisco Chronicle—San Francisco, California—July 7, 1876

HEADLINE: THE INDIAN WAR. REPORT OF A DISASTROUS

ENGAGEMENT WITH THE SIOUX

The Galveston Daily News—Galveston, Texas—July 7, 1876

HEADLINE: THE RED MAN'S REVENGE
The Atlanta Constitution—Atlanta, Georgia—July 7, 1876

HEADLINE: THE DEFEAT AND DESTRUCTION OF
GENERAL CUSTER AND HIS COMMAND
The Colorado Springs Gazette—Colorado Springs,
Colorado—July 8, 1876

HEADLINE: GENERAL TERRY'S REPORT OF GENERAL RENO'S
DISASTROUS FIGHT. SUBHEAD: SITTING BULL NOT ONE OF
YOUR TREATY-MAKING INDIANS.
The Chicago Tribune—Chicago, Illinois—July 9, 1876

HEADLINE: CUSTER'S LAST FIGHT.
GENERAL TERRY'S OFFICIAL REPORT
The New York Times—New York, New York—July 9, 1876

I n Missouri on July 9, in addition to running new stories about the Battle of the Little Bighorn, newspapers reported on the latest train robbery by a gang of thieves. The Sunday edition of *The Kansas City Times* featured three major stories. The first ran with the headline MILITARY MASSACRE and detailed the first official report about the battle. The second featured continuing coverage of the upcoming political elections. The third big story fell under the headline ORGANIZED OUTLAWS and a series of subheads that provided the reader with an outline of the story: ANOTHER TRAIN ROBBERY SUCCESSFULLY CONSUMMATED AND THE THIEVES ESCAPE. THE MISSOURI PACIFIC RAILROAD TRAIN STOPPED BY

TWELVE MASKED THIEVES AND THE EXPRESS SAFES ROBBED OF $25,000. HOW MODERN HIGHWAYMEN MANAGE A DANGEROUS TASK WITHOUT SHEDDING BLOOD. As was usually the case, several details in the initial story were wrong.

The New York Herald, which received the scoop of a lifetime with the story of the battle, showed its readers two different experiences on two consecutive days. On July 6, in the prominent position in the upper left-hand corner of the front page, it ran the story of the Battle of the Rosebud. The narrative was generally positive and the subheads made it sound like a victory for General Crook's troops. In the same space on July 7, it ran the story of Custer's defeat under the simple headline THE MASSACRE.

Over the course of twenty-two hours on July 6, telegraph operator J. M. Carnahan transmitted fifteen thousand words written by Clement Lounsberry. When *The Herald* started receiving the story, managers sent reporters to the Centennial Exposition in Philadelphia to talk to General Sherman and General Sheridan. The generals initially dismissed the claims that Custer and part of his regiment had been wiped out. The story was simply too wild to be true. But as they started receiving official intelligence, they were forced to confirm the event.

The impact of the news can't be understated. It hit the American psyche like a sledgehammer. It was unthinkable that the country's number one Indian fighter and a sizable portion of his famous regiment could be destroyed. On July 7, three days after the one hundredth anniversary of the adoption of the Declaration of Independence, the country was forced to embrace the reality. The grand campaign that seemed to begin in promising fashion with General Crook's battle at Rosebud Creek now looked like a disaster. Crook's men were still camped in northern Wyoming. General

Terry's men were camped on the Yellowstone as they rested, recovered, and waited for more troops and more supplies. And the hostiles were still on the loose.

A week later, in mid-July, two events met the definition of *underreported*. Wild Bill Hickok, the most famous gunfighter in the West, arrived in Deadwood, and a pitcher made baseball history in St. Louis.

In Deadwood, *The Black Hills Pioneer* noted in its July 15 edition the arrival of a wagon train that carried a celebrity. The notation was a single line that was buried in the Local News section on page 4. It read: "Calamity Jane has arrived." There was no mention of Wild Bill, but he made a splashy entrance nonetheless.

A reporter wrote that Hickok and several others rode down the middle of Main Street on fine horses. Hickok and Charlie Utter were clad in buckskin suits, and their long hair flowed behind them. People stopped to watch the impromptu parade, and others noted that the cheers that sprang up from the viewers were not for celebrities like Wild Bill and Calamity Jane.

The rough and rowdy miners of Deadwood cheered for the group that historian James D. McLaird described as "ladies of easy virtue." Several such ladies were part of the wagon train, along with the expected assortment of prospectors, gamblers, hustlers, and merchants. Before the entourage stopped at a saloon, the ride down the main thoroughfare would have been an assault on the senses.

Main Street was a ragged, downhill quagmire of mud, muck, and manure. The stench would have been an eye-watering bouquet of slaughtered animals, live animals, cigar smoke, burning kerosene, burning coal, freshly cut lumber, cheap perfume, cheaper whiskey, and the unwashed bodies of hundreds of men. The sounds of clanking pianos drifted out of the saloons and mingled with laughter, shouts, and curses. Horses, mules, and oxen crowded the street that was already packed with wagons, carts, and carriages. Ditches, trees, and stacks of logs turned the road into a slalom course that forced travelers to dodge left and right.

By midsummer, several structures in town were made entirely of wood, but many, like Al Swearingen's Cricket Saloon, were framed with wood and topped with canvas roofs. Still others were basic canvas tents that had yet to elevate themselves to a level of permanence.

As Hickok and the parade rode through town, they eventually reached the section that became known as the Badlands. The area of Main Street beyond its intersection with Wall Street was home to most of the dens of vice and vulgarity. That area was already home to the No. 10 Saloon, owned by William Nuttall and Carl Mann, and Swearingen's Cricket Saloon, and it would eventually be home to establishments like the Bella Union Theatre and the Gem Variety Theatre. Hickok stopped at the No. 10 and met Carl Mann. The proprietor asked Hickok to make the No. 10 his headquarters, and Hickok obliged.

Shortly after the wagon train set up camp along Whitewood Creek outside town, Hickok began the routine that dominated the remaining weeks of his life. A young man who traveled with the wagon train wrote about the routine in his memoir many years later. His name was Joseph Foster Moore Anderson, and he was twenty-two when he made the trip to Deadwood with Hickok and Calamity Jane. He wrote that Bill began his day with target practice.

Hickok fired two pistols at a cottonwood tree until they were both empty. Then he took a shot of whiskey and strolled into town for breakfast. The first meal of the day was probably at the Grand

Central Hotel, where the best cook in town, a universally respected Black woman called Aunt Lou Marchbanks, ran the kitchen. Then, more often than not, Hickok walked down to the No. 10 to play poker and drink whiskey.

In terms of taking money from miners, whether it was at a poker table or a hardware store, there was no better time to be in Deadwood than June and July of 1876. Later estimates said that miners pulled more than a million dollars' worth of gold out of the ground per month in those two months. Newspapers began calling the Black Hills the "richest 100 square miles on Earth," and saloon operators and savvy gamblers could get rich nearly as quickly as miners who struck it lucky. But Wild Bill Hickok had no intention of mining, and his luck at the poker table had run out years ago.

Hickok turned thirty-nine years old two months before he arrived in Deadwood. He wasn't old, but he felt like it. He had packed several lifetimes' worth of adventures into his thirty-nine years, and now he felt worn out. His wife, Agnes Lake, waited in Cincinnati for news of his success in Deadwood, but he showed no interest in searching for gold.

As the days passed, his drinking became heavier, and his losses at the poker tables deepened. He was forced to watch his back at all times against glory seekers who would shoot him to raise their own profiles and thugs who were afraid he was in Deadwood to bring law and order to a lawless town. The experience of arriving in the boomtown went from hopeful to exhausting in short order, and his hours of drinking and gambling didn't help.

Hickok said to Charlie Utter, "I feel like my days are numbered. My sun is sinking fast." It was the first of two worrisome premonitions that Bill talked about with Charlie. The second came at the end of July, when it was just a couple of days away from becoming a prophecy.

The second event that felt underreported, with the benefit of hindsight, happened in St. Louis, Missouri. On the same day that *The Black Hills Pioneer* noted the arrival of Calamity Jane, George Washington Bradley, the starting pitcher for the St. Louis Brown Stockings, threw the first no-hitter in National League history.

He pitched three consecutive shutouts against the Hartford Dark Blues, and the third earned him a place in the record book. The *St. Louis Globe-Democrat* reported the news the following day, July 16: "For the first time in the annals of the League, nine innings were played without a single base hit being placed to the credit of one of the teams. The Hartford's utterly failed to do anything whatever with Bradley's twisters."

The next day, July 17, Buffalo Bill Cody killed a Cheyenne warrior and, in the process, created a legend.

A week before the fight, the Fifth Cavalry, with Cody as the chief scout, received orders to join General Crook's command in northern Wyoming. Crook and the Wyoming Column had been sitting at their base camp along the banks of Goose Creek since the Battle of the Rosebud in mid-June. In early July, as the wider world learned about the Battle of the Little Bighorn, Crook had been ordered to retaliate against the hostiles who'd killed Custer.

Crook had been requesting supplies and reinforcements since the moment he set foot in camp after his battle. Some of those reinforcements were the Fifth Cavalry. But before the Fifth could make it to northern Wyoming, it received orders to make a detour.

The regiment received a report from Camp Robinson at the

Red Cloud Agency in northwestern Nebraska that one thousand Cheyenne were about to leave the reservation to join Sitting Bull's village. The Fifth veered east to get in front of the Cheyenne and turn them back toward the agency. At dawn on July 17, the action began.

The cavalrymen had reached Hat Creek in what is today the Oglala National Grassland. They set up an outpost to cover the direction from which they expected the Cheyenne to arrive. Trooper Chris Madsen, who became a U.S. marshal and earned fame as one of the Three Guardsmen with Heck Thomas and Bill Tilghman, stood on a nearby bluff as a signalman. Cody had been out reconnoitering with a few scouts in the earliest light of day, and he rode up to Madsen to tell him that the huge group of Cheyenne was about to move. The report was correct; between eight hundred and one thousand Cheyenne were camped beyond the hills. At nearly the same time, a lieutenant at the outpost noticed the same thing.

At about 5:00 a.m., the Cheyenne rode into view. It was one of the few times that the U.S. Army successfully crept within striking distance of a war party while remaining undetected. But the stealth didn't last long. The warriors spotted the wagon train of supplies that accompanied the cavalry. They began feverish rides around the hills to signal to the rest of the group that soldiers were nearby.

But before a battle could begin, the soldiers saw two couriers in the distance who were riding toward the outpost with messages for Colonel Wesley Merritt, the commander of the Fifth Cavalry. Seven Cheyenne warriors dashed away from the others to attack the couriers. Cody asked to take some men and engage the warriors to save the couriers. Merritt gave the order, and Cody led eight men toward the Cheyenne.

The two groups clashed when they crested a hill. According to

Madsen, who had an excellent view from his hilltop observation post, both groups seemed surprised, as if they hadn't seen each other until that moment. But the two men in the lead kept their cool.

Cody was out in front of the troopers, and Yellow Hair was in front of the Cheyenne. Both men raised their guns and fired at each other as they charged. The shots rang out at nearly the same time, but only Cody's bullet did damage. The shot passed through Yellow Hair's leg and slammed into his horse. The pony crashed to the ground and took Yellow Hair with it.

A moment later, Cody's horse stepped in a prairie dog hole and stumbled. Cody jumped off his horse, dropped into a kneeling position, and fired again. Yellow Hair fired his second shot a split second before Cody, but again, it went wild. Cody's second shot found its mark, this time with deadly precision. It hit Yellow Hair in the head and killed him instantly.

The soldiers in Cody's group chased the remaining warriors, and that was the extent of the fighting near Hat Creek. The Fifth Cavalry marched in formation to the top of a hill to prepare to engage the rest of the warriors, but the Cheyenne fired an inconsequential volley and then scattered in all directions. The cavalry pursued the warriors back to the Red Cloud Agency, but no more shots were fired. The regiment accomplished its mission of stopping a host of warriors from joining Sitting Bull's village, which still roamed free somewhere in southeastern Montana. But the moment that achieved legendary status happened back at the spot where Buffalo Bill Cody killed Yellow Hair in the close-range gunfight.

When the Cheyenne warrior was dead on the ground, Cody scalped his opponent. Buffalo Bill participated in fourteen engagements against Native American warriors. The fight with Yellow

Hair was the only one in which he scalped a man. It was a highly unusual practice in the army, and it helped elevate the fight to mythical proportions. In subsequent years, the story of the fight was embellished and exaggerated to the point where it bore almost no resemblance to the real thing—and many of those embellishments came from Cody himself.

In some versions, Buffalo Bill and Yellow Hair fought in hand-to-hand combat with tomahawks and knives. In others, the two men fought a duel with their rifles that began on horseback and ended on foot.

Cody's version evolved over time and typically included a moment before the scalping when he stabbed Yellow Hair with a bowie knife. But the punctuation mark at the end of the story was always the same, and Buffalo Bill repeated it countless times in his Wild West show many years later as he reenacted the fight for live audiences. When he removed Yellow Hair's scalp and held it up, he shouted: "The first scalp for Custer!"

It's a pretty safe bet that Cody didn't utter the line that he repeated into immortality over the next couple of decades, but ironically, he was probably right. It was likely the first clash between U.S. soldiers and Native American warriors since the Battle of the Little Bighorn, even though there were just two combatants and a grand total of four gunshots. Buffalo Bill Cody could have been the first military man to exact a measure of revenge for the losses of the Seventh Cavalry.

After the Fifth finished its assignment near the Red Cloud Agency, it marched back to Fort Laramie to replenish supplies and grab a few hours of rest. Then the regiment hit the trail again to make the long ride to Camp Cloud Peak, General Crook's temporary base on Goose Creek in northern Wyoming. When the regiment reached

Crook's command on August 3, one day after one of the most notorious murders in the Old West, the final month of the great campaign of 1876 was about to begin.

While Buffalo Bill led the Fifth Cavalry north to meet the Wyoming Column, and his good friend Wild Bill drank and gambled in Deadwood, troubles mounted for the James-Younger Gang in western Missouri.

After the Rocky Cut robbery, the outlaws scattered to lie low. Three posses from communities in the area around the robbery searched for the thieves, but, as usual, they had no luck. Notably, the posse from Sedalia was led by Bacon Montgomery, the former Union officer whose unit killed Archie Clement, Jesse's good friend and fellow member of Quantrill's Raiders, in December 1866.

Now, at the end of July, the James-Younger Gang was on the verge of a serious setback. Neither the gang nor Hobbs Kerry knew it, but Kerry was being watched. St. Louis police chief James McDonough heard rumors earlier in the year of Kerry's desire to rob the Granby Mining and Smelting Company. He sent detectives to investigate, but they didn't find evidence of an immediate plan and couldn't stay in Granby indefinitely. In June, McDonough intercepted a letter written by Kerry that outlined his attempts to meet the James-Younger Gang. But it didn't include actionable intelligence, so McDonough was forced to continue waiting. After the Rocky Cut robbery, McDonough sent his men back to Granby.

On July 26, Hobbs Kerry returned to town and started recklessly spending money. The detectives watched him for a few days to see if he would interact with any other known criminals or inadvertently expose himself as one of the Rocky Cut robbers. When neither happened, the detectives asked for permission to arrest

Kerry. With Kerry's letter in hand and Kerry's sudden infusion of cash, the detectives possessed enough evidence to arrest him and question him in the hope that he would "squeal," as the *St. Louis Republican* newspaper phrased it.

The request was granted on August 1, the second-to-last day of Wild Bill Hickok's life.

Hickok believed his end was truly near in Deadwood, and he wrote his final letter to his wife, Agnes Lake. It was tender and romantic, like most of his missives to her. It said, in part: "Agnes darling, if such should be we never meet again, while firing my last shot, I will gently breathe the name of my wife, Agnes. And with wishes even for my enemies, I will make the plunge and try to swim to the other shore."

And at the end of July, he reportedly said to Charlie Utter: "Charlie, I feel this is going to be my last camp, and I won't leave it alive."

Two days into August, his words came true.

17

MURDER AT THE NO. 10 SALOON

On the night of August 1, 1876, Wild Bill Hickok experienced a rare lucky streak at a poker table in the No. 10 Saloon. He and the other men at the table forced a player to retire. When the busted player wandered away, a loafer named Jack McCall took his place. McCall was a twenty-five-year-old native of Louisville, Kentucky, who roamed the West throughout the 1870s. His odd appearance, highlighted by crossed eyes and a nose that had clearly been broken at some point in his life, earned him the nickname "Crooked Nose Jack."

When Jack slithered into the chair at the poker table, he was already drunk, and he kept drinking as he played. He was overmatched and lost hand after hand until his money was gone. Hickok took pity on the younger man and gave him some money to buy breakfast. By the time the game broke up, it was close to dawn on August 2.

While Hickok sat at a poker table in Deadwood, Hobbs Kerry sat in a jail cell in Granby, Missouri. He had been arrested that day, August 1, and detectives were currently trying to get him to admit that he had participated in the Rocky Cut robbery. And, more importantly, they wanted him to identify the other robbers. But for the moment, Kerry held strong. He denied any knowledge of or involvement in the robbery. His strength, however, wouldn't last long.

In Montana Territory on August 1, Major Marcus Reno and a decent percentage of the soldiers in the combined Montana-Dakota Column were getting drunk. There wasn't much else to do. The column had camped at the junction of the Yellowstone and the Bighorn for most of July and then marched east to the junction of the Yellowstone and the Rosebud. There, they found a small store that had been erected by an enterprising merchant. The man had whiskey for sale, and the soldiers happily indulged. The officers played games of baseball and raced horses during the day, and nearly everyone debated the performances of the commanders in the battle. The criticism of Reno, both publicly and privately, was withering.

But now, in early August, reinforcements arrived. New recruits joined the Seventh Cavalry, and Colonel Nelson Miles arrived with six companies of the Fifth Infantry. The force adopted a new name, the Yellowstone Column, and prepared to march out onto the plains once more to find Sitting Bull and Crazy Horse.

A little after dawn on Wednesday, August 2, Hickok left the No. 10 and headed back to his camp along Whitewood Creek to go to sleep. Later that morning, he rose, took a bath, and dressed in some of his finest clothes. He and Charlie Utter were known as oddities for their interest in bathing once a day. That level of cleanliness was laughable to some, but no doubt appreciated by others. Hickok met Utter, and they walked into town to have breakfast at around noon, when many people were having their second meal of the day.

That day, two men who became prominent citizens of Deadwood, Seth Bullock and Sol Star, arrived to start their hardware business. Bullock grew up in Ontario, Canada, and settled in Montana when he was eighteen years old. At the age of twenty-four, he was a member of the territorial senate. At twenty-six, he was the sheriff of Lewis and Clark County. One year later, just a week after his twenty-seventh birthday, he arrived in Deadwood with his business partner, Sol Star.

Star was born in Germany and moved to Ohio when he was ten years old to live with an uncle. After the Civil War, he drifted west, like many young men, and ended up in Helena, Montana. He became friends with Bullock, and in the summer of 1876, they decided to seek their fortunes in Deadwood. Unlike most men who flocked to the camp, they wanted to be merchants and to put down roots in the Black Hills.

They set up Star and Bullock Hardware on the southwest corner of the intersection of Main Street and Wall Street. Their store was roughly 150 feet from the front door of the No. 10 Saloon, where Hickok was about to spend the final hour of his life.

At about three o'clock in the afternoon, Hickok headed for the No. 10. He walked in and chatted with his friend Harry Young at the bar. Hickok met Harry seven years earlier in Hays City, Kansas. Hickok had been the marshal of Hays City for about three months when Young drifted into town in September of 1869. When Harry arrived, he had forty dollars in his pockets. After a single night of entertainment, less than two dollars remained. He bumped into Hickok and lamented his losses. Hickok helped Harry get a job as a wagon driver. Harry spent the next six months hauling freight, and never forgot the generosity of Wild Bill Hickok.

Now, seven years later, Harry poured a shot of whiskey for Hickok in the No. 10 Saloon. Bill gulped the shot and headed for the poker table. A game was in progress between three men: Carl Mann, the co-owner of the saloon; William Massie, an old riverboat captain; and a seventeen-year-old named Charles Rich. Rich sat in the chair that had its back to the wall, the spot that was said to have been Hickok's coveted position.

The lone empty chair left Hickok exposed to the back of the saloon. He asked Charles Rich to change places with him, but Rich refused. Hickok didn't push it. He sat down and started to play. The first hour of the game went about as badly as it could. Hickok lost every hand and was forced to ask Harry Young for a loan of fifty dollars. Harry gave him the loan, and Hickok muttered his final words, an expression of frustration about his recent loss to Captain Massie. "The old duffer broke me on that last hand," Bill said.

The game started back up, and Jack McCall entered the saloon at around 4:00 p.m. He didn't sneak in through the back door and creep up behind Wild Bill. He walked in through the front door, and Hickok would have been able to see him the whole way. But no one viewed McCall as a threat, and his appearance in the saloon didn't raise any alarms. More likely, it was seen as an annoyance.

McCall idled at the bar for a few minutes as Charles Rich dealt the next hand to the players. The men examined their cards and made their bets. While they studied the game, Jack McCall slinked around behind Hickok. At about 4:10 p.m., McCall pulled out a .45-caliber revolver and put it to the back of Hickok's head. He pulled the trigger and shouted, "Damn you, take that!" The bullet slammed into Hickok's head at point-blank range. It exited below his right cheekbone and burrowed into Captain Massie's left wrist across the table.

Hickok toppled sideways out of his chair and slumped to the floor. McCall waved the gun at the other men in the saloon and continued to pull the trigger, but every other attempt ended in a misfire. The only round McCall successfully fired was the one that killed Wild Bill Hickok.

McCall raced out the back door and hurried around to Main Street. He leaped on a horse, but the saddle was loose, and he slipped off. He scrambled to his feet, ran down the street, and ducked into a butcher's shop. He hid in the store as chaos erupted in Deadwood. Word of the murder spread quickly, and a mob of citizens tracked McCall to the butcher's shop. They captured him and placed him under guard until they could decide what to do with him. The decision was to hold a hasty trial the next day.

On Thursday, August 3, a miner's court convened to try to bring some sort of justice to the situation, but it was probably a lost cause from the outset. Deadwood was an illegal town. It sat on Lakota land and thus was not part of a state or territory of the United States. The trial had no legal standing, so if McCall were found guilty, there was no way to punish him under the law. The citizens would simply need to agree to carry out a punishment—or not.

During the trial, McCall claimed he killed Hickok out of revenge. He said Hickok killed his brother in Abilene when Hickok was the marshal of the famous cow town. The claim was a lie. McCall didn't have a brother. But the men of the jury had no way of knowing, and they accepted McCall's defense. In the minds of many at the time, revenge was a justifiable reason for killing. The jury found McCall not guilty, and he was free to go.

McCall wasted no time making his exit. He jumped on a

horse—which some said was provided by Al Swearingen—and rode out of Deadwood.

While the trial played out, Charlie Utter held a funeral service for his good friend Wild Bill Hickok. For hours, people filed past Hickok's casket to pay their respects to the celebrated lawman and gunfighter. Strangely, Calamity Jane was not among them. Her whereabouts at the time are unknown.

James Butler Hickok was larger than life, a legend in his own time, and yet somehow killed in a dingy saloon by a no-account drifter with crossed eyes and a crooked nose. Hickok was buried in Deadwood's original cemetery beneath a headstone that was commissioned by Charlie Utter. It read:

> WILD BILL J.B. HICKOK,
>
> KILLED BY THE ASSASSIN JACK MCCALL IN DEADWOOD,
>
> BLACK HILLS, AUGUST 2ND, 1876.
>
> PARD, WE WILL MEET AGAIN IN THE HAPPY HUNTING GROUND
>
> TO PART NO MORE. GOOD BYE.
>
> COLORADO CHARLIE C.H. UTTER.

Late in the afternoon, while mourners said goodbye to Wild Bill, Buffalo Bill Cody led the Fifth Cavalry into Camp Cloud Peak, the base where the Wyoming Column had been sitting since the Battle of the Rosebud six weeks earlier. It was 160 miles west of Deadwood, near the present-day city of Sheridan, Wyoming. The newly reinforced column would spend another week in camp before it finally marched out in search of the hostiles.

In Granby, Missouri, on the night of Hickok's funeral, lawmen transported Hobbs Kerry north to Sedalia. Kerry had managed to stay quiet about his involvement in the Rocky Cut robbery for two days, but when he reached Sedalia, he started talking. He gave a full confession, including the names of the seven other robbers. It was the first time in ten years that an associate of the James-Younger Gang gave up the famous outlaws.

Members of the gang had been arrested at various times, but none had breathed a word to the law about Jesse or Frank or the Younger brothers. Ten days from now, every detail of Kerry's confession would appear in the newspapers. But by that time, the gang members had long since learned about Kerry's loose lips. The gang was on the run through the hills of central Missouri and seriously considering leaving the state altogether.

On August 10, the Yellowstone Column and the Wyoming Column merged into the largest force of American soldiers on the northern plains. The new army boasted four thousand men, and it trudged through southern Montana. Heavy rainstorms drenched the soldiers and animals and created thick mud that made travel slow and treacherous. The army crossed the Tongue River and then made it to the Powder River, the favored hunting grounds of the Lakota and Cheyenne.

Sitting Bull's village and Crazy Horse's village spent time in the Powder River country after the Battle of the Little Bighorn, but both continued to elude the army. Each village could have been the size of the army expedition, and each moved freely with no threat from the soldiers. Sitting Bull led his people north toward Canada, and Crazy Horse led his people east toward the Black Hills.

The army's search grew more difficult. Nerves frayed, and tensions rose within the ranks.

* * *

The heat on the outlaws in Missouri escalated quickly. Hobbs Kerry confessed on August 3. By August 6, newspapers were hinting at the possibility of a confession. On August 9, they reported it outright. On August 11, the day after General Crook and General Terry began their combined march to find the hostiles, a twelve-man posse raided Samuel Ralston's farm. Samuel was Frank James's father-in-law. Not surprisingly, Samuel never approved of his daughter Anna marrying an outlaw, but Frank took care to keep his illegal activities away from the Ralston family. The posse found nothing at the farm.

Two days later, on August 13, the details of Hobbs Kerry's arrest and confession appeared on the front page of the *St. Louis Republican* newspaper, among others. The rumors and hints were true. Hobbs Kerry named the other seven men who participated in the Rocky Cut robbery: Jesse James, Frank James, Cole Younger, Bob Younger, Clell Miller, Charlie Pitts, and Bill Chadwell. Soon enough, those seven men, plus Jim Younger, who had refused to go on the Rocky Cut job, would leave Missouri and head north to Minnesota.

A raid in Minnesota had been in the works for an unknown length of time. It wasn't a spontaneous reaction to the betrayal by Hobbs Kerry, but Kerry's confession could certainly have accelerated the timeline.

In Dodge City, a key player was also about to head north. Bat Masterson caught gold fever and decided to go to Deadwood while the weather was still passable. He had survived the first major cattle season in Dodge as he recovered from the gunshot wound he sustained in Sweetwater in January.

By virtually any metric, the season was a success, and it wasn't quite over yet. A few straggling herds would still arrive in September. But by October, it would be done. When the numbers were tallied, a quarter of a million cattle passed through the stockyards in Dodge that season. And the violent crime that typically came with those numbers was way down. The number of arrests skyrocketed, but the number of violent crimes plummeted. The small army of new lawmen in Dodge did their jobs well.

The more well-known incidents in the history of Dodge City would happen over the next three years, and now, with the season on the wane, Bat bade goodbye to his friend Wyatt and went in search of riches. Wyatt replaced Bat on the police force with a new arrival, his younger brother Morgan.

As the summer faded, so did the prospects of success for the army's campaign against the tribes of the northern plains. Toward the end of August, after less than three weeks on the trail together, the Wyoming Column split from the Yellowstone Column. Reportedly, there was friction between General Crook and General Terry, and Crook decided to chase Crazy Horse's village on his own. He was so confident that his men would catch the village in a matter of days that he left his supply wagons with Terry.

Crook's men marched away with just a few days of rations in their saddlebags and none of their Shoshone and Crow scouts. The scouts were fed up with the slow, plodding progress of the army and the age-old inability to find the enemy.

The Wyoming Column also lost the services of its famous scout,

Buffalo Bill Cody. Cody switched to the Yellowstone Column for the last two weeks of his final campaign as an army scout. When the two columns split, the Yellowstone marched northeast. It continued to look for Native American camps while, at the same time, slowly drifting toward the home of the Seventh Cavalry at Fort Lincoln.

Cody thought he was going to leave the campaign on August 22, but as he started his trip to the East Coast, he learned some intelligence about possible villages in the area. He took the news back to Terry and ended up staying with the column until the end of the expedition.

While Terry, Cody, and the Yellowstone Column patrolled an area to the northeast, Crook led the Wyoming Column east along the trail of a village. The men were headed toward Dakota Territory, about one hundred miles north of Deadwood. They didn't yet know it, but they were about to experience the worst march of their lives. Afterward, many would call it "the Horsemeat March" or "the Starvation March."

The James-Younger Gang left Missouri sometime in the middle of August. There are so many conflicting stories about the dates and modes of travel that it is impossible to know the truth about the trip. But there seems to be enough evidence to say that the eight men in the gang were in the cities of Minneapolis and St. Paul on August 24, the same day that Buffalo Bill Cody reunited with General Terry to deliver new intelligence. Jim Younger rejoined the gang for the upcoming raid in Minnesota, which made the full lineup: Frank and Jesse James; Cole, Jim, and Bob Younger; Charlie Pitts; and Bill Chadwell. Chadwell was a native of Minnesota, so the gang hoped to rely on his firsthand knowledge as much as possible.

The gang split up but stayed close. The outlaws booked hotel rooms in Minneapolis and St. Paul. They used fake names and moved around the cities in small groups. But other than the fake names, they made no attempt to disguise themselves, and they began to leave a trail of interested observers in their wake. Up here in Minnesota, they might as well have been from a different planet. They looked, talked, and acted differently from everyone else.

They tucked their pants into knee-high boots. They wore long spurs and long linen dusters, which marked them as men from points farther south. Their Southern drawls were unmistakable, and they didn't take their hats off when they entered a dining room. They had a good time drinking and gambling, which earned plenty of notice from bystanders.

But the trip wasn't all fun and entertainment. They were there to rob something—probably a bank, but they hadn't decided on a target. The gang scouted potential robberies in Red Wing, St. Peter, Madelia, and maybe Mankato. The men bought expensive new horses and saddles that were admired by people in the area. They bought .44-caliber bullets for their guns, which surprised one local gunsmith. Few of his customers used such a large weapon.

At some point during the reconnaissance process, Jesse may have scouted the murder of Samuel Hardwicke. Hardwicke was the lawyer from Clay County, Missouri, who had helped the Pinkertons when they organized the raid that injured Jesse's mother and killed his eight-year-old half brother. Jesse knew Hardwicke's exact address in St. Paul because the newspapers printed it after Hardwicke moved to Minnesota. But for whatever reason, Jesse didn't make a move against Hardwicke.

Two days before the end of August, a killer was caught in Wyoming. Jack McCall was on the run for twenty-three days after he murdered

Wild Bill Hickok, but his luck ran out in Laramie on August 29. His acquittal by an informal court of miners in an illegal community didn't protect him when he cleared the Black Hills. An arrest warrant was issued, and he was caught by a U.S. marshal. The marshal took him to Yankton, the capital of Dakota Territory. His second trial would happen at the end of the year, and it would have the full weight of the American justice system behind it, and its result would be final.

As the calendar flipped from August to September, the James-Younger Gang narrowed the list of possible robbery targets to a single name. Towns like Red Wing were crossed off the list because they were too small and didn't have banks. Others, like Mankato, were too large and had too many banks. As the gang continued to search in a sweeping arc south of Minneapolis and St. Paul, it became increasingly clear that one town possessed the perfect combination of elements: Northfield.

18

THE NORTHFIELD RAID

Northfield, Minnesota, sits on the Cannon River about forty miles south of St. Paul. In 1876, it was home to two thousand people. Its population was slightly larger than Dodge City's and significantly smaller than Deadwood's, though Deadwood's population steadily dropped as the mines played out. The great value of Northfield, from the perspective of an outlaw gang, was that it had just one bank, the First National. All the money in town would be stored in one place.

From the perspective of the James-Younger Gang, the First National Bank of Northfield possessed an added bonus: it was deeply connected to a former Union general from the Civil War. The gang could rob a bank and strike a blow against its old enemies at the same time.

The general in question was Adelbert Ames. He was a native of Maine and fought all four years of the Civil War. He commanded the Twentieth Maine regiment for a year before passing the baton to Colonel Joshua Lawrence Chamberlain, the man who became a legend at the Battle of Gettysburg. Ames rose to the rank of major general and became a U.S. senator and the military governor of Mississippi after the war. While he was a senator, his father and brother helped start the First National Bank in Northfield.

After Ames left the governor's office in March of 1876, he joined his father and brother in running a flour mill in Northfield. The company owned one-quarter of the First National, and Ames's father was the vice president and his brother was one of the directors. The close connection of the Ames family to the bank was more than enough motivation for the James-Younger Gang to select it as the target, but there was an additional layer of motivation, as well. Cole Younger wrote in his autobiography in 1897 that the gang believed Union general Benjamin Butler was also an investor.

Butler was reviled throughout the South because of his time as the military governor of New Orleans. He was a Massachusetts lawyer and politician by trade, and he owed his officer's commission during the Civil War to his political connections rather than military training or experience. He tried and failed to achieve success on the battlefield on several occasions and was removed from command for the second, and final, time five months before the end of the war. In 1876, he was in his ninth year as a U.S. congressman from Massachusetts. But more importantly for the James-Younger Gang, Butler was one of Adelbert Ames's former commanders, and Ames was married to Butler's daughter, Blanche.

So the First National Bank of Northfield, Minnesota, was an inviting target for several reasons, but the gang still needed to do its due diligence. Jesse and Clell Miller spent a day or two reconnoitering the area around the town in early September. When they talked to residents in the region, they portrayed themselves as cattle buyers.

In one instance, they spoke to a farmer and pretended to be interested in buying land outside town. They tried to get a sense of the resistance they might face if they conducted an armed holdup of the bank. The farmer assured them that the good people of Northfield were peaceful, law-abiding citizens. It sounded like the townsfolk wouldn't put up much of a fight, which was exactly what the outlaws wanted to hear.

Around the same time that the gang planned its robbery, the bookkeeper of the First National stood inside the bank vault with the president of Carleton College. The bookkeeper, Joseph Lee Heywood, demonstrated the new chronometer lock on the safe that had recently been installed to upgrade security. The time lock could be set to engage and disengage at specific hours. The new feature had been reported in the local newspaper, the *Rice County Journal*, which prompted the president to stop by and see it for himself.

In addition to Heywood's job at the bank, he was also treasurer for the town and the college. Heywood and the president, James Strong, were both New Englanders, and as they stood in the vault, Strong relayed a story from his home state of Vermont. Late in 1864, during the final months of the Civil War, a unit of Confederate soldiers infiltrated St. Albans and robbed three banks in one day. There were between eighteen and twenty-two robbers, and they disguised themselves as ordinary citizens. They studied the town, which was double the size of Northfield, and the banks, one of which was the First National Bank of St. Albans.

On the day of the robbery, the soldiers essentially took control of the town. They progressed through their targets and netted more than $200,000. But as the raid wore on, the townspeople started to fight back. A shootout erupted, and a posse chased the bandits out of town. Within a day, fourteen robbers were caught and $87,000 was confiscated. The remaining $150,000 was never found and presumably made its way south to the Confederacy.

When Strong finished his tale, he turned to Heywood and asked if the bookkeeper thought he would hand over the money if he found himself in a similar situation. Heywood was a thirty-nine-year-old husband and father to a five-year-old girl. He was a Civil War veteran who was at the siege of Vicksburg. He thought about the question and then said, "I do not think I should."

Strong's story about a gang of Confederates storming a town and robbing its banks was amusing, with the benefit of the passage of twelve years. But it was also a *wartime* story. Things happened in war that were unfathomable in peacetime. That didn't mean bank robberies were a thing of the past, of course. Far from it. The newspapers were thick with stories about outlaws robbing anything that could be robbed—but not in Northfield. Despite the installation of the new time lock, few people thought that a robbery would happen in a sleepy little town in the middle of farm country.

At the same time two members of the James-Younger Gang scouted Northfield, the Yellowstone Column gave up its quest to avenge the deaths of Custer and the men of the Seventh Cavalry. It had been seven weeks since the Battle of the Little Bighorn. It had been fifteen weeks since the Seventh Cavalry marched out of Fort Lincoln to begin the campaign. And the new Yellowstone Column had been marching for the past month without seeing any significant sign of its enemy. General Crook led his Wyoming Column away from the combined army several days ago, and now General Terry was at a crossroads.

Terry received a report about a large group of Sioux who were somewhere between the Yellowstone River and the Missouri River in the northern reaches of Montana. At that point, he had three basic choices: One, he could continue to follow the Yellowstone until it merged with the Missouri. It would mean marching at least another seventy miles north and hoping that the column miraculously spotted reliable signs of the village.

Two, he could leave the comfortable and familiar banks of the Yellowstone and begin a search of the barren lands between the two rivers. But the vague reference to the village being somewhere in that area meant that it could be anywhere in a landscape of hundreds of square miles. And as every soldier on the expedition had painfully learned, villages moved every few days. Without solid intelligence and at least some sort of trail to follow, the search for a Native American village could quickly look like a dog chasing its tail.

Three, he could quit the expedition. His men were tired and disgruntled, and their home of Fort Lincoln was on a straight line to the east. Even though he was the commander and his troops would have to follow his orders, he would probably need to craft a powerful and eloquent argument to convince them to start an uncertain journey without staging a mutiny.

Terry didn't know which village was somewhere north of him on the plains, but it didn't really matter. It was actually Sitting Bull's village, and it was on its way to Canada. But the knowledge probably wouldn't have changed Terry's mind.

On September 5, Terry made his choice. He disbanded the Yellowstone Column and ended the campaign. Captain Thomas Weir put it best, with one of the all-time great sarcastic lines. He said, "As the Sioux have failed to find us, we are going home."

The Seventh Cavalry had traveled in a giant loop over the past three months and was now within striking distance of home. It would march back to Fort Lincoln and scout for camps along the Yellowstone on the way. Colonel Nelson Miles's Fifth Infantry would remain on the Yellowstone for the winter and chase any hostiles in the area. The Montana Column faced a trek of roughly 350 miles to return to Fort Ellis near Bozeman, Montana.

The campaign was a military failure, and its results weighed heavy on the minds of the soldiers, especially the men of the Seventh Cavalry. But it accomplished its ultimate goal. The U.S. government used the battles in June of 1876 as pretext to strip the Sioux of much of the land that had been ceded to them in the Fort Laramie Treaty of 1868.

While the Yellowstone Column broke up, representatives of the American government informed a group of chiefs at the Red Cloud Agency that they had lost the Black Hills. The coveted land, and the richest gold deposits in North America, now belonged to the United States.

Meanwhile, General Crook's Wyoming Column was in the middle of a march that became one of the worst trials of his soldiers' lives. Sporadic winter storms already plagued the northern plains. Cold rain and hail turned the ground into a sea of muck that stuck like glue to boots, hooves, and wagon wheels. When the rain stopped, thick fog enveloped the column. By September 5, the day Terry disbanded the Yellowstone Column, Crook's men were dangerously low on rations. They were starving and desperate, and they began to kill and butcher their horses for meat.

On September 7, Crook knew the situation was dire to the extreme. Even after killing many of their horses for food, the troopers might not survive a march to the nearest outpost or town. Crook ordered 150 men to ride south to Deadwood and bring back food for the rest of the column. The unit started its ride at the same time that eight outlaws started the robbery that ultimately destroyed the most famous outlaw gang in the country.

At about 10:00 a.m. on Thursday, September 7, four bandits rode into Northfield. At least one shop owner remarked on their fine horses and long linen dusters, and they likely drew attention from others in town. By 11:00 a.m., all eight outlaws were in town for one final reconnaissance patrol. Some of their number stopped for an early lunch at a local restaurant and ate ham and eggs while they discussed politics and the upcoming elections.

According to Cole Younger, the outlaws rode out of town in the early afternoon and reunited on a road two or three miles from Northfield. They discussed the robbery one last time, formed a loose plan, and then headed back to town.

In the First National Bank, the day progressed like any other, though the business was short-staffed that day; there were three employees behind the big L-shaped counter instead of four. Book-keeper Joseph Heywood was the senior man in the bank, and he doubled as the cashier. The regular cashier, George Phillips, was in Philadelphia to visit the World's Fair. Heywood sat at the cashier's desk in the part of the counter that was directly in front of the vault. Frank Wilcox, the assistant bookkeeper, stood at his station on the long side of the L-shaped counter. And Alonzo Bunker, the teller, stood near the teller's window in the corner of the L that faced the front door.

Most of the counter was guarded by tall wooden frames with glass inserts that acted as windows. If a bandit wanted to climb over one of the frames to reach the vault, he would have to grab on to the top, haul himself up like he was doing a pull-up, throw a leg over the top rail, drop onto the counter, and then hop down to the floor. But the wood frames only partitioned the straight edges of the L-shaped counter. The rounded corner where the two sides met to form the teller's window was wide open.

The day had passed quietly thus far, and Heywood looked forward to taking his wife and daughter to a show that evening. An Australian magician was in town, and his show would begin by sending two hot-air balloons into the sky at 6:45 p.m. Heywood was sure his wife and daughter would like to see the balloons, and then maybe they would stick around for the performance afterward.

Behind Heywood, the vault was unlocked but closed. He had checked the safe at the beginning of the day, as always. It sat against the back wall of the vault, and the new time lock had worked as advertised. It unlocked itself at the appointed hour, but Heywood kept the safe closed, just like the outer door of the vault.

A little after 2:00 p.m., the day changed dramatically.

A debate will likely persist forever about the role each outlaw played during the first half of the robbery that afternoon. No two versions of the Northfield Raid are the same, so determining the roles of the robbers becomes an exercise in the process of elimination. In previous bank robberies, the gang divided its force to do two things at the same time: execute the robbery inside the bank and control the crowd outside the bank. If Cole Younger's memory is trustworthy, he said the gang split into three groups and entered the town in waves.

The first wave was the group of three men who performed the robbery. The second wave was the group of two men who stayed outside and controlled the crowd. And the third wave was a group of three who rode in at the end to help with the escape. Cole specified that he and Clell Miller were the second wave; they were on crowd-control duty. He also said that Jim Younger was part of the third wave. There could be some logic in that move. Jim had refused to go on the Rocky Cut robbery, and he reportedly expressed last-minute reservations about the Northfield Raid. It was probably too risky to trust Jim with the important jobs of conducting the robbery or controlling the crowd.

The idea of trust also applies to Charlie Pitts and Bill Chadwell. They were the new guys. They had vouched for the traitor, Hobbs Kerry. And they had been relegated to background duties during the Rocky Cut robbery while the core of the gang did the heavy lifting. It seems unlikely that a close-knit group like the James-Younger Gang would have trusted Pitts and Chadwell with the most serious roles of the Northfield Raid. So it seems most likely that the first wave comprised Jesse James, Frank James, and Bob Younger. The second wave was Cole Younger and Clell Miller. And the third wave was Jim Younger, Charlie Pitts, and Bill Chadwell. If so, then Jesse, Frank, and Bob rode into Northfield at about 2:00 p.m.

They crossed Iron Bridge over the Cannon River and trotted into the town square. The square dead-ended at Division Street, where a left turn would take them north toward Carleton College and a right turn would take them south into the heart of Northfield. Jesse, Frank, and Bob turned right toward downtown and the First National Bank.

As they rode through the town square, Adelbert Ames strolled along the river toward his family's flour mill. It sat along the edge of the water near the bridge and opened onto the square. Ames carried a letter that he intended to mail to his wife, and he noticed the three men on fine horses who wore linen dusters. In a few minutes, he would understand their presence in town, but at the moment, he didn't give them much more than a passing glance.

J. S. Allen, who owned one of the hardware businesses that faced the town square, watched the three men ride past his front door. They looked like hard men, and he was immediately concerned. George Bates was also worried. He stood in a store across from the bank, and he noticed the three riders as they turned onto Division Street. Elias Hobbs, the town marshal, also saw the three men, but he wasn't as concerned as Bates or Allen. He had believed a couple of the men earlier in the week when they said they were cattle buyers.

When Jesse, Frank, and Bob turned onto Division Street, it was a short distance to the bank. The First National was the first business on the right that faced Division Street, and it was wedged between the back of a long, narrow general store and an undertaker's shop. The three men dismounted, tossed the reins of their horses over the hitching posts, and split up. Two of the three drifted up the sidewalk toward the corner of the street where they could look out onto the town square. The third man hovered near the horses.

Directly across the street from the bank, Henry Wheeler lounged in a chair outside his father's drugstore. He was twenty-two and home from the University of Michigan on a break. He watched the three men dismount in front of the bank and assumed they were cattle buyers.

In the hardware store next to the Wheeler and Blackman drugstore, the owner, W. H. Riddell, stared at the newcomers through his window. Like fellow hardware store owner J. S. Allen, Riddell was worried by the look of the men. His worry would explode into full-blown alarm in a few seconds.

On the corner where Division Street met the town square, the two robbers watched Cole Younger and Clell Miller walk their horses over Iron Bridge and into the square. The men on the corner turned and strode back toward the bank to begin the robbery.

Allen watched two more men in linen dusters (Cole and Clell) ride into town, and now he knew something was very wrong.

Frank, Jesse, and Bob reunited in front of the bank. They had the full attention of several residents on Division Street, but they were going through with the robbery anyway. As Cole and Clell trotted up to the bank, the three robbers stepped inside. Cole and Clell dismounted and tried to act casual, but the ruse ended as quickly as it started.

Allen marched down the street toward the bank. His suspicion was rising, and he was determined to see what was happening. As he drew level with the bank, Clell Miller grabbed him by the shirt collar and yanked him backward.

Miller growled, "You son of a bitch, don't you holler."

Clell didn't have to worry about Allen hollering. Across the street, W. H. Riddell watched the scuffle and did it for him.

The front door of the First National Bank swung closed behind Frank, Jesse, and Bob. They weren't aware of it, but the situation was already deteriorating on the street behind them. They reached under their linen dusters, drew their revolvers, and pointed them at the three men behind the counter.

Alonzo Bunker, the teller, stood near the open space in the counter that acted at the teller window. Frank Wilcox, the assistant bookkeeper, stood behind Bunker along one side of the L-shaped counter. And Joseph Heywood sat at the cashier's station in front of the vault.

The outlaws jumped over the counter through the teller window and landed next to the employees in a flash. One of the outlaws shouted, "Throw up your hands, for we intend to rob the bank! If you holler, we'll blow your goddamned brains out."

The bandits forced Wilcox and Bunker to drop to their knees and then demanded to know which man was the cashier. Joseph Heywood spoke up and said the cashier wasn't in. One of the robbers, later thought to be Frank James, leveled his gun at Heywood and told him to open the safe. Heywood coolly replied that it couldn't be opened. It was on a time lock. Frank shouted that that was a lie. They knew all about the time lock. Clell Miller had seen the newspaper article about the new security feature. In fact, he ripped it out and now carried it in his pocket. And the robbers didn't believe the safe would be locked during business hours anyway.

Frank decided to open the safe himself. He stepped into the vault, and Heywood jumped out of his chair and tried to slam the vault door shut. One of the other robbers pulled Heywood back. And while the attention of the bandits was locked on Heywood, Alonzo Bunker inched toward his teller window. On a ledge below the counter, he kept a small Smith & Wesson pistol. On his knees, he was nearly eye-level with the weapon. If he could get to it, he could help—

The outlaw who guarded Bunker and Wilcox noticed Bunker's gradual movements and snatched the pistol before Bunker could reach for it. That outlaw was probably Bob Younger, and now Frank yelled at Bob to take whatever he could from the teller's drawers. Bob found a small box that contained some bills and a few coins. He stuffed them into a grain sack and then yanked open a drawer. It held only stationery, and he jammed it shut with a frustrated shove. He stopped looking at that point, but if he had opened the drawer next to it, he would have found $2,000.

The outlaws' fury rose, and the violence inside the bank escalated at nearly the same time that gunshots boomed outside the bank.

W. H. Riddell and Henry Wheeler shouted the alarm. Riddell stood at the door of his hardware store, and Wheeler stood in front of his father's drugstore. The businesses were side by side, and Riddell and Wheeler would have been just a few feet from each other. They watched Clell Miller manhandle J. S. Allen, and they realized the bank was being robbed.

When Riddell and Wheeler screamed about a robbery, Cole Younger leaped into the saddle, drew a revolver, and fired at Riddell across the street. The bullets slammed into the front of Riddell's store. Cole yelled, "Get in there, you son of a bitch!"

In front of the bank, J. S. Allen twisted free of Clell Miller's grasp and sprinted toward the town square. He blared the alarm that robbers were attacking the bank as he ran around the corner to his hardware store. Citizens rushed through the square toward Division Street, and Allen handed them guns as they passed his store.

For Cole and Clell, the scene was spiraling out of control. They fired in the air and at the businesses across from the bank. They shouted for people to clear the street.

Theodore Miller, the undertaker whose shop was right next to the bank, walked through his shop to the front door. Like many other people in town, he initially believed the shooting and shouting was part of some kind of show, possibly connected to the magician's performance that was scheduled for later that day. But when Cole or Clell screamed at him to get back inside and fired a shot that smashed through his door, Miller retreated in a hurry.

Henry Wheeler dove into his father's drugstore as the outlaws sprayed bullets around Division Street. He needed a gun, but there was no weapon in the store. As his mind raced, he remembered that he had seen an old rifle at the Dampier Hotel. The hotel was just two doors north of his father's store, where Division Street met the town square. Wheeler charged out of the back door of the store and turned left to sprint through the alley that ran behind the business on Division Street.

While Henry rushed out of his father's drugstore, George Bates aimed a shotgun at the outlaws. Bates stood in the entrance to a clothing store next to Wheeler's drugstore. He leveled the shotgun at the bandits and pulled the trigger, but it wouldn't fire. He threw the shotgun aside, grabbed a pistol, and then discovered the pistol wasn't loaded. He thought he might be able to intimidate the bandits by pointing the gun at them and shouting that he had them dead to rights. But it quickly became apparent that it wasn't the greatest plan ever conceived by the mind of man. Bates ducked for cover as bullets continued to crash through windows and pepper doorframes.

In the town square, in yet another hardware store—yes, North-field had at least three hardware stores within 150 feet of each other, but only one bank—Anselm Manning snatched a Remington rifle out of the front window and rushed toward Division Street.

The robbery was probably five minutes old, and downtown Northfield was utter chaos when Jim Younger, Charlie Pitts, and Bill Chadwell galloped across Iron Bridge and into the town square.

Fire bells and church bells rang out the alarm all over town. At Carleton College, two blocks north of the square, the Dean of Women heard all the noise but didn't know what to make of it. Then two women rushed into her office. They had run from Division Street and were out of breath. One of them finally sputtered,

"Keep the girls off the street," and then fainted. The dean leaped into action. She rounded up all the girls and herded them up to the third floor of the dormitory. They grabbed all the fire axes in the building and huddled together, ready to defend themselves if necessary.

In the bank, one of the outlaws—likely Jesse—pulled a bowie knife and pressed it to Joseph Heywood's throat. The razor-sharp edge drew blood, and Jesse roared at the bookkeeper to open the safe. Alonzo Bunker and Frank Wilcox looked on in horror, but Heywood somehow squirmed out of Jesse's grasp. He tried to escape, but Frank slammed the butt of a gun into his skull. Heywood crashed to the floor. Frank fired a shot over Heywood's head that sounded like the thunder of a cannon in the small space. Gun smoke blew out of the barrel and clouded the room, and Bunker thought Heywood had just been killed.

Bunker bolted for the back door of the bank. The door was open, but blinds hung in the way. Bob Younger fired at Bunker as he ran, but he only hit the blinds. Bunker smashed through the blinds as he fell into the alley behind the building. He turned left and sprinted south across an empty lot toward Fifth Street at the end of the block. Bob stepped out of the back door and took careful aim. He fired, and the bullet tore through Bunker's right shoulder. Bunker staggered, but kept running.

The situation in the bank went from bad to worse. One employee was gone (Bunker); one was still subdued on the floor (Wilcox); and the other (Heywood) was stubbornly refusing to open the safe. As the outlaws reassessed the situation, they became keenly aware of the gunfire outside on Division Street.

The dynamic outside was changing. It wasn't just the gunfire of their fellow gang members who tried to intimidate the towns-people. It started to sound like an all-out battle.

In the town square, a farmer named Elias Stacy grabbed a shotgun from hardware store owner J. S. Allen and raced toward the bank. Lee & Hitchcock General Store sat on one corner of the town square and Division Street, and an outdoor staircase ran up the side of the general store to a dentist's office on the second floor. The staircase was a solid wooden structure whose bottom step was flush with the front of the store. So when Elias Stacy reached the edge of the general store, he took another step and leaned around the staircase to look down Division Street. He spied two outlaws in the middle of the street who fired in different directions.

Stacy eased the shotgun around the side of the staircase. He took aim at Clell Miller as Clell was scrambling up onto his horse. Stacy squeezed the trigger and blasted Miller, but the gun was loaded with birdshot instead of buckshot. The force of the smaller pellets knocked Miller off his horse and stung his face, but it didn't kill him.

In the square behind Stacy, three new outlaws galloped into town firing their guns and shouting at the tops of their lungs. Jim Younger, Charlie Pitts, and Bill Chadwell thought they would race into town, howling and shooting, and scare the hell out of the townspeople to cover the escape after a successful robbery. Instead, they rode straight into an urban combat zone.

On Division Street, Cole Younger whipped around at the sound of a shotgun blast and saw Clell Miller in the dirt with blood trickling down his face. For a moment, Cole's old friend looked like he might be in bad shape. But Miller climbed into the saddle and appeared ready to ride. Reinforcements arrived in the forms of Jim, Charlie, and Bill, but the action also grew hotter by the second.

Anselm Manning, a hardware store owner, ran along one side of the town square and made it to the corner where Elias Stacy stood. When he peered around the wooden staircase, he saw rider-less horses standing outside the bank. Manning drew a bead on one of the horses and fired. Bob Younger's horse dropped dead in the street. Manning hopped back behind the stairs to reload his rifle. It jammed, and he rushed back to his store to fix it.

Directly across the street from Manning and Stacy, Henry Wheeler ran through the back door of the Dampier Hotel. He located the old .50-caliber rifle and shouted for the hotel clerk, Charlie Dampier, to find some cartridges. Dampier handed him four rounds, and Henry bounded up the stairs to the third floor. He dashed into a room that had a window that overlooked Di-vision Street. Now he had to load the weapon. The single-shot breechloader was a relic from the Civil War that required Henry to stuff a paper cartridge with gunpowder and the bullet into the chamber and then situate the percussion cap. With the tedious process complete, he now prayed it would fire.

Henry leaned out of the window and took aim at Jim Younger. He was breathing hard, and his hands were shaking. He tried to focus on Jim, and then he squeezed the trigger. The rifle answered with a crack and sent the bullet screaming toward the outlaw, but it missed. It kicked up dust in the street. Henry reloaded, and this time, he leaned the gun on the windowsill to steady his aim. He sighted down the barrel at Clell Miller. He fired, and the shot hit Miller in the left shoulder like a sledgehammer.

Miller fell off his horse for the second time in just a few seconds, and it would be the last time. He struggled up to his knees, but the bullet had demolished the artery under his shoulder blade, and he collapsed to the dirt as his heart gave out. Henry Wheeler, the twenty-two-year-old medical student, had just killed the first man in the Northfield Raid.

South of the gun battle, bank teller Alonzo Bunker burst out of the alley that ran behind the businesses on the west side of Division Street. He ran across Fifth Street and nearly collided with Nellie Ames. Nellie's husband, John, was Adelbert's brother and one of the directors of the bank. Nellie was driving a small, one-horse carriage, and she heard popping sounds coming from Division Street. She couldn't tell if they were fireworks or gunshots, but then Alonzo Bunker ran past her with blood streaming down his back. He shouted that he'd been shot, and he kept running south, away from the gunfire.

Another man yelled at her to get out of the street or she'd be shot. She started to step down from the carriage, but then men on horseback charged into the intersection in front of her. They wore linen dusters and fired pistols in different directions. Nellie's eyes locked on the biggest man. He was large and muscular, but then movement on her left drew her attention.

Several men clambered up a stairwell from a basement saloon. They stumbled out into the sunlight and a blistering firefight. The last man up the stairs was a Swedish immigrant, Nicolaus Gustavson, who understood very little English and was completely drunk. He weaved toward the horsemen in the intersection.

Cole Younger—the large, muscular man—wheeled his horse around and yelled at Nellie to get out of the street, but she was transfixed. Cole's blood was up, and he was done with the scare tactics. Nicolaus Gustavson stumbled toward him, and Cole shot him in the head. Gustavson toppled over backward and lay motionless in the street.

Nellie could do nothing but stare. Then two men rushed into the street and dragged her away from the carriage. They carried her into a nearby store to get her out of harm's way.

Across the town square from the shootout, Adelbert Ames didn't know that his sister-in-law was in a store on the other end of the street fight. He was in his family's flour mill, where he had been since he noticed three men in linen dusters ride into town several minutes earlier. A man rushed into the mill and told Ames about the battle on Division Street.

Ames hurried outside and strode across the square. He found Anselm Manning and Elias Stacy huddled behind the outdoor staircase that ran up the side of the general store. Manning had cleared the jam in his Remington rifle and was back at his post. Ames was unarmed, but he stayed near Manning despite the chaos on Division Street. Four men on horses galloped back and forth and fired their pistols and shouted and cursed. One outlaw lay in the dirt, and presently, the biggest outlaw on horseback jumped down and tended to him. As he did, Manning steadied his rifle and took aim.

Cole Younger knelt beside Clell Miller. Cole couldn't help his old friend, so he grabbed Miller's pistols and gun belt. The gang would clearly need every weapon and round of ammunition to get out of this fight. Before Cole stood, he felt a punch to his left hip and then searing pain. But it could have been worse. Anselm Manning had fired the shot, but the bullet ricocheted off the outdoor staircase before it slammed into Cole's hip. The bullet lost some of its power and didn't cripple Cole the way it might have otherwise.

Cole hobbled back into the saddle and spun toward the bank. The sounds of gunfire from pistols, rifles, and shotguns blared at full volume, but Cole's voice cut through the cacophony. He screamed, "Come out of the bank!"

Inside the bank, the robbers heard the panic in Cole Younger's voice, and they knew it was time to go. Bob and Frank vaulted over the counter and hurried toward the front door. Jesse was enraged at Joseph Heywood's quiet stubbornness. Years earlier, Jesse wrote in one of his letters to *The Kansas City Times,* "A man who is a damned fool enough to refuse to open the safe or a vault when he is covered with a pistol ought to die."

Now, Jesse made good on the threat. Before he jumped over the counter, he shot Joseph Heywood in the head. The bullet hit Heywood in the left temple and splashed his blood across the cashier's desk. Frank Wilcox, the assistant bookkeeper, remained frozen in place. He knelt near the counter, terrified beyond movement. Jesse hopped over the counter and ran for the front door. When he was gone, Wilcox broke his trance and raced out the back door, leaving the body of Joseph Heywood alone in the bank.

Outside, Anselm Manning tried to steady his shaking hands. His aim had been a little off when he'd targeted Cole Younger, but the bullet struck the outlaw anyway. Now, Manning chambered another round, leaned around the staircase, and looked for another target. With Adelbert Ames watching over his shoulder and speaking words of encouragement, Manning took aim at one of the outlaws on horseback. His hands still trembled, but he squeezed the trigger. Manning thought he saw his targeted outlaw wince in pain, and then he and Ames pivoted out of sight while he reloaded.

In front of the bank, Bill Chadwell reeled in the saddle. He clutched at his horse's neck to stay on the animal, but his strength failed, and he fell to the street. He pushed himself up onto his hands and knees but then folded into a heap. Manning's bullet struck him right above the heart. In the space of a few seconds, two members of the gang were dead on Division Street.

Around that time, Jesse, Frank, and Bob Younger emerged from the bank. They ran out into a firestorm. Bullets and shotgun pellets flew in all directions. Windows shattered. Wood splintered. Stone crumbled. Clell Miller and Bill Chadwell lay dead in the dirt near Bob Younger's dead horse. Division Street was a perfect war zone, and the most direct gunfire came from about fifty feet up the block next to the general store on the corner. Men with rifles and shotguns were unloading on the gang from that spot.

When Bob Younger exited the bank, he turned left and hurried up the block toward the shooters on the corner. Cole likely screamed at his younger brother to shut down the gunfire coming from that direction, and Bob followed the order. He rushed up the street toward Anselm Manning and Adelbert Ames. The outdoor staircase on the side of the general store provided cover for Manning, and near the base of the stairs sat a large wooden box. Bob ducked behind the box and tried to get an angle on Manning. For a moment, their duel looked like a comical scene from a B-movie western.

Bob held his pistol cocked and ready to fire, but he couldn't find a clean shot on Manning. The outdoor staircase was in his way. He peeked over the box and poked his head around the side. A few feet away, Manning did the same thing: he leaned out from the staircase and monitored Bob, then ducked back out of sight. For a few tense seconds, nothing happened. Then Cole shouted at Bob to shoot through the staircase. Bob blasted the stairs, and jagged wood chips flew through the air. But Manning and Ames remained unharmed.

On the street behind Bob, a bullet clipped Jim Younger's shoulder. He spun in the saddle but stayed upright. Jesse and Frank fired at their attackers as they climbed onto their horses. They were just seconds away from leaving when Bob suffered the worst injury of the raid.

From the third-floor window of the hotel across the street from the bank, Henry Wheeler had a better angle on Bob than Manning did from street level. Henry shifted his old Civil War rifle and fired his third of four rounds. Bob jumped as Henry's bullet crashed into his right elbow.

The impact shattered Bob's elbow. His right arm now dangled uselessly, and painfully, by his side. But he switched his pistol to his left hand and kept firing at Manning.

Behind the staircase, Manning knew he couldn't win the fight in this fashion. He retreated around the corner to the front of the general store and tried to think of a new plan. There was a door at the back of the long, narrow store that opened onto Division Street. It was behind Bob Younger, and Bob likely hadn't paid attention to it during the gun battle. If Bob Younger stayed where he was, Manning could pop out of the door and get the drop on him. Manning ran inside and hurried through the store.

On the street, Bob was done with the duel. He staggered away from his position behind the wooden box. His right arm was a bloody mess, and his horse was dead in the street. Cole spurred his horse and hurried to his brother. Cole reached down, grabbed Bob's left hand, and hauled Bob onto his horse. With all the outlaws mounted, they pointed their horses south and galloped down Division Street.

Two blocks later, they cleared the downtown area. Less than a mile after that, they were out of Northfield. The robbery and the gun battle lasted no more than ten minutes, but the trial-by-fire was just beginning for the James-Younger Gang. The robbery netted $26.60 or $26.70, depending on the version of the story. Even if the gang had been assured of receiving all the gold in the Deadwood mines, it might not have been enough to incentivize them to endure the pain that they would experience over the next two weeks.

⊹⊱ 19 ⊰⊹

THE MANHUNT

As the outlaws rode south, the people of Northfield grappled with the aftermath of the raid. Anselm Manning had stepped out of the side door of Lee & Hitchcock's general store just moments after the bandits escaped. Henry Wheeler ran down from his third-floor window of the Dampier Hotel. Debris from the gunfight littered Division Street. Two dead outlaws and one dead horse lay in the dirt.

Nicolaus Gustavson lay on Fifth Street. The bullet from Cole Younger had not killed him. It pierced his skin and scraped the side of his skull. He survived for a few days, but he eventually passed away from the trauma of the wound.

James Strong, the president of Carleton College, helped collect the body of his friend Joseph Heywood from the bank. He drove Heywood's body home in a carriage. Heywood's wife, Lizzie, had heard about the robbery and the shootout and the possible murder of her husband, but now it was real.

Less than an hour after the gang fled, John Ames (Adelbert's brother) dictated a telegram about the raid. The telegraph operator tapped it out and sent it far and wide. The message read: "Eight armed men attacked bank at 2 o'clock. Fight on street between robbers and citizens. Cashier killed. Teller wounded. Two robbers killed. Others wounded. Send us some men and arms to chase robbers."

The news raced across the wires to towns and villages south of Northfield—along the possible path of the outlaws—and to the big cities of Minneapolis and St. Paul. Within minutes of receipt, hundreds of lawmen began mobilizing to rush to the area. Townspeople organized posses to search the roads, trails, and bridges. But they lacked the most crucial piece of information for a manhunt: the identities of the robbers.

The people of Northfield didn't know who had robbed them. The town was mayhem after the raid. People streamed in from everywhere to see the damage and the dead outlaws. The bodies of Clell Miller and Bill Chadwell were searched for clues to their identities, but they carried nothing of use in that regard. Speculation was rampant, but there was no confirmation.

Two hours after the robbery, trains left Minneapolis and St. Paul headed south. They were packed with detectives and well-armed volunteers. In towns all over southern Minnesota, telegraph operators ran to the leaders of their communities with news of the raid.

But that didn't happen in Dundas, the first stop on the road southwest of Northfield. The telegraph operator wasn't at his station when the gang rode through town.

On the edge of Dundas, a village of eight hundred people, the outlaws stopped at the Cannon River and washed their wounds. They fashioned a crude sling for Bob Younger's right arm. His elbow was gruesome, and it caused him excruciating pain. The gang pressed on after the brief stop, and the men attracted a few looks from passersby in town. But since no one in Dundas knew about the robbery, the outlaws cruised through town without trouble.

Beyond Dundas, the road turned west, and the gang encountered a man with two horses and a wagon. Bob Younger had been riding double with Cole, and he needed his own mount. The man didn't want to give up one of his horses, so an outlaw whacked him over the head with a pistol and stole a horse. When Bob crawled onto the animal and the men trudged onward, they experienced the first of many recurring problems that nagged them throughout the escape.

The area was full of farmers, and farmers had plow horses that weren't accustomed to spurs or riders. The lack of good horses slowed the gang's progress nearly as much as its injuries. But Bob's new horse was better than nothing, and the men continued west toward an area called the Big Woods. It was three thousand square miles of trees, lakes, streams, and marshes, and it was about to become the gang's personal hell.

The bandits passed the hamlet of Millersburg, which was just a speck on the road and didn't have a telegraph line. At about 6:00 p.m., they reached the town of Shieldsville, about fifteen miles from Northfield. Sunset was no more than an hour away, and the coming darkness would be both a blessing and a curse. It would help hide them and allow them to rest, which they badly needed. They were sore and exhausted, and Bob's elbow wound had bled ferociously for most of the escape. He, more than anyone, could use a break. But the darkness would also hinder their progress, and it might not stop pursuers who were familiar with the area.

In Shieldsville, the outlaws stopped their horses at a water trough. They might have relaxed, but only for a moment. The men knew they were being trailed. They knew a manhunt was under way. But they didn't know that the first posse had already made it to Shieldsville. The urgent telegram that had raced out of North-field at 3:00 p.m. made it to the town of Faribault a few seconds later. A group of four or five men threw some guns into a wagon and rode to Shieldsville to intercept the gang. When they arrived and saw no outlaws, they went into the nearest saloon . . . and left their guns in the wagon.

A few seconds after the gang used the water pump, the Fari-bault posse walked out of the saloon. Maybe it was a coincidence or maybe they had been warned by someone in town, but they now faced off with the James-Younger Gang, and they didn't have their guns. The outlaws pulled their pistols and instructed the posse to stay back. Then the outlaws blasted the water pump and galloped out of town.

Roughly five minutes later, a larger posse reached Shieldsville and joined the men from Faribault. Now that the new posse was more than double the size of the gang, the manhunters chased the outlaws. Four miles outside town, the posse spotted the outlaws in the distance. The bandits were crossing a ravine, and the posse lobbed some long-range rifle shots. The bullets did little damage, but one caused Bob Younger's horse to buck and jump. Bob top-pled off the animal and crashed to the ground. The pain in his elbow must have been exquisite. The gang returned fire and ended the pursuit, but Bob's horse was gone, and he was forced to ride with Cole again. The gang disappeared into the woods and left the posse behind.

As night fell, the outlaws were blessedly shielded from sight, but they were also disoriented. They were strangers in a strange land, and their store-bought maps of the area were useless. They ran into a local farmer and forced him to guide them through the unfamiliar territory. They finally found shelter for the night at a farmhouse near a town called Waterville. If the farmer who owned the spread knew about the raid, he concealed it well. He didn't cause trouble for the outlaws, and they didn't cause trouble for him.

The men settled in for the night and tried to sleep. It's safe to assume that September 7, 1876, was the longest, most difficult day for the gang since the Civil War. They had ridden into Northfield approximately twelve hours earlier and decided to rob the bank. Since then, nothing had gone right. And this was only day one. There were six more to come before the breaking point, and then there was another week beyond that.

While the gang tried to rest at the farmhouse near Waterville, the manhunt grew and expanded. More than two hundred men now scouted the roads, trails, bridges, fords, and river crossings. For the outlaws, the growing manhunt was bad, but it wasn't the worst problem. The men would reach back into their old bushwhacker days and use their evasive tactics to stay ahead of their pursuers. But they couldn't do anything about the rain.

For the next two weeks, southern Minnesota saw near-constant rain. It became the chief torment of six men who were on the run.

The bandits rested very little that night, despite their exhaustion, and they were in the saddle early the next day. Around noon on Friday, September 8, they rode toward the Little Cannon River about thirty miles southwest of Northfield. The bridge over the river was guarded by a posse, and the gang moved toward a crossing downstream from the fortified spot.

As the outlaws started to cross the river, a shotgun boomed near them. The ford was being watched by three men. But the farmer who fired the shot succeeded only in scaring his own posse. The gang briefly retreated into the woods, and then, when nothing further happened, they rode across the river and disappeared into the dense timber on the other side.

A half an hour later, the outlaws found a farm and tried to convince a German farmer to loan them two new horses and saddles. When the man justifiably hesitated, the outlaws stopped talking and pulled their guns. They took the farmer's son as a guide, and when he was done helping them, they sent him home. On his way back, the boy met a man who told him about the Northfield Raid, and the boy realized he had just helped the most-wanted men in the state. One last posse spotted the bandits before darkness fell on September 8, but the outlaws melted into the trees and vanished like ghosts.

The gang avoided hundreds of pursuers for a full day while continuing a line of movement to the southwest. They set up a crude camp in the woods and prepared for a night that promised to be more miserable than the last. They rigged shelters by draping their coats over tree branches, but it wasn't nearly enough to protect them from the rain.

Throughout the day on September 8, news of the Northfield Raid spread far and wide. That morning, the story dominated the front page of *The Minneapolis Tribune*. The page featured seven columns of text, and the four in the center were dedicated to the robbery. As fascinating as the story was to the readers, the bandits were unnamed. No one knew it was the work of the infamous James-Younger Gang.

But in the upper left-hand corner of the paper, right next to the story of the raid, there was news about a man who might have been equally infamous at the time. William Tweed, better known as Boss Tweed, was arrested in Spain and set to be extradited to the United States.

Tweed was one of the most corrupt politicians in American history. Throughout the 1860s, he ran the notorious political ring called Tammany Hall in New York City. He and his cronies were finally swept out of office in 1871 after embezzling millions of dollars' worth of city funds. He was tried, convicted, and sent to prison, but he escaped in 1875. He fled to Cuba and then to Spain, where he was arrested by Spanish police in early September 1876. By November, he was back in an American prison, and he died there two years later.

If the outlaws had been able to see the newspaper, they would have learned some information about their hunters. They had already encountered posses of locals, but hundreds of lawmen and volunteers streamed into the area immediately after the raid and throughout the day on September 8.

Detective Mike Hoy led a team that took a special train from Minneapolis. Detective John Bresette led a squad from St. Paul. They had the unenviable task of attempting to separate fact from fiction in the flood of reports that came in from points southwest of Northfield. And their mission wouldn't become easier over the next few days, and it wasn't helped by the fact that they hated each other.

Saturday, September 9, was bleak for both the hunters and the hunted. The skies dumped incessant rain. That morning, the outlaws decided to abandon their horses. The animals were thoroughly used up, and the men had been forced to dismount several times over the past day and a half to avoid searchers. The gang decided that it could move just as fast on foot. But of course, that decision added a new challenge to their misery. Their riding boots were not meant for hours of walking in these conditions, and they tore up the feet of the outlaws. But the decision wasn't entirely without benefits.

The Big Woods region was home to thousands of feral hogs, in addition to every other form of wildlife. The hogs tore up the ground and obliterated the trail of the outlaws. When the posses thought they had identified the correct path, they realized they were only crossing each other's tracks as hundreds of men scoured the same ground. The constant rain made everyone miserable, and most of the manhunters didn't know the area. They suffered the same major problem that the outlaws suffered: their maps were painfully unreliable. In essence, everyone was lost, everyone was tired, and everyone was miserable.

The outlaws and the manhunters weren't the only people in the upper Midwest who experienced those conditions. If the bandits thought they were suffering, it was nothing compared to the soldiers of the Wyoming Column. On the edge of Dakota Territory, 450 miles west of the manhunt, General Crook's men were on the edge of starvation. A detachment of 150 men had been ordered to hurry south to Deadwood to find food. Instead, they found the Lakota.

Two thousand soldiers had been surviving on meat from their horses for days. The weather system that had plagued them with rain and hail throughout the first week of September could have been the same one that now dumped its misery on southern Minnesota. Many, if not most, of the men of the Wyoming Column were on foot. They trudged south toward Deadwood, and their advance detachment hurried ahead of them to secure food in the booming gold camp.

On September 8, the detachment discovered a Native American village near a spot called Slim Buttes. It was a Minneconjou camp that was led by Chief American Horse, the man who had killed Captain William Fetterman in the infamous Fetterman Fight ten years earlier during Red Cloud's War. American Horse was born into the Oglala band of the Lakota, like Crazy Horse. And like the famous warrior, American Horse was a prestigious Shirt Wearer. He was reportedly leading his village to a reservation, likely the agency of his old friend Red Cloud.

At dawn on September 9, while members of the James-Younger Gang mounted up to begin their second full day on the run, the detachment of soldiers attacked the Minneconjou village. The troopers overwhelmed the village of forty lodges, but not before runners escaped to find help from other villages in the area.

During the attack, American Horse led a few warriors and a group of women and children into a deep ravine near the camp. The ravine acted almost like a cave. It provided good defensive cover, and American Horse's people dug in and waited for reinforcements. Crazy Horse's village was no more than twelve miles away, and American Horse expected his friend to sweep in with hundreds of warriors and wipe out the small force of white soldiers who had attacked the camp. But then the main body of the Wyoming Column arrived.

The rest of Crook's two thousand men reached the village about midmorning and quickly secured the site. They ravaged the camp and found five thousand pounds of meat that was being stored for the winter. They also discovered a pair of heavy gloves that belonged to Captain Myles Keogh and the flag of Keogh's I Company of the Seventh Cavalry. It was clear that the villagers had been at the Battle of the Little Bighorn.

When the initial elation at the discovery of food had passed, Crook ordered his men to focus on dislodging American Horse's people from the ravine. The troopers poured relentless gunfire onto the position. The handful of warriors returned fire through the onslaught and refused to leave their makeshift fort. After a prolonged stalemate, Crook halted the firing. Two of his scouts approached the ravine and attempted to convince American Horse to surrender. By that point, multiple people in the ravine were dead or wounded, including American Horse. The chief suffered a grisly gunshot wound to the abdomen, and he knew he wouldn't last long.

American Horse appeared at the mouth of the ravine. He offered to surrender if the survivors in the cave would be spared. Crook agreed, and American Horse led the people out of the ravine. Two surgeons attempted to operate on the chief's wound, but the damage was too severe. American Horse, a celebrated warrior and leader, died a short time later.

Crazy Horse rode through the hills with reinforcements, but as they approached the village, they were surprised to see 2,000 soldiers instead of the 150 men who'd made the initial attack. Regardless, the warriors charged the site and galloped straight into the teeth of 2,000 rifles. The troopers allowed the warriors to come within range and then opened fire with a thunderous volley. The bombardment scattered the warriors in all directions. The contingent remained in the hills and traded fire with the soldiers as daylight slowly faded, but when night fell, the warriors drifted back to their camps. The Battle of Slim Buttes was done, and so was the campaign on the northern plains in the summer of 1876.

The next morning, Crook made no effort to follow Crazy Horse's camps. His men were too exhausted and too dispirited to continue the expedition. They now had enough food to quell their starvation, and they marched south until they made it to Custer City. That was the end of the road for the foreseeable future. They made camp and settled in to rest and recuperate.

While Crook battled Crazy Horse for the second time in three months and the James-Younger Gang slogged through the Big Woods, William Arthur Cummings made baseball history for the second time. Cummings had already earned a place in baseball lore by inventing the curveball. Then, on September 9, 1876, he became the first pitcher to win two complete-game victories in the same day. His Hartford Dark Blues beat the Cincinnati Red Stockings 14–4 and 8–4 in a doubleheader in Hartford.

Cummings wasn't the only pitcher to make history in early September. Four days before Cummings won two complete games in the same day, George Bradley added his name to the record book for the second time that season. He threw the first no-hitter in major league history on July 15. On September 5, he recorded his sixteenth shutout of the year when his St. Louis Brown Stockings beat the New York Mutuals 9–0. The record of sixteen shutouts by a pitcher in a single season has been equaled once, by Pete Alexander in 1916, but never surpassed.

A thousand miles to the west, the James boys and the Younger brothers neither knew nor would have cared about Candy Cummings's history-making performance. Their trek through southern Minnesota grew worse by the hour. The only bright spot, though they didn't know it, was that the horrible weather caused most of the manhunters to quit and go home. The outlaws had no intention of quitting, but they desperately wanted to go home.

As the gang slowly worked its way southwest, the men scavenged food from fields or stole it from farmhouses. They rested for the second half of the day on September 9 and resumed their march after nightfall. They stopped frequently to rest and then set up a camp around daybreak on Sunday, September 10.

Reportedly, there were more than five hundred men searching for the six bandits. Special trains shuttled lawmen and volunteers to the search areas. Telegraphs operated twenty-four hours a day. The governor of Minnesota offered a $1,500 reward for the capture of the gang. John and Adelbert Ames put up $500 on behalf of the First National Bank. Both numbers would climb substantially over the next few days. But the resources weren't enough. Or maybe they might have been if there hadn't been cases of poor leadership.

On the morning of September 10, two boys spotted the outlaws near a town called Marysburg, about twelve miles west of Waterville. The boys hurried to tell their important news to Minneapolis detective Mike Hoy, but he ignored them. Hoy and Bresette continually issued conflicting orders to their respective groups of searchers. These orders opened holes in the dragnet, and the outlaws slipped right through. And even when the commanders trusted their reports, the trail of the outlaws was nearly impossible to follow. The weather conditions and the lack of success steadily reduced the number of searchers.

On the afternoon of September 10, as the gang made slow progress westward, Joseph Heywood was honored as a hero and laid to rest in the Northfield cemetery. Nearly a thousand people attended the ceremonies, despite the rainy weather.

Thirty-five miles southwest of Northfield, the gang paused for a while at Madison Lake. After dark, they made another nine miles of hard marching and were rewarded with their first reason to rejoice in three days. They found an abandoned farmhouse about three miles from the small city of Mankato. It was their sanctuary for the next three days.

The gang holed up in the abandoned farmhouse Sunday night, September 10, through Tuesday night, September 12. They dressed their wounds, stayed out of the rain, and tried to figure out what to do next. While they relished several days of rest and respite from the rain, the manhunters finally discovered their horses in the woods east of Marysburg.

It was Tuesday morning, and the searchers were initially delighted by their find. But as they examined the scene more closely, they learned that the animals had been there for days. The gang had abandoned them Saturday morning, and the belated discovery was another blow to the manhunt. Later on Tuesday, hope brightened again when a report of suspicious men came in from an area near Mankato, but another downpour cursed the hunters and obliterated any trail. It wouldn't have mattered anyway. The supposedly suspicious men weren't the outlaws.

By Wednesday morning, September 13, Detectives Hoy and Bresette had had enough. They had been scouring the area around Northfield and searching the Big Woods for six days, and neither man had come close to glimpsing the fugitives. They loaded their volunteers onto trains and began the disappointing trip back to the Twin Cities. But their dark moods changed that very afternoon when they received their first real lead on the outlaws.

Thomas Jefferson Dunning was a hired hand on a farm north of Mankato. Around 6:00 a.m. on Wednesday, he walked outside to begin his morning routine. He started to bring in his boss's cows for milking when he was startled by six haggard-looking men. The outlaws used their standard lie: they said they were a posse chasing robbers, and they accused Dunning of being one of the bandits so that he was instantly thrown off balance. He stammered that he was no such thing, but the men pulled their pistols and tied his hands behind his back.

They instructed Dunning to show them the way to Mankato, and they began to march. Dunning repeatedly proclaimed his innocence, but the men were interested only in geography. They asked about the roads around Mankato. They asked about the two major rivers in the area. Were there places to cross? Could they swim across if they had to?

As they walked, Dunning slowly understood the situation. Jesse was the most talkative of the gang, and he eventually told Dunning about the raid. After three-quarters of a mile, they decided the farmhand was more trouble than he was worth. They left him standing in the road as they moved a short distance away to discuss his fate. There were only three options: shoot him, tie him to a tree, or let him go.

Jesse and Frank wanted to shoot him. It was the only way to guarantee his silence. Cole opposed the shooting, as Jesse knew he would. They were always on opposite sides. Bob seemed to be the deciding voice. Bob also opposed the shooting, so they made a soft compromise. They allowed Dunning to leave unharmed and unrestrained, but they made him swear to keep their secret. If he didn't, they said they would know it. They would hunt him down and kill him, no matter how long it took.

Dunning hurried back to the farm. For a while, he thought about keeping the secret, but in the end, he knew he couldn't. He told the farm owner about his experience. The man immediately leaped onto a horse and galloped to Mankato. While he rushed to town, the fugitives picked their way through the woods toward the same destination.

When the farmer reached Mankato and spread the news, the manhunt kicked into high gear. The town crackled with energy. The streets buzzed with excited chatter and bustled with people who rushed to be part of the chase. Local volunteers formed picket lines and tromped through the fields and the woods. Sheriffs from seven counties near Mankato formed posses and hurried to the area. The telegraph line lit up with the first reliable report in days.

Detective Mike Hoy learned the news at about 10:00 a.m. as he and his team stepped off the train in Minneapolis. They immediately regrouped to rush to Mankato, but they were forced to wait for four and a half hours until the 2:30 p.m. train.

Detective John Bresette and his team fared better. They were only thirty-five miles north of Mankato when they heard the report. They were on a train headed home to St. Paul, but they rushed off at the stop for the small town of Blakeley and impatiently waited for the next train headed in the opposite direction.

The gang reached the outskirts of Mankato while the reinvigorated manhunt exploded to life. With posses of lawmen and locals crisscrossing the region, the fugitives needed to make an important decision: Should they go through Mankato or around it? If they went around it, they would continue to be at the mercy of an unfamiliar landscape. If they went through it, they would be walking straight into the heart of the manhunt. But they would also be able to follow a set of railroad tracks through town and across the Blue Earth River on the other side.

The outlaws had spent their lives choosing the daring option, and now would be no different. They chose to go straight through Mankato. It was the last thing the manhunters would expect. But to attempt such a move, they needed darkness. The outlaws hunkered in the woods and waited for nightfall.

Ninety-nine percent of the plan to go through Mankato worked perfectly. But the one percent that didn't led to the end of the most famous outlaw gang of the Old West.

THE END OF AN ERA

Around midnight, the gang began its trek through Mankato. It was a dark night. The moon and stars were shrouded by clouds that continued to dump rain on southern Minnesota. Although the conditions were as miserable as ever, they helped the outlaws.

The men quietly sneaked through town until they made it to the railroad bridge over the Blue Earth River. The manhunters had guarded every crossing in the previous week, and the outlaws expected to find watchers at this one, as well. But as they studied it, they didn't see any guards. Cautiously, the outlaws walked across the bridge in a single-file line, six barely perceptible silhouettes in the pouring rain.

Two men and a boy were stationed out of sight to watch the bridge. The boy spotted the bandits and rushed to a larger group of guards, who watched an old wagon bridge. News of the sighting spread quickly, but not quickly enough to help the searchers. The outlaws had crossed the railroad bridge and disappeared into the woods on the other side. The combination of rain and impenetrable darkness forced the manhunters to wait for daylight to begin their pursuit.

After the fugitives crossed the bridge, they stumbled into a watermelon patch. They devoured as many as they could before continuing west along the tracks. Later, they discovered a chicken coop and grabbed a few birds for breakfast. They walked three miles past the bridge and set up camp at the base of a ridge.

As a murky dawn broke on the morning of September 14, the men built a fire to roast the chickens. They tried to hide the flames by rigging their coats and blankets into a tarp, but the smoke still drifted up through the trees. They were dangerously close to Mankato and they could only hope the smoke wouldn't give them away.

In the town at first light, Detective Mike Hoy led a group over the railroad bridge to find the trail of the outlaws. The searchers found footprints in the mud and followed them along the railroad tracks. But Hoy initially rushed past the spot where the gang moved away from the tracks and down into the woods. A keen-eyed member of the posse spotted the new trail, and then they saw the smoke rising out of the timber.

Hoy shouted for the men to follow him, and he bounded down into the trees . . . and that was all the warning the gang needed to escape again. If Hoy had taken the time to quietly encircle the gang, the manhunt would have ended that morning. But Hoy's attempt to be the hero who caught the bandits backfired, and he wouldn't receive another chance.

The outlaws heard the commotion and raced deeper into the woods. They stayed ahead of their pursuers, but at great cost. They were forced to abandon their food and some of their coats, blankets, and bridles. Despite their close call, and their pain and exhaustion, they eluded the searchers for the rest of the day.

The fugitives continued to use their old evasive tactics: they walked through streams and stepped on rocks to avoid leaving footprints; they walked in each other's tracks; they doubled back on their trail to confuse the signs. And they were aided by the relentless rain, though it was one of many elements that led to the breaking point that night.

The gang hit its lowest point when it made camp on the evening of September 14. Bob Younger performed an incredible feat of strength and stamina to make it this far, but he was in terrible shape. His mangled arm forced him to move more slowly than the others, and the gang could move only as fast as the slowest man. After days of rain, strenuous physical exertion, and living in the woods, it would also be a small miracle if he didn't have a raging fever. The area around the gang was swarming with manhunters, and Bob couldn't move at the speed that was needed to outrun them. It was time to make one of the most difficult decisions of their lives.

The James boys and the Younger brothers had known each other for fifteen years. They had fought in the Civil War together. They had been outlaws together. They had traveled countless miles together and experienced fantastic highs and endured difficult lows. But they couldn't stay together any longer. Cole and Jim Younger obviously were not going to abandon their brother. And Charlie Pitts was loyal to the Youngers. The best hope—maybe the *only* hope—for Jesse and Frank to make it home was to go on alone.

That night, Jesse and Frank probably exchanged a short, heartfelt goodbye with their comrades, and then they slipped away into the cold, rainy darkness of the Big Woods.

* * *

Around midnight near Lake Crystal, about fourteen miles southwest of Mankato, a man on guard duty had a brief encounter with two men on a black horse. He rushed into the town of Lake Crystal to alert the rest of the searchers, and they later found tracks that suggested the riders were the James boys.

Sometime in the predawn hours of September 15, Jesse and Frank stole two gray mares from the farm of a Baptist minister named Joseph Rockwood. They had reliable horses for the first time since they had fled Northfield, and the animals were about to do some hard riding. At 6:00 a.m., they stopped at a farm and bought a few supplies from the wife of the farmer. She thought they looked a little rough around the edges, but they were nice, so she helped them.

At about the same time, Joseph Rockwood discovered that his horses were missing. He hurried to Lake Crystal with the news, and the searchers had to confront the possibility that they were chasing two groups instead of one. All day, frantic reports came in of two men on Rockwood's mares. But the manhunters, which included Detectives Hoy and Bresette and their teams, were always a step behind.

While one half of the manhunt focused on the two phantoms on the gray mares, the other half continued to search the woods southwest of Mankato. There were no more reports of stolen horses, so the possemen assumed that the remaining four outlaws were on foot. If the assumption was true, then the outlaws shouldn't be too difficult to catch. But as the *Rice County Journal* put it later in a wonderfully sarcastic article, that was easier said than done:

Here were six men hunted in a land comparatively strange to them. . . . The best detective talent was employed. The best woodsmen engaged in the hunt. Citizens of every class deserted all else, and took up their arms. Yet almost in the face and eyes of eager pursuers, they have passed through carefully laid traps. . . . Probably no men were ever more desperately set upon, nor more intrepid daring ever displayed by mortals. Houseless, footsore, hungry and poorly clad, they have passed on, and their miraculous escape excites more wonder than did their daring attempt at robbery.

The four remaining outlaws—the three Younger brothers and Charlie Pitts—were on foot, as the searchers suspected. While the James boys rode southwest on Joseph Rockwood's horses, the quartet walked in the same general direction. But the next week illustrated the stark difference between the two groups.

When Pitts and the Youngers made camp on the evening of September 15, they had trudged just a few miles toward the town of Madelia. The James boys traveled more than forty miles that day. While Pitts and the Youngers stayed in camp for two days and suffered through rainstorms that seemed endless, the James boys made it to the edge of Minnesota.

On the night of September 15, Frank and Jesse bunked with a German farmer who had not heard about the raid. They left at 7:00 a.m. the next day. That afternoon, Saturday, September 16, they stopped at another farm and told the woman at the homestead that they were on the trail of horse thieves. She gave them food, which they ate in the saddle before setting off again.

All day, they were essentially bracketed by the squads of Detective Hoy and Detective Bresette. The lawmen and their posses monitored likely routes along a southwesterly course, but the out-laws zigzagged through fields and rarely used established roads.

Bresette's team didn't learn about the encounter with the woman at the farm until sunset. He and his men were forced to wait until the next morning to resume their pursuit. Bresette's team found the trail of the gray mares, but by that time, the outlaws were more than seventeen hours ahead of the posse. The manhunters continued the chase, but it was quickly becoming an exercise in futility.

At the same time Bresette restarted the pursuit on the morning of September 17, the James boys were dozens of miles ahead at a farm northeast of Luverne. It was the home of Charles and Sarah Rolph. Charles was away from home, and the outlaws asked Sarah for break-fast. She happily obliged, having not heard about the raid ten days earlier. Jesse and Frank were so stiff and sore when they struggled down from their horses that they were forced to make an excuse about a wagon accident to explain why they were in such rough shape.

When they finished their meal, they thanked her and paid for the food. They hauled themselves back into their saddles with great difficulty and trotted away toward the southwest. They were no more than twenty miles from the border of Dakota Territory, which meant they had covered approximately one hundred miles in the past two days. But the hard traveling had used up their horses, and they moved at a slower pace when they left the Rolph farm.

A short time later, Sarah Rolph's brother visited the house and told the couple about the robbery. They were understandably shocked, and Charles raced into Luverne to tell the county sheriff about the experience. The sheriff quickly rounded up some men and went in pursuit. That afternoon, the small posse spotted the outlaws and closed within rifle distance, but the sheriff's nerve gave out. He chose not to start a gun battle with the killers. Instead, he followed them at a distance, which was another fateful mistake by law enforcement. The posse lost the outlaws after dark and never saw them again.

That night, Jesse and Frank crossed into Dakota Territory and stopped at the farm of a Swedish immigrant named Andrew Nelson. By that point, the gray mares had performed a herculean task, and the James boys could ask no more of them. They swapped the mares for two black horses in the stable. Nelson had a mind to protest, but the pistols under the outlaws' coats convinced him otherwise. The joke would be on them anyway. When they rode away on the horses, they realized they had a serious problem: one of the horses was completely blind, and the other was blind in one eye. Somehow, they guided the animals for twelve miles before they stole a pair of gray geldings.

The geldings carried them through Sioux Falls in the middle of the night. The brothers asked for directions from a stagecoach driver at about 3:30 a.m., and they thought it best to stay out of sight after that encounter. They had been traveling for the better part of ninety hours, and now they hid and rested during the day on Monday, September 18.

Behind them, across more than 150 miles of territory, messages burned up the telegraph lines. They alerted every town in the area to the presence of the outlaws. Posses rode through the countryside all day but never spotted the brothers. The new manhunters were part of a growing club. It seemed no one was capable of cornering either group of bandits. The searchers were able to track the movements of the pair of fugitives who were racing southwest, albeit belatedly and without any hope of catching them. But the other four were virtually ghosts. There had been no substantial information about them since the near-miss outside Mankato four days earlier. And with so few positive results, and so many failures, September 18 became a day of reckoning.

While both groups of fugitives stayed out of sight, Detective Mike Hoy of Minneapolis and Detective John Bresette of St. Paul quit their pursuit. They had been soundly beaten by the boys from Missouri, and they were savaged in the press for their failure.

Late in the day on September 18, the James boys resumed their ride, though they traveled only until dusk. They spent the night with a Norwegian farmer who had no reason to suspect they were robbers. The next morning, Tuesday, September 19, they continued south from the Sioux Falls area. They came across two men in the road who were driving teams of horses. Jesse and Frank stole the two best horses and gave the men the pair of gray geldings.

The brothers wanted to cross the Big Sioux River from Dakota Territory to the northwest corner of Iowa as soon as possible. They reached their goal a short while later. But as they splashed across the river, they were spotted by a posse of eight men. Three members of the posse raced ahead of the others, though it's hard to understand their intent. The James boys dashed up to the top of a bluff, dismounted, and fired at their pursuers. The three men immediately retreated because, as unlikely as it is to believe, they were unarmed.

The group of eight decided to wait for more reinforcements rather than continue the chase, and Jesse and Frank galloped away. When a larger posse finally arrived, the James boys had a sizable lead, and they were about to be aided by the weather. A storm rolled in and washed away the outlaws' trail. It was another in a long line of missed opportunities for the searchers.

By early afternoon the next day, September 20, the brothers were closing in on Sioux City, Iowa. Several miles north of town, they encountered Dr. Sidney Mosher. He had received an urgent telegram that a woman was seriously sick on a farm northeast of the city. He grabbed his medical bag and rode in the direction of the farm. After a time, he feared he was lost. He spotted two men on the road who were headed toward Sioux City, and he asked them for help.

Dr. Mosher thought they looked like intelligent men, though they had clearly been out in the wilds for quite some time. Their clothes were covered with dirt and grime, and the taller of the two men wore boots that were full of holes. The doctor asked the men if they lived in the area, and if so, did they know how to reach the farm he was trying to find?

Jesse and Frank responded yes to both questions, but they failed when they tried to give Mosher directions to his destination. The doctor knew about the raid and the hunt for the robbers, and he asked Frank and Jesse if they were searching for the killers. They said they were, and they asked Mosher if he had any information. The doctor had plenty. He filled them in on the posse from Sioux City that was looking for the robbers at that very moment.

Jesse and Frank stopped the ruse. They told the doctor they were part of the Northfield gang, and they took the doctor prisoner. The brothers forced Mosher to ride with them until 7:00 or 8:00 p.m. Then they dismounted, and Frank exchanged clothes with the doctor. When he gave the doctor his pants, there was a distinct bullet hole in the right leg. Jesse swapped coats with the doctor, and then it was time to leave. They pointed the doctor in the direction of a speck of light way off in the distance. They told him to head toward the light and not to look back.

When Dr. Mosher reached the source of the light, he found a house that belonged to a German farmer. He nearly collapsed from exhaustion in the man's home, and then told him a fantastic tale about the last few hours of his life. By then, the James boys were long gone.

The next day, Thursday, September 21, exactly two weeks after the raid, the doctor rode back into Sioux City and told his story to the authorities. Unlike many other sightings, he possessed actual proof that he had met the fugitives: he was wearing their clothing. The bullet hole in the pants convinced everyone.

Once again, messages buzzed over the telegraph lines alerting towns and railroad depots that the bandits were in the area and probably headed south. But from that point forward, there were few, if any, verified sightings.

On the same day the James boys disappeared into Iowa, the Younger brothers and Charlie Pitts lost their battle with the man-hunters. Over the past week, while Jesse and Frank escaped the entire state of Minnesota, the other four outlaws had struggled to escape the Big Woods.

They had pushed west for five days and nights. They were starving. They were exhausted. Their boots were destroying their feet. They had been soaking wet for so long that they probably started to question whether they would ever be dry again. But they eventually emerged from the hell that was the Big Woods. They were out on the prairie west of the dense timber, and at about 7:00 a.m. on September 21, they approached a farm a few miles north of Madelia.

The owner of the farm, Ole Sorbel, was in the road milking a cow in front of the family's home. Jim Younger and Charlie Pitts said a cheerful good morning to Mr. Sorbel as they walked past the house. Sorbel's seventeen-year-old son, Oscar, carried pails of milk near the barn when he saw Jim and Charlie. Oscar knew all about the robbery in Northfield and the manhunt for the bandits. He had interacted with some local men who were on the lookout for the outlaws.

It was easily the most exciting thing that had ever happened in the area, and the moment Oscar saw Jim and Charlie, he was convinced they were two of the robbers. When the two strangers passed the house, Oscar hurriedly whispered as much to his father. Oscar's father said they seemed like nice men, and he instructed his son to go back to work. Oscar returned to his milking, but he couldn't contain his curiosity. He set aside his pail and hustled down the road after the men. But they had entered a stretch of woods, and he wouldn't follow them in there.

When he returned home, he found out that two more men had stopped by the house, one of whom appeared to have his arm in a sling under his coat. Oscar was certain that the four men were the robbers. He begged his father to let him ride to Madelia to warn the lawmen who were searching for the bandits. Finally, his father gave his consent. Oscar climbed onto an old horse and began the eight-mile trip to Madelia.

The roads were sludge, thanks to the incessant rain, and at one point the horse tripped and flipped Oscar into the mud. An hour later, Oscar arrived at the Flanders House hotel, the headquarters of the manhunters. He shouted his news, but he was covered in mud from head to toe, and most people thought he was crazy. Watonwan County sheriff James Glispin did not. He immediately organized a posse and rode out to find the robbers.

In the woods beyond the Sorbel farm, Bob Younger was ready to collapse. His arm had started to heal in the past two weeks, but not in a good way. He couldn't straighten it, and he couldn't use his right hand at all. As the foursome approached the marshes near Lake Hanska west of the Sorbel farm, Bob said he couldn't go any farther. He told his companions to leave him, but of course they wouldn't.

Then, at about 11:00 a.m., they heard riders behind them. They turned to see four men galloping in their direction. Sheriff Glispin was in the lead, and he shouted for them to halt. The outlaws ignored him and began splashing through the marshes. The four manhunters fired shots at the runners, but they missed, and the bandits were soon out of range. The horses couldn't follow the fugitives through the marshes, so the hunters backtracked and rode two miles out of their way to continue the pursuit. But in that time, more men joined the posse.

The group made up ground, and soon the men located the bandits. The fugitives were hurrying toward the brush along the banks of the Watonwan River. The outlaws fired at the posse as they retreated toward the river. The posse returned fire, but soon they lost sight of the outlaws in the thickets near the water.

The Youngers and Charlie Pitts were down to their last option. They had to wade into the freezing-cold river and try to cross to the other side. The water swallowed them up to their chests and forced them to hold their guns over their heads, but they made it to the south bank.

As they staggered out of the water and hurried across the prairie, they were spotted by a farmer's wife. She shouted the alarm to a hunting party on a nearby road. A man and his son grabbed their shotguns and began walking down the hill toward the river. They blocked the path of escape, and the outlaws retreated to some tall weeds near the river.

Sheriff Glispin's posse—now forty men—had been forced to ride a mile downstream to cross the river, but now they converged on the thickets where the outlaws would make their last stand. The possemen spread out and locked up the area. Men were stationed on both sides of the river, and the gang was now surrounded. Captain William Murphy called out for volunteers to walk into the thickets and flush out the bandits.

Murphy, like many Civil War veterans, was referred to by his military rank long after the war was done. Six men agreed to go with Murphy: Sheriff Glispin, Thomas Vought, Charles Pomeroy, Benjamin Rice, George Bradford, and S. J. Severson. They dismounted, formed a line, and marched toward the thicket.

The Youngers and Charlie Pitts crouched in the willows, some of which were five feet high. Charlie spotted Sheriff Glispin moving toward him. He allowed the sheriff to get within fifteen feet, then he jumped up and aimed his pistol at Glispin. Glispin swiveled toward Charlie with his single-shot rifle. They fired at nearly the same time. The sheriff's bullet slammed into Charlie's chest. He pitched forward and crashed to the ground, dead on the spot.

Glispin dropped to a knee to reload his rifle. The Youngers leaped to their feet and began firing. Possemen on both sides of the river opened up on the thickets. Gunfire roared in all directions. Then Captain Murphy went down. He was shot on the right side of the stomach. His hand flew to the wound. He expected to see blood, but there was none. The bullet had scored a direct hit on his briarwood pipe. The only mark on his body was a slight bruise.

In the weeds, the Youngers were in the middle of an onslaught. Jim was hit in the right leg. Then his head snapped around as a shot smashed into the left side of his upper jaw and lodged in the roof of his mouth near the back of his throat. He fell to the ground, unconscious, with blood gushing from his face.

Buckshot peppered Cole Younger. Then he took a devastating wound: a ball struck him in the head behind the right eye. He fell beside Jim with blood pouring from his nose and mouth. Bob was hit in the chest, and now the revolver in his left hand clicked on empty cylinders. He was the last man standing, and the injury to his right arm prevented him from reloading. He shouted for the manhunters to stop firing. He would surrender. It was over.

News of the surrender reached Northfield that evening, Thursday, September 21, exactly two weeks after the raid. The townspeople went wild. That night, they lit a bonfire in the middle of the town square, the same town square the outlaws had ridden through on the day they changed Northfield forever.

A band played, and people fired guns in the air and set off fireworks to celebrate. The jubilation was well deserved, and expected, but not fully complete. The James boys were still out there somewhere. Over the next two days, there were supposed sightings near small towns in central Iowa and rumors that the boys were traveling through Nebraska. The brothers never talked about the raid or wrote about it in letters, newspaper articles, or memoirs. They took the truth to their graves.

On Saturday, September 23, one day after the traditional end of summer, the hunt for Frank and Jesse James was officially called off.

Three days later, and four hundred miles northwest of Northfield, the Seventh Cavalry finally made it home to Fort Lincoln. The weary soldiers had been gone for 131 days, traveled hundreds of miles, and experienced unparalleled loss. There were undoubtedly tearful reunions for officers and wives, but there were no triumphant cheers. There was no rousing music. The men bathed and changed their clothes, and a few gathered to talk and to attempt to relax. The campaign was now genuinely done, but its ramifications had barely started.

One month later, almost as an afterthought in the wake of one of the most turbulent summers in American history, the National League played the final game of its inaugural season. Most teams wrapped their seasons in late September or early October, but Hartford and Boston still needed to close out the year. Hartford won 11–1 in Boston. It was Candy Cummings's sixteenth win of the year. He finished with a record of 16–8, and his team finished second in the standings. Prior to 1883, the champion was the team with the most victories, and that honor went to the Chicago White Stockings.

The season was an unquestioned success, but even the National League was not immune to the chaos that plagued so much of the country that year. The events of the summer of 1876 reverberated the following year and likely would for all the years to come.

EPILOGUE

Two and a half weeks after the National League finished its season, America went to the polls to choose its next president. The election that followed was regarded as one of the most controversial in American history. It took five months to determine a winner between Republican Rutherford B. Hayes and Democrat Samuel J. Tilden. Congress formed an electoral commission to investigate the election, and the commission determined that Hayes won the election by an electoral vote count of 185–184. Hayes was sworn in as the nineteenth president of the United States on March 5, 1877.

The first season of the National League was a success, but it had its difficulties. The Philadelphia Athletics and the New York Mutuals were expelled from the league after the season. They struggled mightily and experienced financial problems. And that was a sign of things to come for the young league. The size and makeup changed frequently over the next few years, but the league clung to life. It remained the only professional league to stand the test of time until the American League began in 1901.

Al Spalding played just two seasons in the National League. He was a dominant pitcher for the Chicago White Stockings in 1876 and switched to first base in 1877. He retired in 1878 at the ripe old age of twenty-seven. He became the club secretary and protégé to owner William Hulbert. He became club president and owner in 1882 when Hulbert passed away, and from that point forward, he was the most influential owner in the sport (as well as a sporting goods magnate). He helped popularize the game in America and around the world and was inducted into the National Baseball Hall of Fame as an executive in 1939.

But for all his positive contributions, there was also a downside. He was an ardent supporter of the hated reserve clause, the provision in a player's contract that allowed owners to limit salaries and restrict a player's freedom to switch teams. In essence, it prohibited free agency, and it remained in effect for one hundred years.

Two of Spalding's classmates in the Hall of Fame class of 1939 were William Arthur "Candy" Cummings and Adrian "Cap" Anson. Cummings's career in the National League was brief, but he was honored with an induction primarily because of his historic contribution to the game: the curveball.

Cap Anson's story has two sides, like that of Spalding's. On the field, his greatness was unquestioned. He was the Babe Ruth of his era in terms of both production and celebrity stature. But the downside was that he used his power and influence to keep players of color out of the game. Anson retired in 1897 after twenty-seven years in baseball, twenty-two of which were in the National League with the Chicago White Stockings. It took another fifty years for an African American player to break the color barrier and permanently integrate the sport of baseball.

The Centennial Exposition closed November 10, 1876, three days after Election Day. It was a phenomenal success by any standard, and an estimated ten million people traveled to Philadelphia during the six months of the World's Fair.

Eight days later, on November 18, the Younger brothers were sentenced to life in prison. Cole and Jim survived the grievous gunshot wounds they sustained during the final shootout with the Madelia posse. Bob received medical attention for his mangled arm, and they all went to the Minnesota state prison at Stillwater. Bob died in prison of tuberculosis. Cole and Jim were paroled in 1901. Jim took his own life one year later, and Cole passed away peacefully in 1916.

The James boys made it home to Missouri and then moved their families to Nashville, Tennessee. They stayed in the Nashville area for three years while they allowed the heat to die down from the raid that quickly became one of the most notorious in U.S. history. By 1879, Jesse was bored with the quiet life and wanted to restart the gang. He moved back to Missouri and formed a new outfit, but the group was a shadow of the old James-Younger Gang. Three years later, in April of 1882, Jesse was murdered by one of the new recruits, Robert Ford.

Frank James participated in one last robbery with Jesse. It was the Blue Cut train robbery on September 7, 1881, exactly five years after the Northfield Raid. After that, Frank gave up the life of crime. He rekindled his friendship with Cole Younger when Cole returned to Missouri after his release. They briefly traveled with a stage show called *The Cole Younger and Frank James Wild West Show*. Frank passed away in 1915, one year before Cole.

On December 4, while the Youngers began their third week in prison, the second trial of Jack McCall began in Yankton, Dakota Territory. McCall was captured in Wyoming on August 29 and returned to Dakota to face a formal trial for the murder of Wild Bill Hickok.

Two days later, with Hickok's brother Lorenzo in attendance, McCall was found guilty. He was sentenced to hang, and the execution was carried out March 1, 1877, four days before Rutherford B. Hayes took the oath of office.

After the murder of Wild Bill, Calamity Jane began claiming she was in a romantic relationship with the famous gunfighter and lawman. It wasn't true, of course, but the people of Deadwood enjoyed the story. A life of hard drinking took its toll, and Jane passed away on August 1, 1903, one day short of the twenty-seventh anniversary of Hickok's death. She was buried next to Wild Bill in Mount Moriah Cemetery in Deadwood, and their graves have been the sites of pilgrimages ever since.

Agnes Lake survived Hickok by thirty-one years. She passed away in 1907 and was buried in Cincinnati, Ohio, next to her first husband, William Lake Thatcher.

Deadwood continued to boom throughout 1876. The following year, in the summer of 1877, millionaire industrialist George Hearst bought the Homestake Mine, the grandaddy of them all. It became the longest-operating and most profitable gold mine in the Western Hemisphere. That same year, Al Swearingen opened the Gem Variety Theatre, the saloon that was arguably the most infamous joint in town. And that's saying a lot.

Sometime in the second half of 1876, Mark Twain published the novel that made him famous: *The Adventures of Tom Sawyer*. Twain had met the real Tom Sawyer in San Francisco in 1863. Tom seemed to have had more adventures than Twain could count, and Twain loved listening to Tom's stories. Thirteen years later, when Twain needed a name for his main character, he borrowed the name of his friend from San Francisco.

In the autumn of 1876, future president of the United States Theodore Roosevelt watched his first game of American football. On November 18, he stood on the edge of Hamilton Field in New Haven, Connecticut, and watched Harvard battle Yale in the second-ever contest between the two schools. Roosevelt was a freshman at Harvard, and he was captivated by the game. He never participated, but he helped save the sport in 1905 while he was president.

Football's brutality was appalling, and the level of violence caused many to call for the game to be outlawed. President Roosevelt held a summit at the White House with prominent college football coaches and urged them to make sweeping changes. One of the many new initiatives was the creation of the National Collegiate Athletic Association—the NCAA—that governs the sport to this day.

On that rainy afternoon in November of 1876, a sophomore named Walter Camp made a good impression during his limited minutes for Yale. Camp became the most influential man in the earliest years of the young sport. He is credited with numerous innovations, including the creation of the line of scrimmage, the quarterback position, and the eleven-man team.

Buffalo Bill Cody turned his fight with Yellow Hair into a theatrical sensation. After General Alfred Terry ended the expedition on September 5, Cody returned to the stages of the East and began work on a new play. He performed it later in 1876 and throughout 1877. It was called *The Red Right Hand; or, Buffalo Bill's First Scalp for Custer.*

Wyatt Earp and Bat Masterson patrolled the streets of Dodge City together for four cattle seasons. In 1878, John Henry "Doc" Holliday arrived in Dodge and added some lively color to the mix. After the 1879 season, Wyatt, Doc, and most of the Earp clan moved to Tombstone, Arizona. Eighteen months later, on October 26, 1881, Wyatt, Doc, and Wyatt's brothers Virgil and Morgan participated in a relatively well-known gunfight.

Wyatt and Bat returned to Dodge one last time, in 1883, to assist their friend Luke Short. They helped form the Dodge City Peace Commission with other noted lawmen and ultimately avoided a shooting war in town.

The Battle of the Little Bighorn became one of the most analyzed events in American history. It would be a daunting task to try to count the newspaper articles, magazine articles, academic papers, and books that have been written about the battle and the 1876 campaign against the tribes of the northern plains. A complete wrap-up of the events after 1876 would be equally daunting, but there are a few things to note . . .

A court of inquiry convened in 1879 to hear testimony about

the conduct of Major Marcus Reno during the battle. Days of testimony by surviving soldiers and civilians produced the foundational narrative for the Battle of the Little Bighorn. The court found Reno innocent of any wrongdoing, though his reputation had already been ravaged by three years of publications that held the opposite opinion.

Libbie Custer devoted the rest of her life to promoting her husband as a hero.

Crazy Horse remained free for nearly a year after the Battle of the Little Bighorn. He fiercely believed in avoiding white society, but he surrendered at Camp Robinson near the Red Cloud Agency in May of 1877. Four months later, he was killed by a soldier on the reservation. He remains the most prominent Native American leader of the second half of the nineteenth century who was never photographed.

Sitting Bull stayed out of reach of the U.S. Army for five years. He led his people to Canada, but by 1881, they were isolated and starving. He surrendered, was held as a prisoner of war for two years, and then moved to the Standing Rock Reservation in Dakota Territory. He traveled with Buffalo Bill Cody's Wild West Show for a season in 1885. Sitting Bull was killed in a controversial incident in 1890, two weeks before the Wounded Knee massacre, where three hundred Lakota were killed by the U.S. Army on the Pine Ridge Reservation.

The summer of 1876 was a brief, frozen moment in American history. It was a time when a host of things overlapped that would never overlap again. Some would, but not all. It had frontier towns where quintessential Old West lawmen walked the dusty streets. It had boomtowns where lawlessness reigned. It had cattle drives that would inspire countless books and movies in the years to come. It had wagon trains *and* railroads. It had the peak of the first generation of bank robbers and train robbers. It had full-scale battles between Native American armies and U.S. armies. It added a new career choice for certain Americans: professional athlete. It was possible to make a living by playing baseball before 1876, but the formation of the National League solidified it for all time.

The summer of 1876 was also the beginning of the end in many ways. It was the beginning of the end of freedom for Native American tribes within the borders of the United States. The previous year, in 1875, the last band of Comanche and their leader, Quanah Parker, surrendered in Texas. In 1877, Chief Joseph of the Nez Percé helped lead his people on an incredible journey to elude the U.S. Army and remain free, but eventually, he and his people surrendered. That same year, Crazy Horse and his band surrendered. Sitting Bull and his followers held out for another four years, and by the time they surrendered, the Indian Wars, as they were called, were all but done.

There were still clashes throughout the 1880s, particularly in the Southwest, where Geronimo kept the army busy for a few years, but none of the fighting resulted in any meaningful changes for any of the tribes. Their futures were the reservations, and there was no way out of it. Ultimately, that was one of several legacies of the Battle of the Little Bighorn.

It was the greatest victory of warriors over soldiers, and the result horrified the American nation, but it did nothing to change America's resolve to expand westward. If anything, the loss at the Little Bighorn pushed the military to act harder and faster.

The battle has name recognition that is in the same realm as the Battle of Gettysburg and the Battle of the Bulge. Americans might not be able to list many details about any of the three, but they have probably heard of them.

Another legacy was related to the concept of celebrity. Performers like actors and singers had always held various levels of celebrity status, but that was expected. They made their livings by portraying characters or versions of themselves for the benefit of entertainment. But by the 1870s, America clearly yearned for real-life idols.

George Armstrong Custer was an idol and a celebrity because he was viewed as the nation's number one Indian fighter. Wild Bill Hickok was an idol and celebrity because of his adventures as a scout, a lawman, and a gunfighter. Jesse James was America's first outlaw celebrity. The publication of dime novels brought fanciful tales of these men, and many others, to the masses. The novels turned the men into heroes, even if their real-life actions were the opposite of heroic, as in the case of Jesse James.

And Buffalo Bill Cody took the dime novels one step further with his Wild West show. He actually *showed* people the adventures of western heroes. The spectators weren't constrained by merely reading about adventures, they could *see* them. When Cody's show toured the world and dramatized the West for sold-out crowds, it showed them the West of the 1870s.

But in a span of six weeks in the summer of 1876, Americans experienced the tragic loss of two of their idols. It was a new type of feeling, the loss of a celebrity. Most Americans didn't personally know Custer or Hickok, but the status of both men transcended personal acquaintance. In later years, the same treatment would be given to lawmen like Wyatt Earp and Bat Masterson, and outlaws like Jesse James, Billy the Kid, and Butch Cassidy and the Sundance Kid.

When television became widely popular in the 1950s, the entertainment industry reached back to the 1870s for inspiration. Producers created shows like *The Lone Ranger, Gunsmoke, Wagon Train, The Rifleman, Rawhide, The Life and Legend of Wyatt Earp, Bat Masterson, Have Gun—Will Travel,* and dozens more.

The Old West era is generally viewed as the period between 1865 and 1900. And in that era, the year 1876 stands alone. It has healthy competition from most of the other years in its decade, but the events of the summer help set it apart. No other Native American battle compares to the Little Bighorn. No other outlaw gang compares to the James-Younger Gang. Wild Bill Hickok was one of a kind, and so was Deadwood. And no other frontier town could boast of a collection of lawmen like Dodge City's.

When we look for incredible stories from the Old West, and when we look for inspiration for books, movies, and television shows, it's no coincidence that we continue to look to 1876.

ACKNOWLEDGMENTS

This book started with an epiphany in the spring of 2019. In hindsight, the realization seemed so obvious that I was surprised I hadn't thought of it before. I had started a podcast called *Legends of the Old West* a year earlier, and over the course of that year, I produced series about Red Cloud's War, Wyatt Earp, Deadwood, and Jesse James. I had read books about the Battle of the Little Bighorn, and I knew some of the early history of Major League Baseball because of other podcast work.

So, in the spring of 2019, it hit me: some of the most well-known events of the Old West, which featured some of the most well-known people of the Old West, all happened in a short space of time. It might make a great book to weave all those stories into a single narrative.

A year and a half later, I was standing in the driveway of a rented house in Deadwood, South Dakota, when I mentioned the idea to Steve Wilson. The mention wasn't planned, but it unexpectedly led me down an exciting road.

At the time, Steve worked for Apple Podcasts. My sister, Mandi, and I own and operate an audio production company called Black Barrel Media, and we were talking with Steve about ways to grow our business. I don't remember how it happened, but I gave him the quick pitch of the book idea. He graciously offered to introduce me to Kathy Doyle, the vice president of content development for Macmillan Publishers.

I did the quick pitch for Kathy, and she organized a meeting with Laura Clark, vice president and associate publisher at St. Martin's Press. Laura recapped the idea for executive editor Marc Resnick, and Marc requested a proposal for the project. I wrote the proposal. St. Martin's said yes; Marc said yes; and here we are, about a year and a half later, as I'm writing these words. So the first round of thank-yous goes to Steve, Kathy, Laura, and Marc. Marc, thanks for guiding me through this process. I've written virtually every other type of printed work, but never a nonfiction book. Thanks for your help and expertise.

In Deadwood, special thanks go to Dr. David Wolff, Rose Speirs, and Ty Sanford. Dr. Wolff was a professor at Black Hills State University and has written extensively about the early eras of Deadwood's history. He answered several questions during the writing process, and I'm grateful for his help. Rose is the director of communications for Deadwood History Inc., the keepers of the flame of Deadwood history. My sister and I have known Rose for several years. She's great and is always ready with a helping hand. She introduced me to both Dr. Wolff and Ty Sanford. Ty is a member of Deadwood Alive, the group that re-creates Deadwood's famous—and infamous—moments for visitors. Ty is also a wealth of local knowledge, and he's become a good friend over the years.

Thank you, of course, to my family: my sister, Mandi; my mom,

Jane; and my dad, Bill. Their support was unwavering and crucial to the process, especially when I ignored everything around me to finish writing this book.

I should probably thank coffee producers everywhere. They will never know the depths of their contributions, but their product was as vital as air, food, and water.

Last, but certainly not least, I want to thank the loyal listeners of the *Legends of the Old West* podcast. They stayed with the show through all the experimentation and evolution as I tried to figure out, in real time, how to produce one of these things. Without their love of the Old West and their support of the podcast, this book would not have been possible. Thank you. Thank you very much.

SELECT BIBLIOGRAPHY

BASEBALL

National Baseball Hall of Fame
Society for American Baseball Research
Retrosheet

BATTLE OF THE LITTLE BIGHORN

Ambrose, Stephen E. *Crazy Horse and Custer: The Epic Clash of Two Great Warriors at the Little Bighorn.* New York: Simon & Schuster, 1975.

Bolen, Robert D. *The Lakota Sioux Indians: A History of the Siouan People.* Fort Boise Publishing Company, 2012.

Carter, Robert A. *Buffalo Bill Cody: The Man Behind the Legend.* New York: John Wiley & Sons, Inc., 2000.

Donovan, James. *A Terrible Glory: Custer and the Little Bighorn, the Last Great Battle of the American West.* New York: Back Bay Books / Little, Brown and Company, 2008.

Drury, Bob, and Tom Clavin. *The Heart of Everything That Is: The Untold Story of Red Cloud, an American Legend.* New York: Simon & Schuster, 2013.

Greene, Jerome A. *Slim Buttes, 1876: An Episode of the Great Sioux War.* Norman, OK: University of Oklahoma Press, 2012.

Grinnell, George Bird. *The Fighting Cheyennes.* New York: Charles Scribner's Sons, 1915.

Hardorff, Richard G. *Washita Memories: Eyewitness Views of Custer's Attack on Black Kettle's Village.* Norman, OK: University of Oklahoma Press, 2008.

Marshall, Joseph M., III. *The Journey of Crazy Horse.* New York: Penguin Books, 2005.

Philbrick, Nathaniel. *The Last Stand: Custer, Sitting Bull, and the Battle of the Little Bighorn.* New York: Penguin Books, 2010.

William F. Cody Archive at the Buffalo Bill Center of the West, codyarchive.org.

Wyoming State Historical Society, wyohistory.org.

DEADWOOD, WILD BILL HICKOK, CALAMITY JANE

Bryant, Jerry L., and Barbara Fifer. *Deadwood's Al Swearingen: Manifest Evil in the Gem Theatre.* Helena, MT: Far Country Press, 2018.

Bryant, Jerry L., and Barbara Fifer. *Deadwood Saints and Sinners.* Helena, MT: Far Country Press, 2016.

Clavin, Tom. *Wild Bill: The True Story of the American Frontier's First Gunfighter.* New York: St. Martin's Griffin, 2019.

Parker, Watson. *Deadwood: The Golden Years.* Lincoln, NE: University of Nebraska Press, 1981.

Parker, Watson. *Gold in the Black Hills.* Pierre, SD: South Dakota State Historical Society Press, 1966; new material, 2003.

Rosa, Joseph G. *Wild Bill Hickok: The Man & His Myth.* Lawrence, KS: University Press of Kansas, 1996.

Wolff, David A. *The Savior of Deadwood: James K. P. Miller on the Gold Frontier.* Pierre, SD: South Dakota State Historical Society Press, 2021.

DODGE CITY, WYATT EARP, BAT MASTERSON

Clavin, Tom. *Dodge City: Wyatt Earp, Bat Masterson, and the Wickedest Town in the American West.* New York: St. Martin's Griffin, 2017.

DeArment, Robert K. *Bat Masterson: The Man and the Legend.* Norman, OK: University of Oklahoma Press, 2014.

Tefertiller, Casey. *Wyatt Earp: The Life Behind the Legend.* New York: John Wiley & Sons, Inc., 1997.

JESSE JAMES, THE NORTHFIELD RAID

Gardner, Mark Lee. *Shot All to Hell: Jesse James, the Northfield Raid, and the Wild West's Greatest Escape.* New York: William Morrow, 2013.

Stiles, T. J. *Jesse James: Last Rebel of the Civil War.* New York: Vintage Books, 2003.

Yeatman, Ted P. *Frank and Jesse James: The Story Behind the Legend.* Nashville, TN: Cumberland House Publishing, Inc., 2000.

INDEX

ABOUT THE AUTHOR

Sneaky Big Studios

Chris Wimmer is the creator, host, and lead writer of *Legends of the Old West*, a long-form narrative podcast that tells true stories of the American West. He has a master's degree in journalism from the Walter Cronkite School of Journalism and Mass Communication at Arizona State University and has won numerous local, state, and national awards for his writing. *The Summer of 1876* is his first book.